BE A BLESSING
Jewish Wisdom on Celebrating Life

MORDECHAI BAR-OR
Translated from the Hebrew
by Jessica Setbon

gefen נפן
publishing house בית הוצאה לאור
JERUSALEM ◆ NEW YORK Est. 1981

Scripture quotations are modified from *The Holy Scriptures According to the
Masoretic Text*, published by the Jewish Publication Society in 1917.

Cover design: Tsofit Tsachi
Typesetting: Optume Technologies

ISBN: 978-965-7801-57-4

1 3 5 7 9 8 6 4 2

Gefen Publishing House Ltd.
6 Hatzvi Street
Jerusalem 9438614,
Israel
972-2-538-0247
orders@gefenpublishing.com

Gefen Books
c/o Baker & Taylor Publisher Services
30 Amberwood Parkway
Ashland, Ohio 44805
516-593-1234
orders@gefenpublishing.com

www.gefenpublishing.com

Printed in Israel
Library of Congress Control Number: 2024947922

Contents

Contents

Foreword
Rabbi Yitz Greenberg

This book appears in English in a time of troubles for the Jewish people. Israel is embattled. The evil axis of Hamas, Hezbollah, and Iran poses an existential threat. A worldwide upsurge of antisemitism is targeting our Diaspora Jewish communities. We are tempted to focus our religious worldview on a unity based on sharing the fate of a persecuted people.

This book offers a healing, life-affirming alternative to a religious approach based on solidarity, imposed by external enemies. The vision of blessing consciousness presents Judaism as the religion of living an abundant life. The text guides us to purpose and mission in life through embrace of existence and living an expansive way of life of creativity and joy. Bar-or enriches the book by offering images and models that draw upon the poetic and mystical insights of the kabbalistic tradition (which most modern theologians do not access). Broad in structure and vision, richly detailed in the warp and woof of daily living, this book brings an inspired and inspiring voice to uplift Jewish life at a critical moment.

We live in a unique era in which the Jewish story holds special significance. Alongside the dangers to the very existence of the Jewish people, Judaism possesses a distinct vision for healing a broken world. Furthermore, Judaism and the Jewish people must bring the celebration of life to the world!

I recommend this book strongly to all who seek a positive Jewish identity and a fulfilling way of living the Jewish heritage.

Rabbi Irving (Yitz) Greenberg
Senior scholar in residence at Hadar Institute; President, J.J. Greenberg Institute for the Advancement of Jewish Life

Preface to the English Edition

The English edition of this book differs from its original Hebrew counterpart, on several levels. Written initially for Israelis at the crux of a pivotal societal crossroads, the book delves into Israel's tumultuous life, brimming with events that challenge the fabric of its society and the bonds uniting diverse communities. It presents Israelis, divided in opinion, a unified vision for the future, anchored in a covenant of destiny.

In October 2023, while Israel found itself ensnared in a profound schism that drastically divided its society, Hamas waged a brutal terror attack, prompting the Iron Swords War. These events, inevitably, demand elucidation. Can Israel sculpt a vision in which dissent is not just tolerated but harnessed to forge a society of worth? The Hebrew book questions Israel's core battles – not merely for Jewish survival, but for survival with a purpose.

The English edition, however, targets a global audience, predominantly non-Israeli. While it touches on Israeli issues with global implications, it primarily asks: What unique value does Judaism bring in this modern era? Beyond its storied history, does Judaism, and do Jews, offer something vital to a rapidly evolving world?

This work explores fundamental questions: Why continue the Jewish journey in a world ripe with democracy, humanity, and other positive values? It introduces fresh perspectives on the richness and celebration of life through a Jewish lens. Moreover, the book envisions a collaborative future for Diaspora Jews and the State of Israel, inspiring both communities to bring this vision to fruition.

It's also a compelling read for anyone intrigued by the future of Jews and Judaism. While much is written about the Jewish past and its humanitarian contributions, this book questions the necessity of Jewish continuance in the twenty-first century. What shape could meaningful dialogues with other religions and diverse cultures assume?

Amidst sweeping transformations in the Western world, where foundational beliefs and paradigms in economics, communication, technology, and family structures are shifting, this book examines Judaism's potential contributions. In addition, I've infused the narrative with thought-provoking questions and practical suggestions.

I hope you find this journey worthwhile, as I have.

Mordechai Bar-Or
Jerusalem
Elul 5784/September 2024

Acknowledgments

I wish to express my thanks.

I pause briefly in this feeling of thankfulness, as it extends beyond its immediate subjects. In gratitude, there is a wondrous element that bursts beyond the confines of time and space. *Todah*. Gratitude.

This book is dedicated to my parents. It honors the blessed memory of my father and teacher, Meir Brayer, a man of great heart and simple giving, who symbolized for me how at any stage and age, one can touch life anew and embrace love.

My mother, Shoshana Singer, passed away on the day the Hebrew edition of this book was published. The book dialogues with her remarkable life in a broad embrace. From my parents, I received a love of life and the power of *niggun*, Jewish melody, in carrying life's fragments.

I am grateful to my elder sisters, Chava and Ruth. Growing up with their presence and perspective has enriched my understanding of my life's path. We have been fortunate to profoundly heal our bond.

Thank you to my teacher and study partner Rabbi Dov Berkovitz. Dov has walked with me on life's path and introduced me to the Torah of the Tree of Life.

Thank you to Yumi (of blessed memory) and his wife Hedy Shleifer, who opened new doors of understanding and listening in the Imago process.

A special thanks to my dear friend Tzvika Gilat. Beyond being a study partner in blessing consciousness, he has expanded my understanding of the space for human frailty in my life and teachings.

Avner Haramati challenged me to expand the question of the internal Jewish blessing to the broader blessing of the sons of Abraham, and partnered with me in a new and exciting project. Thank you.

My thanks to Alan Barkat, for his wisdom and dear friendship.

Acknowledgments

Thanks to the Lippman-Kanfer Foundation, and to Joe Kanfer who leads it, for bringing me to the first gathering of Ve'heyeh Berachah, and for his assistance in publishing the English version.

Thanks to Sally Gottesman, a longtime friend from New York, who helped publish the book in both editions.

Many friends from the Diaspora have walked with me for years in a spirit of trust and deepening connection. Some of them contributed to the publication of the book in English. I would like to especially thank Michelle and Ben Belfer-Friedman, Irene Susmano, Roger Low, the Friend family, Evan Schlessinger, Randy Levitt, Debbie and Jeff Swartz, Lisa and Josh Greer, Selwyn Gerber, Bob Immerman, Julie Gadinsky, Ariella Riva Ritvo-Slifka, and Tricia Gibbs. Thank you very much. May you be blessed.

My thanks to Gila, the mother of my children. Her unique personality, presence, and wisdom have brought great blessing to our family.

I began the journey that led to this book at the Kolot Beit Midrash. I am grateful to my colleagues in the organization who permitted me to dream in addition to managing the institute. Thanks to Debra Pell, chair of the board, for enabling this integration.

I have learned from many friends, partners, and students, often through disagreement. I tried to maintain the perspective that these disputes were for the sake of heaven. Thank you for the privilege.

Thoughts of my children and their spouses make my heart swell with joy. I am deeply grateful for their presence in my life. To Noga and Yonatan, Shira and Noam, Eitan and Tal, David and Renana. My beloved ones. My children also commented on chapters in the book. I hope this book will further strengthen our connection.

My eighteen grandchildren bring me joy, learning, silliness, and healing. It's hard to describe the wonder they are.

Thanks to the editor of the Hebrew edition, Roy Horn, and special thanks to Yedioth Books, who published the book in Hebrew.

Thank you to God, for His abundant kindness to me that allows me to move into new realms, and for opening new gates for me.

Introduction

This book emerges amidst times that can only be described as unexpectedly turbulent. For many, the dawn of the twenty-first century heralded a shift from a legacy of mere survival to an era rich with meaning and enhanced quality of life. There was a widespread optimism, a belief that the shadows of great wars were receding, paving the way for a brighter epoch. Across the globe, nations and individuals shifted focus toward measuring quality of life, hinting at a transformative course ahead, particularly for future generations.

Then the world was rocked by the unforeseen ravages of the COVID-19 pandemic, a stark reminder that we must adapt to coexist with such global crises. Additionally, we are bearing witness to a distressing and avoidable conflict in Eastern Europe, power-hungry leaders, and a mounting sense of instability across various life domains. It's becoming increasingly clear that many paradigms we deemed unshakeable are on the brink of upheaval. Critical aspects of life such as economic frameworks, the pervasive impact of technology, family dynamics, and more stand at a pivotal junction.

In Israel, these global upheavals were mirrored and magnified by a devastating invasion by Hamas and a harsh war that erupted amidst a holiday celebration. The Jewish people are now confronted with the daunting task of reconstructing their state, all while grappling with profound questions about their vision, purpose, and the resilience of their society.

Human existence, particularly within the Jewish context, is an unceasing summons to mindfulness, an existential invitation to discern and fathom our individual and collective roles in the ever-shifting tableau of life.

For me personally, the onset of the COVID-19 pandemic coincided with a pivotal moment in my journey. It amplified my foray into the unknown, a feeling that has shadowed me since my departure from leading the Kolot Beit

Midrash[1] after two decades of stewardship. This newfound realm of uncertainty, emerging after years of creation, assuredness, action, and the mirage of control, sparked a distinctive odyssey of awareness for me. It was as if the pandemic peeled back the layers of routine, revealing a deeper, more intricate dance of existence, urging a deeper contemplation of my path in a world that's constantly in flux.

The pandemic's timing was eerily synchronous with my mental state. I wasn't alone in this inward focus – it became a universal necessity. Technology, with Zoom as a prime player, enabled life to trudge on. Yet this digital lifeline didn't alter my conviction about the importance of self-reflection. I was curious to discover what insights would surface from a journey inward, from a different mode of engaging with my thoughts.

This introspective voyage, though challenging, led me to a realm of consciousness deeply intertwined with existential queries: Why do we awaken each morning, both as individuals and as the Jewish people? What truly and earnestly fuels our sense of vitality? Gradually, the book's language and its core proposition took shape: to reencounter and savor the fruit of the Tree of Life, as Adam and Eve were destined, and to embody the concept of *ve'heyeh berachah* – "and be a blessing," what we will call "blessing consciousness," as commanded to Abraham at the onset of the Jewish odyssey.

I pondered over the societal blueprint encapsulated in the words that further define Abraham's mission: "and in you will all the families of the earth be blessed" (Gen. 12:3). What social model does this phrase imply, and how does it resonate in our contemporary context? These reflections were the catalysts that shaped the essence of my book.

The Call of Our Age

For many, this epoch stands as an extraordinary juncture to quest for a deeper raison d'être, transcending mere survival. The waning of the COVID-19 pandemic has left in its wake a plethora of existential queries. Those perceiving the pandemic as a call for personal renewal – not just a yearning to revert to the old normal – are delving into profound contemplation.

---

1   Kolot, which I founded in 1997, is an Israeli study center for leadership that bridges Judaism with the contemporary challenges of the twenty-first century in Israel.

Introduction

The relentless surge of technology into our lives heralds radical changes in every facet. Yet we're still grappling with the full scope of this technological revolution; while it has ushered in remarkable efficiency, the hidden costs remain largely uncharted territory.

The breakneck speed of technological advancement starkly contrasts with the sluggish pace of human emotional and spiritual evolution. This efficiency, impressive as it may be, falls short in fostering joy and fulfillment, and certainly does not address our thirst for meaning. Consequently, a pervasive sense of loneliness, a dearth of intimacy and belonging, a void in fulfilling relationships, and challenges in authentic self-expression plague many. But above all, there looms a profound void – a yearning for a sense of life's significance and direction, an assurance that life is not merely an existential march, but a journey imbued with purpose and worth.

The tumultuous landscape of the 2020s marks a pivotal epoch, presenting an unparalleled chance to probe into the core essence of our existence. It beckons us to reassess our approach to livelihood and economics, the nature of our interpersonal communications, our attitudes toward others and those vulnerable in society, the depth of intimacy in our lives, and the equilibrium between giving and receiving. At its heart, it poses the burning question: What ignites the spark of life within us?

Intriguingly, unlike historical crises, the current upheavals have catapulted technology to an unprecedented level of indispensability, bridging communication gaps in a time when human faces were obscured, both literally and figuratively. These contrasts – abundant resources and technological prowess versus the erosion of genuine human connection – serve as poignant hallmarks of our times. Echoing the paradox of ancient Rome, where technological strides did not equate to human advancement, our era mirrors this dichotomy. The introspective shift propelled by the pandemic, juxtaposed with the unbridled freedom we once took for granted, could well be a rare window for us to crystallize our individual and collective aspirations.

The Jewish people find themselves at a critical juncture, grappling with the quest for existential significance in contemporary times. The past century has been a whirlwind of monumental events: the unspeakable atrocities of the Holocaust, the birth of the State of Israel, and an unprecedented gathering of exiles, among other pivotal moments. Yet even after seventy-six years of independence, Israeli citizens continue to bear the weight of mandatory military service. Many are poised to face not only physical but also deep emotional scars, and some even confront the ultimate sacrifice for their nation. This stark reality thrusts open the door to profound inquiries about the essence of Jewish life.

The Jewish-Arab relations crisis that erupted in May 2021, the intense protests against the government by a significant portion of Israel's population in 2023, and most notably, the harrowing pogrom by Hamas and the war begun in October 2023, together with the burst of new-old antisemitism, all beckon a reevaluation of the Zionist vision today and our role within it as Jews. Furthermore, the alarming surge in global antisemitism adds urgency to these existential deliberations, compelling us to confront the fundamental question: What exactly do we, as Jews, stand for in this turbulent era?

The fact that half of the global Jewish population opts to reside outside the State of Israel presents a fascinating and complex conundrum. What does it signify to live in a self-chosen Diaspora? Beyond the State of Israel's pivotal role in their collective identity, what truly binds Jews worldwide? Most critically: Is there a unified vision or dream that Jews across the globe share for their future? Without concrete answers to these queries, the richness of our past alone cannot justify the continuation of intra-faith unions or the perpetuation of our vibrant journey.

In this book, I unveil a vision for the Jewish purpose and destiny in our era – a vision that is simultaneously novel and steeped in tradition. This future-oriented blueprint intertwines with the universal human quest for meaning, aspirations for love and partnership, the significance of family, the transformative power of language in shaping reality, and beyond. The concept put forth in these pages also explores realms of public policy, attitudes toward finance and economics, the dynamics of communication and media, the essence of healthy leadership, and our relationship with the Divine. Together, these diverse threads weave into the grand tapestry of what it means to be part of the Jewish covenant of destiny.

While writing this book, I've been deeply engaged in the initiative called Ve'heyeh Berachah or "Be a Blessing," which centers on these pivotal issues. I've observed an escalating hunger for a holistic approach that harmonizes professional ambition, the search for love and partnership, and a yearning for societal healing – a hunger particularly pronounced among the generation born and nurtured in these times. This emerging need beckons for the birth of a new consciousness, a tool adept at rejuvenating our lives by intricately weaving together our past, present, and future.

Alongside this emergent consciousness, I discern a pressing need to craft a vision, a captivating and provocative glimpse into the future that offers both strength and hope. The foundational tales of the Torah, especially the Garden of Eden narrative, touch upon the core dilemmas of human existence. A considerable portion of Jewish culture, both overtly and subtly, is devoted to elaborating and evolving these stories.

This book endeavors to tread a delicate balance, navigating the dual pathways of personal growth and the conception of a blessed society, while reinforcing their interconnection. It aims to bridge the gap between the personal-communal realm, embodied in "you shall be a blessing," and the universal realm, encapsulated in "in you…will they be blessed."

The Second Generation Pursues Peace

I grew up in a family of Holocaust survivors. "So, you're a second-generation survivor in good shape," a good friend once said to me during a stint in reserve army service in the Jordan Valley, as I shared stories about the home in which I grew up. He then added, "Maybe there are some scratches, maybe even a dent in the chassis, but overall, you've got some good years left on the road." Despite the friendly smiles we shared, he touched a sensitive nerve. Indeed, since my youth, I've felt a certain unease, a subtle pain present within me, hardly noticeable but persistently present. I realized it was connected to my childhood home and my background as a child of Holocaust survivors.

It took me many years to understand the wound of my childhood, the painful foundation that influenced my life. I was born after two daughters, and my parents' joy in having a sole male child was immense. They believed in me and expected greatness from me. They met my basic needs during economically challenging times: clothing, food, good educational frameworks, Chasidic Shabbat songs that touched me deeply. They made a great effort to provide me with a strong foundation for a good life, certainly better than the one they had experienced in Eastern Europe before and during the Second World War. Yet despite this effort, my childhood was marked by a minimal amount of physical warmth from my mother. She was blocked in her ability in this regard. Later, I understood what my mother had endured during those hard times, which perhaps influenced her and led to difficulty in expressing and demonstrating such warmth to her son. This was a painful realization. Over time, I learned that I was not alone in experiencing this lack in childhood – many second-generation Holocaust survivors and others as well deal with the same issues.

Memories from my childhood created a certain void that frequently plagued me. When I encountered the concept of "the empty space" as used by the kabbalistic master Rabbi Isaac Luria (the Ari) to describe divine processes of creation, I felt a physical identification with it.[2] This painful void also steered parts of my life. Genuinely touching the void was and will continue to be key to the quality of my future life.

My childhood pain also harbored sweetness and positive strengths. These forces, along with the pain, propelled me to engage in society, to innovate, to commit, and to establish unique Jewish study centers in Israel for students from all segments of society. These centers contributed significantly to the rejuvenation of Israeli culture. Wounds can carry immense vitality and creativity, yet the outcomes are not always precise. In my life and endeavors, there were moments of pride and condescension. I experienced times of imprecision and flaws. These realizations are challenging to confront and constantly test me. I have learned the importance of seeking forgiveness, including from myself.

I have been granted many blessings in my life. Blessed with a large, dear, and loving family, I cherish a special bond with my children and grandchildren. I was able to forge a deep connection with my parents, honoring them in both deed and spirit. My relationship with my elder sisters has evolved into a touching and emotional bond, a connection that took time and joint effort to build. Such extensive family bonds don't just occur naturally.

---

2   "And behold, then the Infinite One contracted Himself into the central point which is exactly in the middle, and He contracted that light and withdrew to the surroundings of the central point, and then there remained an empty space, air, and a vacant void. And then, from the light of the Infinite, He drew a single straight line, and in the place of the void, He emanated, created, formed, and made all the worlds" (Rabbi Chaim Vital, *Sefer Etz Chaim* 1:1).

Professionally, I've had the privilege of founding and leading unique initiatives. I have taught and learned from students and partners, who have been exceptional companions on my life's journey. I developed tools for facilitating meaningful conversations between secular and religious Israelis. I spent three years managing Gesher seminars and cofounded the Elul Beit Midrash with Dr. Ruth Calderon. After seven years there, I established the Israeli Jewish study center for leadership Kolot and led it for twenty-one years. Throughout this time, I have been part of an endeavor to create a new dialogue between religious and secular communities, working in spaces that seek to intertwine Torah and society, with leaders dedicated to rejuvenating Judaism in Israel.

Genuine Speech

As that remarkable period that spanned more than half of my life drew to a close, I sensed a need for change and a longing to explore a deeper aspect of life. The *Zohar* depicts a state of being in which a person has "voice without speech,"[3] emitting sounds or "voices" but lacking true expression. This absence of speech is the lack of a living expression of our soul's depth and true essence. This can be a difficult experience. For a long time, I woke up each morning and asked myself, when had I last truly "spoken"? When had I last felt the full force of my inner potential?

This kind of expression is not about the gratification of teaching a good class or the success of a viral social media post. True speech is about expressing the deep longing of a soul that has been in exile, yearning to come out into the light. During this time, a particular phrase from the *Zohar* struck a chord with me: "Woe to those people who sleep in their holes." This phrase calls for a unique kind of wakefulness, one that resists the complacency of routine life.

I asked myself, How awake am I really? How closely do I listen to the essence of my soul?

In early 2017, I embarked on a sabbatical. I made my first-ever journey to India and began writing the early drafts of what would become the journey to "be a blessing," the basis of this book. My aim was to shift, even just slightly, from the survival instincts ingrained in me – those tied to both personal childhood pain and cultural pain – to a fresh new path. I did not want to

---

3   *Zohar*, Parashat Va'era.

revert to the familiar but to explore a new-old, untrained part of myself, and to discover what new life movement it could facilitate.

I sought to give the Tree of Life within me, eager to flourish, the space to grow, moving away somewhat from rigid knowledge. The mind solidifies so many aspects within us. It governs our traumas and controls our flow. It embeds itself in the body and retains every detail.[4] My desire was to ease the dominance of the knowledge of good and evil.

During that period, I came across Franz Rosenzweig's letter to his academic advisor Friedrich Meinecke, in which he declined a teaching position at the University of Berlin. He wrote:

> Among the shreds of my talents, I began to search for myself, amidst the manifold for the One. This journey led me deep into myself, to the cellar of my essence, where my talents could not follow. There, I drew close to an old chest…reaching deep inside…striving to touch its very bottom. These were my treasures, my most personal possessions…not borrowed from anyone else.[5]

I read Rosenzweig's letter while in Dharamsala, India, and it made a profound impression on me. A year later, I stepped down from Kolot – my beloved creation that I'd spearheaded for twenty-one years. I had to say farewell to good people, partners, donors, and various energies that had served me in the past but were no longer relevant.

During my sabbatical year, the biblical question of Shemittah, the sabbatical year, resonated with me: "And if you will say: 'What will we eat the seventh year? Behold, we will not sow, nor gather in our increase'" (Lev. 25:20). If I were to release some of the foundational assumptions that had underpinned my life, what would sustain me? If I slightly freed myself from the assumptions that guided my Jewish and human existence, what would become of me? And on a more practical level, how would I support myself?

---

4   For a unique perspective on this topic, see Bessel van der Kolk, MD, *The Body Keeps the Score: Brain, Mind, and Body in the Healing of Trauma* (New York: Penguin, 2015).

5   Franz Rosenzweig, in *Selected Letters and Diary Fragments* (Berlin: Shoken Verlag, 1935), 67.

This existential question found an immediate answer in the subsequent verses: "And I will command my blessing upon you in the sixth year, and it will bring forth produce for three years." I wondered, how was the concept of Shemittah connected to this blessing of abundance, which seems to defy all human and economic logic? These thoughts also surfaced when I sat in the employment office, signing up for unemployment benefits after years of financial security. I knew that only if I were willing to let go of the ground beneath my feet, my foundational beliefs, could I touch a new consciousness and the language of blessing.

A New Consciousness

This book explores a proposal for a new consciousness. What is the difference between a change in values and a change in consciousness? A change in values typically comes from knowledge, from free choice and an ethical system. The values of our foundational narrative are derived from the imagery of the Tree of Knowledge of Good and Evil. Culturally and historically, this understanding is linked to creative endeavors in the fields of arts, technology, and science, as they have evolved to the present time. It also touches on our extraordinary ability to survive as a people and the Jewish people's quest for self-preservation within the surrounding world, which was particularly highlighted during our years in exile.

A shift in consciousness, however, stems from a deeper place, from the kabbalistic concept of *binah* or understanding that originates from the core of the soul. It begins when we play the melody of our inner desires on the strings of our soul, allowing us to hear the inner voice that springs from our inner child. This space enables the Tree of Life within each of us to reveal itself. This is a crucial point. Knowledge/mind is responsible for many of our fears, restrictions, and default choices in life. Deliberate release from the dominance of the Tree of Knowledge in directing our lives allows the Tree of Life to express its "being" – the simple, inherent existence within us.

Many researchers argue that a shift in consciousness of this nature is associated with a different area of the brain than the one used for values. Some even suggest that the brain itself changes with the emergence of a new type of conscious thought. The change in consciousness that I propose in this book is linked to our foundational images: the language of the trees in the Garden of Eden from the foundational myth of the Torah, and daily life's "field of blessing," whose shadow and sounds we will explore extensively in the book.

"Man's origin is from dust and his end is to dust. He earns his bread with his soul's toil, fragile as a shattered clay pot."[6] During these years of exploration, I also learned that there is no person without pain or deep wounds. This holds true even for those who grew up in normative homes and families. The same is evident in the stories of the patriarchs in the Book of Genesis. Abraham's wounds resurface throughout his many trials. The same is true for Isaac, who was bound on the mountain by his father and who did not attend his mother's funeral due to his need of healing, and for Jacob, who fled his parents' home into the deep night in immense fear. I identified many more instances of such pain in these foundation stories. Once I realized that I am not alone in these experiences, this made me more sensitive to the pain around me.

In response to the routine inquiry "How are you?" I began to encourage my close friends to share not just their general well-being but also their pain. Whether in study sessions, collaborative work, or friendships, I urged them to share their pain with precision and gentleness, not as an overwhelming deluge, but in a manner that allows for understanding and empathy.

The awareness associated with the Tree of Life image and its expression in our world seeks to enrich our personalities. It does not intend to erase our memories; instead, it acknowledges and respects our journey, while inviting us to a new path, to be a blessing and "guard the path of the Tree of Life" (Gen. 3:24).

From the individual to the national, the Holocaust brutally reduced life to its barest essence. The gathering and confinement of Jews, the restriction of freedom, the ghettos, the harrowing atrocities brought us to a critical juncture. Survival became the central theme for a nation that lost one-third of its members. The establishment of the State of Israel three years later was akin to the resolute declaration of the Psalmist: "I will not die, but live, and declare the works of the Lord. The Lord has chastened me severely: but He has not given me over to death" (Ps. 118:17–18).

---

6   From the U'netaneh Tokef prayer recited during the High Holidays.

Introduction

The remnants of the Holocaust vehemently clamored for life. But they paid a price.

While after the exodus from Egypt, forty years in the wilderness were necessary for healing and a generational shift before entering the Promised Land, the State of Israel arose amidst the still-fresh wounds of the Holocaust, without a period of healing respite. Yet perhaps it was best this way. My parents, survivors who arrived in Israel in 1947, found themselves in combat in Kibbutz Be'erot Yitzhak near Gaza just a year later.

The State of Israel was born in the shadow of the Holocaust's post-trauma, quickly evolving to accommodate a large influx of immigrants from North African countries, building the foundations of a sovereign nation, a formidable military, and admirable industry. This rapid development was a fusion of survival, creation, and rejuvenation, a pattern that persists to this day.

This book posits that beyond individual human growth, as Jews we must grapple with the question "Why is the Jewish people's existence necessary in the twenty-first century?" Addressing this issue is crucial for strengthening both the Jewish state and the Jewish people globally. It can provide a rationale for our collective identity in a world torn between eroding national identities and promoting universal values of social justice and humanity.

I propose a vision that revisits and revitalizes Jewish purpose for our times. This vision is interwoven with human aspirations for meaning, fulfillment in love and partnership, the importance of family, respect for human dignity, and compassion for the vulnerable, extending to broader themes such as economics, communication, and societal structures.

This concept could inspire a transformation in Jewish life – shifting from a focus on mere survival to a narrative and lifestyle deeply imbued with purpose, vitality, and quality.

The Jewish people must bring the celebration of life into the world.

PART ONE

The Garden of Eden Is Here

According to the *Zohar*, Adam's transgression did not stem from eating from the Tree of Knowledge but rather from neglecting to consume from the Tree of Life first. This interpretation of the foundational narrative offers a profound insight into the essence of life, the distinctiveness of Judaism, and the imperative for repair.

Chapter 1

The Garden of Eden Story – A Microcosm of Ideal Life

From the onset of human civilization, moral and ethical contemplation has been a pivotal aspect of human thought. This distinguishes humans from animals, particularly in the pursuit of a moral code to guide life and the upbringing of children.

The development of morality varies across different cultures and contexts and is primarily reflected in philosophical and religious texts. Understanding the concept of "human" or even visualizing humanity is incomplete without acknowledging our attempts to differentiate good from evil and the continuous struggle to resist evil and embrace good. The saying "Depart from evil, and do good" represents the essence of a person who "desires life" (Psalms 34). Indeed, the Tree of Knowledge of Good and Evil, from which Adam and Eve ate, epitomizes the realm of ethics and free will. It signifies enlightenment and wisdom, embodying the human ability to choose between good and evil.

The compelling nature of the Tree of Knowledge in our lives fostered a focus on permitted and forbidden, pure and impure in Jewish tradition – a whole world of duties and rights. A significant part of the language of the Tree of Knowledge created a special moral obligation toward others, especially the vulnerable, the stranger, and more. This language distinguished between the sacred and the mundane, between Israel and other nations.

Interestingly, the consumption of the Tree of Knowledge was initially forbidden to man. This means that originally, there was an alternative hope for humanity's inception, one beyond the knowledge of good and evil. Can we imagine such a world? In it, we are nourished by eating diverse fruits and drinking from rivers, feeling a divine presence enveloping us – living guided not by the knowledge of good and evil, but solely in the shade of the Tree of Life. Such a world, reminiscent of various utopias, will be discussed later in the book.

The forbidden consumption of the fruit of the Tree of Knowledge had its consequences. Following this act, Adam and Eve were banished from the Garden of Eden. This expulsion marked a shift from harmony to estrangement – between humans and God, between humans and the earth, and between the level of effort and its fruits. Enmity was established between humans and the serpent, a symbol of life's adversities. Furthermore, the relationship between man and woman transformed from unity – "he will cleave to his wife" – to a power dynamic: "and your desire will be to your husband, and he will rule over you" (Gen. 3:16). This significant verse, with its implications for intimate relations, is central in a world shaped by consumption of the fruit of the Tree of Knowledge. This event also influenced many aspects of our lives, including the pursuit of power, cynicism, and a lack of effective communication and empathy, all indicative of a life influenced by eating from the Tree of Knowledge.

Furthermore, perceiving the world and life's purpose only through the prism of good and evil overlooks crucial elements of human existence and experience. When morality is the sole focus, one's worldview can become detached from the realms of meaning, awe, and love, potentially even overlooking the essence of life itself.

In Jewish literature (particularly the kabbalistic masterwork the *Zohar*), the Tree of Life is portrayed as the fundamental source of all life, a symbol of life's vitality. This tree encapsulates the world's mysteries and the essence of life. Followers of the Ari developed a systematic approach to life inspired by the symbol of the tree, representing the essential components of aspiration, desire, and yearning. It signifies a connection to our full potential that does not rely on external validation. In contrast, the *Zohar* refers to the Tree of Knowledge as *ilana demuta*, or the tree of death, signifying not just physical demise but a series of small deaths that occur throughout our lives, shaping our experiences and perspectives.

Consider a practical example: winning a debate without giving due regard to the vanquished side's perspectives and feelings is like a small death. This happens because the mechanics of argumentation and the democratic principle of majority rule can inadvertently quash a valid opinion. Often, in our discourse and our contentious culture, we might unwittingly nullify entire human perspectives. This is especially true in scenarios involving cynicism or shaming for a supposedly noble cause, where the focus shifts away from the individual's life journey and inner dynamics. It's possible to live a life entrenched in the dichotomy of good and evil, yet remain oblivious to the experiences of deep forgiveness and meaningful human intimacy.

As noted, the Garden of Eden narrative marks the dawn of human existence on earth. This setting represented an aspiration for a life filled with abundance, security, and happiness. The Garden of Eden story is also integral to the Jewish historical narrative, encapsulating the core of our existence. This story is not merely an ancient account – it is also a powerful vision for the future. As Gershom Scholem eloquently stated, "The Garden of Eden is both the ancestral past and the utopian image of humanity's redemption."[1]

Do we carry within us, in our physical bodies, some remnant of the Garden of Eden?

On a winter evening in 1994, as my family ate dinner, the phone rang. It was my mother, Grandma Shoshana, calling excitedly: "My sense of smell has returned! It's like the Garden of Eden!" She rediscovered her sense of smell while preparing soup and adding spices. Astonishingly, this sense, which she lost in the dark days of Europe in 1944, miraculously returned to her, exactly fifty years later!

My mother lost her sense of smell while taking refuge in a basement beneath the apartment building where she grew up in Bratislava, Slovakia. The Germans were systematically rounding up Jews, searching every home. My uncle Simcha, a sort of Jewish James Bond, had the foresight to usher everyone from their beds into a cramped twenty-square-meter basement. There, the Singer and Steiner families, along with a few others, found shelter during the harsh winter months. The dire conditions – darkness, damp, and overcrowding – combined to impair the sense of smell of a sixteen-year-old girl.

---

1   Gershom Scholem, "*Valter Binyamin u'malacho*" [Walter Benjamin and his angel], *Od Davar* (Tel Aviv: Am Oved: 1989), 446.

Following my mother's call, I was telling my children about the basement hideout and what little I knew then of my mother's Holocaust stories when the phone rang again. It was my mother, her voice weak, saying, "Mordchelle, not all smells are pleasant…" For my mother, reencountering Eden through her regained sense of smell was a fleeting experience, lasting only a brief moment.

Kabbalistic texts propose that the sense of smell is the only sense that remained unscathed through the Flood and other historical tribulations, preserving its pristine state from Eden. This Eden, which my mother hinted at through her reference to smell, has accompanied my thoughts for many years. In my youth, it was a romantic, childlike idea – a lost Eden, a biblical myth seemingly distant from a child of Holocaust survivors. Yet in adulthood, I see this primeval tale as a narrative capable of lending a unique depth and meaning to our lives, our loved ones, and, by extension, to our broader human connections.

The forthcoming chapters will delve into our primal image, the memory of the Garden of Eden, possibly still imprinted within us. From this foundational perspective, we'll cast light on practical aspects of our world, which will be further developed in the rest of the book.

Ancient Folktales and the Jewish Story of Genesis

On a personal level, growing up in a warm, joyful home versus a somber one makes a significant difference. Did the child in that home receive the fundamental tools for self-acceptance? Was there space for dreaming, or merely the necessities for survival? These and similar questions profoundly influence our adult lives: without directly engaging with them, there is no room for healthy growth, hope, or change. The same principle applies on a national-cultural level: the creation story, with the Garden of Eden at its heart, is central to Jewish culture. The origin stories of humans across different cultures shape the lives of those who grow up under their influence. Myths are narratives about lofty matters, ancient deeds of gods and heroes. In various cultures, these stories elevate humanity beyond the everyday, taking readers into a realm beyond the ordinary.

For instance, *Enuma Elish*, the Babylonian creation story, has beautiful poetic elements, yet it is steeped in egotism, jealousy, deceit, and bloody wars.

The simple quest for good is sometimes entirely absent, and at other times, it flickers dimly at the fringes of consciousness. The gods behave as mortals, differentiated only by their stronger impulses and more brutal actions. The world is born out of conflict, humanity is created from blood, and Marduk rises to supremacy through strife over power and kingship.

In these myths, humanity does not enjoy a privileged status. Hesiod, the ancient Greek epic poet (eighth century BCE), fails to mention the creation of the human race, suggesting that, in his view, it was a minor, universally insignificant event. To Hesiod, humans are but a minor part of a larger system.

The Jewish creation narratives stand out in their stark contrast. A warm, nurturing tone pervades the Torah's stories, with humanity created "in the image of God" (Genesis 1) or from the Creator's "breath of life" (Genesis 2). These statements powerfully impact our understanding of human nature, the significance of our lives, and our responsibility in the world. In this perspective, both humans and the world are constantly evolving, with an ongoing invitation to grow at the core of human existence.[2]

A recurring phrase in Genesis 1 is "and God saw that it was good." The "good" here is not an ethical expression opposing evil. Instead, it reflects a Creator looking upon creation and affirming that the world is alive, vibrant, and full of potential and hope. The creation's goal is a life of meaningful existence. The blessing of fertility and growth at the end of Genesis 1 also centers around life.

In various ancient myths, humans are mere objects, not invited to assume responsibility or leadership. Fear dominates human consciousness. In contrast, the Jewish creation story in Genesis presents humans as subjects, principal actors. This is further emphasized and empowered in the second creation story: the story of the Garden of Eden.

---

2   "The myth is the foundation of religion. Throughout its history, it changes form and takes on new shapes, but it never ends. If it did, religion itself would cease to exist. When God loses His personal, individual, and unique essence, He ceases to be God. A consistent and radical philosophical interpretation will uproot religion from its foundation. Such a danger also arises from the opposite direction. Total materialization and concretization also contradict the myth and negate the essence of religion" (Yehuda Liebes, "Judaism and Myth" [in Hebrew], *Dimui* 14 [Winter 1997]: 6–15).

The Tree of Life in the Garden

Fundamental elements of the Eden story delve into the roots of human existence: the interdependence of creation's elements, the creation of humans from a unique combination of earthly soil and divine breath, the power of rivers and trees, and the abundance of material wealth and existential security. The narrative evolves to encompass themes of solitude and companionship, life and death, temptation, sin, and exile. These weave together to create a rich and unique portrayal of life. This depiction of life in the Garden of Eden can broaden our understanding of the potential for growth in our own lives. Engaging with these foundational elements on our life's journey can contribute to a life of quality and significance.[3]

If entering the garden signifies a specific consciousness, the Tree of Life within it represents the heart or essence. Just as our home can embody the qualities of the Garden of Eden, so may the parents' bedroom resemble the Tree within the garden – the core essence of the home. The *Zohar* views the Tree of Life as representing the essence and zest of life and considers not eating from it as the root of sin: hence, the verse states, "Of every tree of the garden you may freely eat." This refers to the Tree of Life, from which Adam was intended to eat first. His sin was not in eating from the Tree of Knowledge of Good and Evil.[4]

This interpretation suggests that Adam's fall was not due to eating from the Tree of Knowledge, but rather because he failed to eat first from the Tree of Life. The remedy for our world lies in striving to approach life outside Eden with the consciousness of the Tree of Life. To enter this consciousness of Eden with the Tree of Life at its center requires us to shed the familiar and the known. It demands a certain "nakedness" and profound honesty. In entering the garden, we also need to cultivate deep listening, a skill that will influence our ability for effective listening and our overall internal and interpersonal communication.

---

3   This attempt to seek a significant understanding of the foundations of the garden is very central in kabbalistic interpretation and is not characteristic of more rational commentators.

4   *Zohar*, Bereishit 1:771.

Entering garden consciousness necessitates a rejuvenation and expansion of our senses, enabling a transition from mere enjoyment to deeper pleasure. The trees are not simply metaphors for states of consciousness, but actual entities with their own distinct presence. For instance, when one tree's trunk is damaged, a branch may grow thicker to continue or even replace the injured trunk. Trees adapt to their surroundings while maintaining their distinctiveness. This uniqueness is also evident in the shade they cast. A tree in a dense rainforest grows its branches as high as possible, surpassing the shade of others, while an acacia tree spreads its branches wide to create shade for its roots, and in doing so, it offers shelter in the desert for both animals and humans. In discussing these symbolic trees, we consider aspects such as height, branch quality, and the nature of the shade they provide.

Above all stands the Tree of Life, offering guidance and life to "those who grasp onto it" (as in the words of the Jewish prayer [Prov. 3:18]) and find shelter in its shade. The biblical story of Eden concludes with Adam and Eve's expulsion. Jewish tradition views the first sin of Adam as a major oversight, a significant fracture in the initial innocence of humanity. On a conscious level, this act of eating is seen as the root of all sin in the world, and every movement of our lives can be seen as an attempt to rectify it. However, unlike some Christian perspectives, which view this act as the original sin that splits the world and creates existential guilt, the Jewish world seeks to reinvigorate this myth and these foundational images through a fascinating spiritual and cultural discourse: the dialogical dance among the trees of the garden.

Our current lives are lived outside of Eden. We exist in a world defined by knowledge of good and evil, filled with doubt, choice, and creativity. Our world has a profound awareness of these concepts. Free will, desire, and rectification, along with many other foundational ideas, are central in our post-Eden existence, emerging as a result of consuming the fruit of the Tree of Knowledge. Yet the original innocence experienced in the Garden of Eden lingers deep within human consciousness. It's responsible for the feelings of love, the need for security, the capacity for faith and trust. It also fosters hope and sometimes instills in us a yearning for a different kind of existence. Interestingly, some view this primordial quality as offering a richer form of life compared to our familiar world, heavily influenced as it is by the consequences of eating from the Tree of Knowledge.

The narrative of creating Eden and situating humanity within it has evolved into an elusive yearning for us, one that seems unattainable as a lifestyle. The aspiration to return to Eden has influenced numerous cultures and societies, including our contemporary era. Particularly in its inception during the 1960s and '70s, the Western New Age movement echoed a desire to discard the burdens of our existing world and revert to a state devoid of clothing, boundaries, or dualities. While well intentioned, this perspective carries a naive and occasionally oversimplified tone, especially considering the complex realities of our post–Tree of Knowledge world. Recognizing and accepting this reality is crucially significant.

In Jewish tradition, this concept is exemplified by the Sabbatean movement. It perceived itself as returning to an Eden-like existence, where there was no longer a need for laws in general or for adhering to commandments in particular. The Sabbateans posited that the time of redemption had arrived, thereby justifying a return to Eden, free from the constraints imposed upon humanity due to the expulsion.[5] Advocating for the reopening of Eden's gates, they proposed a world in which sexual prohibitions were obsolete, purportedly releasing women from Eve's curse and men from the encumbrances believed to have originated from the Tree of Knowledge of Good and Evil.

Jacob Frank (1726–1791) continued and expanded upon the Sabbatean movement. He was an extremely polarizing figure who attracted a large following. He considered himself the Messiah, bringing new life to the world and destroying the old order. He aimed to liberate the world from the laws of death, often declaring, "In the place we are heading to, there will be no laws, for laws are born of death, and we are connected to life." This sentiment hints clearly at the trees of the garden.[6]

A common thread between these Jewish movements and modern spiritual realms is the belief that God is immanent in humanity, implying that humans have innate intuitions about managing their lives. This was aptly expressed by one of Frank's disciples, Rabbi Nachman ben Samuel Halevi of Busk, who

---

5   See Moshe Attias, *Shirot u'tishbachot shel haShabta'im* (Tel Aviv: Dvir, 1948), 27–28.

6   A literary depiction of this period can be found in *The Books of Jacob* by Nobel Prize in Literature laureate Olga Tokarczuk (New York: Riverhead Books, 2022), 214.

told his wife Feigele: "We are now the chosen of God. God resides in us, and those in whom God resides are not bound by ordinary laws."[7]

Actually, the proximity of this book's ideas to certain movements demands a clear distinction: I argue that there is no return to the Garden of Eden. God's intent, as I see it, was for us to reflect on our eating from the Tree of Knowledge, to accept responsibility, and to rectify "the sin" through renewed work on a conscious relationship between the Tree of Knowledge and the Tree of Life.

In this process, we must confront and rectify evil at its root, but we cannot afford to ignore it. Part of taking responsibility for this new reality involves understanding that since the original consumption in the garden, the seeds of good and evil are embedded in each of us. Just as death is an inevitable part of life, so is the Tree of Knowledge integral to our existence. Recognizing these forces of evil, including the elements of destruction and void within us, paradoxically can lead us to a rejuvenation of life and a deeper understanding of its significance. The Tree of Knowledge is essential to our lives, and its presence cannot be overlooked.

We can broaden our understanding by embracing the wisdom of the Tree of Life, positioned at the garden's core, and integrating it into our complex reality, moving toward a kind of future Eden. This path does not disregard our current world, which is rich in knowledge, duality, ethics, and choice. Instead, it stems from recognizing our world's components, fostering a longing to reconnect with the primordial elements of the Garden of Eden. It's an exploration of an ancient state of being, seeking an eternal connection. Kabbalistic texts convey that the garden continuously sends a stream of enlightenment, *nahar orah*, to those yearning for new insights, enlightening their consciousness. It is believed that these individuals' souls ascend each night to the Garden of Eden for a unique learning experience.[8]

This perspective offers a unique invitation, based on a nuanced understanding: we must recognize and heal the reality of the Tree of Knowledge of Good and Evil, deeply embedded in our existence. From the ladder grounded

---

7   Ibid.

8   Rabbi Moses de Leon, *Sefer Shekel Hakodesh*, Sha'ar Shalosh Aharonot (Los Angeles: Hotzaat Keruv, 1996), 76.

on earth, amidst the reality of knowledge and its crucial role in our lives, the challenge involves rectifying the original transgression associated with this tree, but through the awareness of the Tree of Life. Our focus isn't on reverting to the locked-away Eden, but rather on advancing toward a mature and informed future, one that integrates all aspects of our reality.

A Future Eden – Second Innocence

The idea of a "second innocence" refers to a future vision that revisits the primal elements of Eden while navigating our complex adult reality. Innocence, often associated with the unblemished experience preceding the emergence of knowledge and decision making, is characterized by unadulterated curiosity, untarnished desire, and a sense of open, trusting wonder. This concept can be challenging, as it's typically linked to an earlier, seemingly irrelevant phase of life. At times, an innocent individual is perceived as immature or resistant to maturation. One of the most poignant traits of children is their inherent innocence – the curiosity, trust, and laughter that precede the rationality and decision-making complexities of adult life.

Yet innocence isn't confined primarily to childhood. Some states of consciousness are inherently innocent. Love, for instance, can encompass an element of innocence. Both emotional and physical vulnerability may embody a sense of innocence. Deep insights, moments of awe, experiences in nature – all these can tap into that primal experience. They share a common thread: a connection to an original, unadulterated, and pure essence.

However, as people mature, they often lose some of this innocence. They step into the complexities of life, face various choices, and grapple with duality and the unique creativity it inspires. There are positive elements of our maturation that stem from the partial loss of innocence. Can we, in our adult lives, touch upon these elements of innocence while still embracing maturity, rebellion, and dealing with old wounds? What remains in us of the fresh innocence we may have experienced in our childhoods?

The idea of "second innocence" does not imply a return to the naive innocence of childhood, before maturing. It signifies an evolved developmental phase, which could be described as "maturing beyond maturation." This occurs when an individual is sufficiently aware to recognize his or her own intellectual and emotional limits and is open to what lies beyond these confines.[9] Such a person is adept at accommodating contradictions and oppositions, thanks to a renewed consciousness.[10]

This ability to embrace deficits and fractures comes from the understanding that defects are an integral part of both the world and human existence. In this state of second innocence, people do not judge others for their flaws, recognizing that these same imperfections also exist within themselves, even if to a lesser extent. They can accept others and view them positively, as their comprehensive understanding of reality prevents them from fixating on the negative, allowing them to see the positives. In this phase, an individual encounters mature Tree of Life consciousness and ventures into the acutely aware world.

For the innocent of the first level, the world and life are mysterious due to the inability to comprehend the depths of things. The game of hide-and-seek is appealing to the first-level innocent, who approaches surprise and wonder with gratitude. In contrast, second-level innocents understand the world's complexity and humbly accept the unknown. They acknowledge that there are many things beyond their understanding.[11]

The concept of *oneg* (delight) is a unique sensory experience for the second-level innocent, as it involves recalling the journey of life, distinguishing between mere enjoyment and the deeper experience of delight.[12] This point is crucial, as it suggests that perhaps experiencing *oneg* requires maturity.

The notion of longing is sometimes linked to second innocence. Some yearn for what was, while others long for a future that opens a gateway in the heart to a second kind of innocence.

---

9   The concept of "second innocence" was coined by Akiva Ernst Simon and is one of the foundations of his thought. This concept outlines a state of consciousness in a mature person, enabling independent thinking without being deterred by general enlightenment. It is accompanied by a deep commitment to religious tradition but also the ability for intercultural dialogue. See *Ha'omnam od Yehudim anachnu* [Are we still Jews?] (Bnei Brak: Sifriyat Poalim, 1982), 137.

10 In *Sefer Habahir* (section 137), it is Jacob who is the innocent man who is able to integrate the qualities of his forefathers into his own life – *chesed* (loving-kindness) from Abraham and *gevurah* (strength) from Isaac.

11 I heard a similar idea from my dear friend and colleague Rabbi Ya'akov Nagan.

12 Still, the question of *oneg* in first-level innocence remains open for discussion, learning, and experimentation.

Be a Blessing

John Lennon's famous song "Imagine" invites listeners to envision a different world, one without borders, possessions, or even the concept of heaven. It seeks a return to an Eden-like state. Lennon's beautiful melody elevates us to a higher level of innocence, imagining a future Eden that can be experienced in small ways within our limited world, gradually expanding it. The Tree of Life in Torah is expressed through identifying islands of blessing in our lives. The Sabbath, the sabbatical year, relationships, family, interactions with others, and even a proper understanding of redemption are all fragments of life that can serve as a foundation for us to imagine and dream about expanding the domain of "blessed life" in our existence.

Chapter 2

Paradise and the Garden of Eden

The term *paradise* evokes a sense of leisure, calm, and simplicity in popular culture. It's a common name for holiday resorts, reflecting a universal desire for sunshine and peace. The Garden of Eden that we are exploring, however, is not a paradise in this sense. Rather, it is a biblical narrative offering a distinct perspective on quality of life. While "paradise" often implies pleasure and enjoyment, the Garden of Eden experience is better captured by the notion of *oneg* (delight).

A Place of Delight and Innocence

The Garden of Eden story appears in the second chapter of Genesis, presenting a creation tale that is markedly different from the one in chapter 1. Chapter 1 portrays a world brought into existence through divine speech – a world that is well planned and orderly. The climax of this creation is the formation of human beings in God's image, both male and female, created equally, through a single divine statement and initial thought. This portrayal of creation is linear, marked by an exemplary order.

In Genesis chapter 2, the story of creation is vividly reimagined. Unlike the first chapter's linear and orderly account, this narrative seems to evolve spontaneously, filled with elements of surprise and wonder. The garden, its inhabitants, and even the Creator appear to be discovering and marveling at this new world, learning and sometimes erring along the way.

The thirteenth-century description of life in the Garden of Eden offers a delightful vision: "It was a place designated for *oneg* and will. Its sustenance came from the garden's trees, with waters flowing from the rivers of Eden. The garden's inhabitant was clad in clouds of glory, living completely in immense and great delight…" (Rabbeinu Bachya, Gen. 2:7).

This portrayal speaks of a life rich in leisure, material and emotional prosperity, and personal security, with vast and overwhelming joy.

Similarly, the biblical narrative of the Garden of Eden conjures up a picture of a stable and nurturing environment. Flowing rivers, wondrous trees, and all kinds of nutritious comestibles are readily available for consumption. The presence of God's spirit moves throughout the garden, providing a sense of omnipresent security and comfort.

Living in a world outside the Garden of Eden, it is often difficult for us to comprehend the quality of life that existed within it. To truly understand and feel the essence of life in the garden, we need to approach it with less judgment and choice, allowing the primal elements within us to surface. The Garden of Eden presents images that touch on fundamental questions of our lives – hence the importance of reading them correctly.

A. D. Gordon,[1] addressing a friend in Europe who undervalued the Torah compared to the literary masterpieces of his time, wrote: "Therefore, we do not understand the revealed Torah as it is now. We think that by interpreting it with new ideas formed during our exile, we are elucidating it. But in truth, the opposite is the case – the revealed Torah is actually an interpretation of the hidden Torah within our soul."[2]

These insights, applicable to the entire Bible, are especially relevant to its foundational story, the Garden of Eden. The garden and its imagery are deeply embedded in our souls. Practices such as immersion, solitude, meditation, and love can unlock the ancient memories of our existence in Eden, offering a brief respite from the shackles of knowledge. The journey to the garden is fraught with "the flaming sword which turned every way" (Gen. 3:24), amplifying our innermost fears.

Reflecting deeply on the biblical portrayal of life in Eden can provide answers to crucial questions: What truly nourishes and revives us, and what

---

1 Aaron David Gordon (1856–1922) was a secular Labor Zionist thinker and the spiritual force behind practical Zionism and Labor Zionism. He had a unique relationship with the Bible and Kabbalah.

2 "*Michtavim me'Eretz Yisrael*" [Letters from the Land of Israel], *Kitvei A. D. Gordon* [Collected writings of A. D. Gordon], vol. 2 (Petach Tikva: Hapoel Hatzair, 1930), 364.

causes our soul to wither? These are questions that lie at the core of our consciousness. From the garden's initial innocence, what can we retain in our consciousness as we strive toward a renewed innocence in our lives?

In the following pages, we'll delve into key verses from the second account of creation, before Adam ate from the Tree of Knowledge. We'll attempt to sense the quality of life in the garden and to delineate an existential picture emerging from these verses. In some sections, I've added some questions, inviting the reader to personally connect with the imagery, nuances, and quality of life in the garden.

Elements of Eden

Interdependence and Mutual Responsibility

> No plant of the field was yet in the earth and no herb of the field had yet sprung up; for the Lord God had not caused it to rain on the earth, and there was no man to till the ground; but there went up a mist from the earth and watered the whole face of the ground. (Gen. 2:5–6)

The Garden of Eden was established from a world woven with interdependencies. Plants and herbs in the field depended on rain and human labor. Humans relied on the land and divine rainfall, and later on, man required a companion, a woman. Even the woman, feeling isolated, turned to the serpent for company.

Here we find a narrative about incomplete systems, in which each part hinges on another, necessitating relationships for actualization and survival. This interconnectedness might be the earliest notion of mutual responsibility. In this context, mutual responsibility isn't merely an ethical principle, but a fundamental, natural essence embedded within the world's framework. A person attuned to interconnectedness experiences mutual responsibility as an intrinsic aspect of human identity, inseparably intertwined with the fabric of society.

From this perspective emerges a fundamental and significant point: without the components of creation engaging in reciprocal relationships and connecting with each other, creation itself cannot materialize. Can we construct a world with strong interdependency that is neither constricting nor fostering infantile reliance? This question touches on life across the spectrum – in matters of partnership, honoring parents, relating to the vulnerable, and in community relationships, where responsibility and need must not lead to dependency and loss of individuality. These foundational questions will be expanded upon throughout the chapters of this book.

The Complexity of Human Composition

> Then the Lord God formed man of the dust of the ground, and breathed into his nostrils the breath of life; and man became a living soul. (Gen. 2:7)

The first man in Genesis is composed of two contrasting entities: the dust of the earth and the breath of life breathed into him by God. As Kabbalists have put it, "He who breathes breathes of His own."[3] Dust represents the static, the absence of life, while the breath of life is an expression of divine vitality, imbued with powerful life force, inviting humanity to creativity and vitality. The soul transcends time, embodying eternality, in stark contrast to the earthly aspect of dust that signifies the finitude of our mortality.

God represents the timeless soul, while the primordial serpent emerges from the earth, symbolizing the agent of mortality.

When during our day are we connected to the soul's elements that give us life, and when to the earthly elements that lead to our death? What does reality look like when we are a "living soul"?

Life in the Garden as Humanity's Purpose

> And the Lord God planted a garden eastward in Eden; and there He put the man whom He had formed. (Gen. 2:8)

---

3   The first source to my knowledge that states this idea, albeit in different words, is Nachmanides on Genesis 2:7: "He who breathes into another's nostrils imparts from his own spirit into him." Interestingly, the Ramak (Rabbi Moses Cordovero) in *Shiur Komah* (chapter 51) also gives this idea, citing the Sages. He writes: "He who breathes breathes from his own essence."

Adam was created outside the garden and placed within it.[4] He carries memories from the earth and the previous world, where he was formed and to which he and Eve are exiled following their sin. However, life in the garden represents the Creator's hope for humanity. The very act of living there is intended to instill in humanity a consciousness of full life, manifesting the full potential of our stature.

Do we recognize an area in our lives that is akin to the Garden of Eden? Is God present for us in such a place? Do we give our heart to transitions and feelings in our lives, distinguishing between life outside the garden and entering it?

The Tree of Life in the Garden

> And out of the ground the Lord God made to grow every tree that is pleasant to the sight and good for food; the Tree of Life also in the midst of the garden, and the Tree of Knowledge of Good and Evil. (Gen. 2:9)

The Tree of Life "in the midst of the garden" – at its very center – symbolizes the innermost point, the heart that animates the entire garden. In the literature of the commentators, the Tree of Life assumes the role of a cosmic tree, representing human existence.[5] In kabbalistic texts, it acquires a distinct mythical dimension, portrayed as a tree upon which all human existence depends and from which it draws sustenance.[6]

The relationship between the garden and the tree at its center can be likened to that between the external world and our inner being. Sometimes, this relationship mirrors the contrast between our environment – the greater world – and our private home. At other times, it reflects the relationship between the rooms of our home (the Garden of Eden), seeking to instill security and abundance for the inhabitants, and the parents' bedroom (the Tree of Life within the garden), representing the core of the home, the potential for creating life, the place of intimate communication that enlivens the entire home/Garden. (Chapter 11 will explore how the consciousness of the Tree of

---

4   In Jewish culture, Adam represents a microcosm of all humanity. See *Sanhedrin* 37a.

5   *Midrash Genesis Rabbah* 15:6.

6   *Sefer Habahir* 2:22.

Life in the garden can support the marital journey as a fruitful endeavor that endures throughout life.)

What is the Tree of Life that pulsates at the heart of our existence? In our bodies? In our homes? In our land?

The River and Life

> And a river went out of Eden to water the garden; and from thence it was parted, and became four heads. (Gen. 2:10)

The river, as the garden's lifeblood, carries living waters that quench every part of it. Emerging from Eden, the river symbolizes both physical and conscious security. Its perpetual flow signifies a dynamic present, constantly renewing. Those connected to this river are connected to a life of fluidity and evolution, immersed in a sense of existential abundance. The *Zohar* poetically describes it: "Behold, the river is everlasting, encompassing all, for it is everything."[7]

Beyond its physical aspects, the river also embodies clarity of consciousness. The Hebrew word for river, *nahar*, parallels the Aramaic *nahara*, meaning light or illumination. It represents a synergy of endless abundance and lucid thought, weaving together material wealth and mental clarity. In chapter 8, we explore the mindset of this flowing abundance. Chapter 10 delves into an economy driven by a consciousness of abundance, contrasting it with the dominant economic mindset rooted in the dichotomy of good and evil.

The flow of these waters into the Garden invites a reflective question:

What sustains us in our lives? What sources of abundance irrigate our personal Garden of Eden?[8]

Worthy Work

> And the Lord God took the man and put him into the Garden of Eden to work it and to guard it. (Gen. 2:15)

---

7   *Zohar Chadash* 2:141:2.

8   The garden can also be a woman, as in the Song of Songs (e.g., "I am come into my garden, my sister, my bride" [5:1]), and this image will connect the foundational verses of the garden to the concept of relationships, later in this book.

Man's sole task in the Garden of Eden was to work and guard it. The description of the post-sin punishment, "In the sweat of your face shall you eat bread" (Gen. 3:19), suggests that the work in the garden was effortless. Adam, the first man, walked among the trees as if in a bountiful market, freely picking any fruit he desired.

This work in the garden was not instrumental. It is similar to the satisfaction derived from volunteering, or a unique work environment in which the work itself imparts a sense of purpose and meaning, unrelated to compensation. If slavery in Egypt represents the ultimate degrading labor that turn humans into objects, then the work in Eden symbolizes an immediate connection between humans, their surroundings, and the life-giving sources. The terms *work* and *slavery* can thus signify both the height of enslavement and the pinnacle of joyous devotion.[9]

In chapter 8, I will discuss the intersection points between the concept of the Tree of Life, as proposed here, and fascinating research currently being conducted in the field of positive psychology. I will share a dialogue I had with Professor Martin Seligman, one of the leading researchers in the field.

Where in life do we find enjoyable work? Can we, in the familiar world of employee-employer relationships, create human connections so that all workers feel seen and experience a sense of purpose and meaning?

Eating and the Tree of Life

> But of the Tree of Knowledge of Good and Evil, you will not eat of it; for on the day that you eat thereof, you will surely die. (Gen. 2:17)

Eating holds a central place in the life of the garden. Man is instructed to eat from the trees, but he disobeys and consumes the fruit of the forbidden tree. The curse and punishment center on eating, and even the expulsion from Eden aims to prevent eating from the Tree of Life. Eating involves nourishment and dependency, fulfilling a basic need for survival. Beyond this need,

---

9   See also the *piyyut* "Yedid Nefesh": "Bring Your servant close to Your will. Your servant will run like a gazelle." This is an example of the positive, desired aspect of servitude.

food also offers taste, appearance, and scent, creating a sensual experience. The phrase "you will freely eat" (Gen. 2:16) suggests continual nourishment without scarcity.

If the first man had eaten first from the Tree of Life, all our eating would have been tied to the element of *oneg* (delight); instead, he ate from the Tree of Knowledge, eating that is motivated by enjoyment and dependency.

The concept of food in the spirit of the Tree of Life can add a new dimension to blessings over food, inviting us to be more mindful of what we consume. Chapter 13 in the book will be dedicated to exploring eating from this perspective.

Where can we feel food as an experience akin to the Tree of Life in Eden? What is the relationship between food as a necessity and food as a source of oneg?

Death and Life

> But of the Tree of the Knowledge of Good and Evil, you will not eat of it; for on the day that you eat thereof, you will surely die. (Gen. 2:17)

Eating from the Tree of Knowledge intensified humanity's fear of death, a fear that subtly and overtly influences many aspects of our lives. While the original Tree of Life in Eden promised immortality, the concept of the Tree of Life's consciousness offers aid in confronting the fear of death. Modern society extensively endeavors to fend off death, with a plethora of products and techniques aimed at delaying aging and the inevitable decline of health. However, Tree of Life consciousness suggests a radically different method of dealing with death.

In chapter 15, we will delve into death and the fears accompanying it, and we will see how the Tree of Life consciousness proposed here might somewhat ease the fear of death that governs many aspects of our lives.

What are the Trees of Life of our world, under whose shade the awareness of death is alleviated?

Paradise and the Garden of Eden

Solitude and Loneliness

"It is not good for the man to be alone." (Gen. 2:18)

Contrary to the creation story in the first chapter of Gensis, in which "male and female He created them" (Gen. 1:27), in the story of the Garden of Eden, Adam's partner was created at a later stage. It seems that God wants us to learn to be fulfilled on our own – to experience the possibility of Eden in life – before establishing a relationship with a partner.

However, this creates a paradox. What was the problem with Adam's solitude? If a person is fulfilled by his own essence, why does he need a woman? And accordingly, what is the role of a "helper opposite him" (the *ezer kenegdo* or "helpmeet" of Genesis 2:18) in a world in which a person is fulfilled from his own inner wellspring?

The issue of partnership in our world undergoes new transformations every morning. The relationship between solitude and partnership is one of the fundamental issues of human existence. In chapter 11 of the book, we will discuss this vital issue.

"This Time" – The First Woman

And the man said: "This is now bone of my bones, and flesh of my flesh; she will be called Woman, because she was taken out of Man." (Gen. 2:23)

The woman (*ishah*) was created from Adam's rib. The Bible does not describe any conversation between Adam and Eve, just as Adam does not converse with his own body parts. The existence of the woman allows Adam to become "man" (*ish*), where the woman is like a mirror reflecting himself to him, and he does not see her as a separate entity. This will only change later in the story, after the sin, with the advent of consciousness, duality, and the renaming of the woman as Eve – mother of all living beings. Her being a mother significantly differentiates her from Adam. Perhaps in the garden, there is no childbirth at all, only a very personal experience between Adam and Eve, an intimacy of a unique character. In chapter 11, we will discuss these questions and explore practical tools for deepening couple communication in our world.

Why was the first woman created specifically from the body of man? Can we, in our world where a couple's relationship is built from different family origins, imagine and feel the original concept of "this is now bone of my bones"?

The Snake and Temptation

> And the serpent was more cunning than any beast of the field which the Lord God had made. And he said to the woman, "Yea, hath God said, Ye will not eat of every tree of the garden?" (Gen. 3:1)

Temptation is possible when there is a feeling of lack, which the temptation is supposed to fill. Perhaps the woman sought a purpose beyond being her man's "helpmeet opposite him"? She was created in a context and seeks connection. Only through the woman, the one open to connection, could the serpent reach Adam.

The serpent comes from the dust of the earth, in contrast to God, Who is the root of life in life. There is an existential chasm between the serpent and God. The serpent speaks to the woman, and through her to Adam, in the hope that he will eat from the Tree of Knowledge and discover his individuality, separate from the God of the garden.

Many Chasidic teachings are dedicated to the connection between "serpent" and "messiah," which share the same gematria (numerical value in Hebrew). It seems that on the path of the Tree of Life, we must understand the secret of the serpent as an entity that intends to redeem ourselves, and therefore we need not fear touching the places it represents. In chapters 16–17, we will address man's confrontation with his "vulnerability" as a vital tool for a full life in the shadow of the Tree of Life.

When do we have the ability to be tempted? What is the "serpent" in our lives – those impulses that prevent us from touching the Tree of Life and draw us to know good and evil?

Paradise and the Garden of Eden

Guarding the Path of the Tree of Life

> And the Lord God said: "Behold, the man is become as one of us, to know good and evil; and now, lest he put forth his hand, and take also of the tree of life, and eat, and live for ever." Therefore the Lord God sent him forth from the garden of Eden, to till the ground from whence he was taken. So He drove out the man; and He placed at the east of the Garden of Eden the cherubim, and the flaming sword which turned every way, to keep the way of the tree of life. (Gen. 3:22–24)

The Tree of Life remains behind the flaming, turning sword. However, God's gift to man is that the Tree of Life has "branches" in our world after the forbidden eating. These exist in the dimensions of time, space, interpersonal speech, food, and relationships. Identifying these places in our conscious and dual world and connecting to them can develop in us the taste of a unique quality of life that existed in the garden, where the Tree of Life was central. This taste is derived from giving deep meaning to our personal and societal existence – critical areas for developing a life of *ve'heyeh berachah*, or blessing consciousness.

The intention here is not utopias far off in the heavens, but for a possible reality here on Earth. A profound change in our relationship to money and wealth, to the quality of our speech and listening, and in our interpersonal relationships may point the way toward a future Garden of Eden, which can be touched in our world.

"To keep the way of the Tree of Life," as mentioned in the Bible as a warning not to return to the garden, is understood here as an invitation to personal growth and to create a life vision for Jewish and human existence in our world.

Chapter 3

Life after the Fall

The expulsion from the Garden of Eden marks the dawn of a new era in human history. The first couple, banished from the garden, faced the barrier of the flaming sword, which blocked their return. The garden symbolized a world of security and harmony, abundant with fruit trees and a nourishing river, characterized by unique marital intimacy and the presence of God "in the cool of the day" (Gen. 3:8). This was a world without the knowledge of good and evil, devoid of duality and judgment.

Twenty generations passed from this exile until God's call to Abraham, "*Lech lecha*" (Go forth; Gen. 12:1) to an unknown land. This call emerged from a deep disappointment with human conduct in the created world, prompting God to ask Abraham and his descendants to establish a new human model to serve as an example for the entire world. This "pilot program" of Abraham's descendants continues to this very day.

Throughout the generations leading up to Abraham, we witness fascinating life experiments on our earth, outside the garden. Despite the fact that these experiments ultimately ended in failure, understanding them is crucial, as they provide insight into the world outside the Garden of Eden, a world living under the shadow of the Tree of Knowledge. These stories are in the background of the rectification that God asks Abraham and his descendants to bring into the world, expressed in the mission of blessing consciousness.

This chapter will explore these stories, delving into their nuances and the human arenas in which they occurred. We will try to comprehend what was hoped for, what failed, and what our current story aims to rectify. Like other foundational tales, these stories reflect our vulnerabilities and humanity, making them significantly relevant to all of us. Each of us might find a part of ourselves within them.

Three of the four stories revolve around relationships that are foundational to the concept of family. The first story concerns siblings, the second explores male-female dynamics, and the third delves into parent-child relationships. Indeed, the centrality of family, in all its aspects, forms a cornerstone of our purpose and existence – "to be a blessing". Discussions about what it means to be a "blessed family" are important and vital in our era, as the institution of the family evolves with new interpretations and expansions.

The final story, the Tower of Babel, deals with a productive society attempting to create a unique start-up. These stories touch upon fundamental questions of our lives in this era.

The Brothers' Blessing as a Basis for Fraternal Love

The first story occurring outside the Garden of Eden is a tale about brothers, ending in fraternal conflict and the murder of the younger brother, Abel. What is so significant about this primordial story?

The bonds between brothers and sisters in a family are typically the longest relationships in an individual's life, starting from birth and often extending well past the parents' demise and old age. This relationship dynamic is intricate, varying over different life stages and uniquely experienced by each sibling. Several factors, including individual personality, childhood experiences, each sibling's position in the family, the family's composition (sons/daughters, age gaps), and especially the parents' role, significantly influence the nature of sibling relationships. The values instilled at home, the extent of parental involvement in their children's interrelations, and their approach to parenting are immensely impactful in shaping the fabric of sibling bonds.

The comparison between sibling dynamics and intimate relationships is intriguing. In a traditional marriage or companionship, the central question is how to connect two individuals from different backgrounds into one home. The very terms *man* and *woman* embody the aspiration for connection and unity. In contrast, sibling stories often start with a common origin and parentage but diverge into separate life paths. The natural trajectory of siblings is parallel lines that don't necessarily intersect – almost the opposite of a marital journey.

Mutual responsibility, fraternal love, and the ability of siblings to create an open encounter between themselves are not automatic. There are often significant differences among siblings: birth order, varying levels of success, self-image differences, and possible parental favoritism, to name a few. The challenge lies in recognizing the uniqueness and separateness of each sibling while maintaining their bond. Where the hope for intimacy characterizes romantic and marital relationships, solidarity should define sibling relationships. It's important not to confuse these concepts – intimacy and solidarity.

The story of Cain and Abel opened the gates of hope for a healthy and proper meeting between brothers, as an expression and symbol of human brotherhood on a societal level.[1] But this hope was unfulfilled, and it ended in bloodshed.

The Birthright as a Blessing

Cain, as the archetypal elder brother, receives a significant name. Continuing his father's tradition but differing from his shepherd brother, he works the soil outside the garden. The name Cain in Hebrew is connected to the word *kinyan*, or ownership. Perhaps Abel, in choosing a new profession, was already aware of the economic importance given to the firstborn, who traditionally received a larger inheritance in ancient culture. Cain, as the firstborn, is burdened with extra responsibility.

Where does this consciousness of the firstborn as a source of responsibility originate? In the language of blessing, it comes from the understanding that the firstborn, with all his strength and sense of primacy, must see himself as a conduit. Being the first fruit of his father invites him to serve as a messenger and a vessel for transmitting the previous generation's abundance, rather than adopting a position of power and control. Perhaps this is the simple idea behind the redemption of the firstborn, inherently linked to God due to the firstborn's primacy. This understanding turns the firstborn status into a blessing. The firstborn role is an invitation to work properly with the gift of abundance that it entails.

---

1   There is a gap between the centrality of siblings in our emotional lives and the limited attention they receive in psychological literature and in individual therapy.

If Cain had connected with the Tree of Life consciousness and seen the blessing in his firstborn status, he could have corrected his father's sin of eating from the Tree of Knowledge. He would not have been perturbed by God's preference for Abel's offering. Someone connected to the Tree of Life feels fulfillment from his or her role and is therefore less influenced by the external world.

The story intensifies when God asks Cain, "Where is Abel your brother?" Cain's response – "Am I my brother's keeper?" – is pivotal. God tried to expand Cain's awareness before the murder, but Cain did not absorb the message. Afterwards, God invited Cain to take responsibility for the murder. Had Cain done so, the human story might have changed. In both opportunities given to him, before and after the murder, Cain showed a lack of appreciation for blessing in relation to property, responsibility, and admitting mistakes.[2] Thus, from Cain, no blessing could develop for the continuation of human existence.

If the concept of social alliance is rooted in sibling relationships, then in a blessed society, the "other" is your brother, whom you are obligated to protect. The Torah answers the question "Am I my brother's keeper?" unequivocally: yes! Protecting your brother is fundamental to your existence.[3]

Sons of Elohim – Daughters of Man

The second story deals with the relationships between men and women.

> And it came to pass when men began to multiply on the face of the earth, and daughters were born to them, that the sons of Elohim saw the daughters of men that they were fair, and they took them wives, whomsoever they chose. And the Lord said: "My

---

2 For further exploration of the concepts of admitting mistakes and the foundation of blessing, see chapter 13, on repentance, and chapter 15, on lack and the Tree of Life.

3 For example, "Do not take from him interest or profit, but fear your God, and let your brother live with you" (Lev. 25:36); "When your brother, a Hebrew man or a Hebrew woman, is sold to you" (Deut. 15:12); "And I cut asunder mine other staff, even bands, that I might break the brotherhood between Judah and Israel" (Zech. 11:14); "You shall not abhor an Edomite, for he is your brother" (Deut. 23:8). "If two were traveling in a desolate place...and one of them dies, his companion does not inherit him. But if he was treating him as a brother, his companion inherits him" (Tosefta, *Bava Batra* 8:2).

spirit will not abide in man forever, for that he also is flesh; therefore will his days be a hundred and twenty years." (Gen. 6:1–3)

Many have pondered the question of the identity of the "sons of Elohim" and
the "daughters of men." It's difficult to settle on a single interpretation, as
Elohim is understood in some contexts as a name for God.[4]

Rashi provides a straightforward understanding: "sons of Elohim" refers
to "the princes and judges." According to this interpretation, the "sons of
Elohim" are earthly men, leaders with power and influence.[5] They misused
their power by taking women by force, "whomsoever they choose" – without
regard for their condition, and above all, without their consent.

God initially sought to place His spirit to dwell within man. In the creation
of the Garden of Eden, He envisioned a unique template for life, establishing
within it the means for man to work with this divine essence, in harmony
with the various facets of existence. This, of course, includes man's relationship with woman. God intended for man to recognize woman separately, to
respect her in the most fundamental sense.

In other words, it was specifically in the creation of woman as a partner to
man that the challenge emerged to see her as distinct from him, possessing
her own separate identity. The troubling behavior of the sons of Elohim, who
exploited the daughters of men, led the Creator to shorten human lifespans
from 500 to 120 years. Perhaps this limitation and the proximity of mortality
would awaken men to use their power and masculinity responsibly.

On a spiritual level, the sons of Elohim seek eternal life, symbolically represented by the Tree of Life in the garden. They recognize that they cannot
return to the garden and thus seek alternative ways to confront death and the

---

4   The influence of mythology can be observed from two angles in this narrative. On one
     hand, there's a subtle reference to the myth of divine offspring (a polytheistic theme) and
     a link to mythological tales in which gods marry human women. On the other hand,
     there's a demythologization happening here: these are lesser divine beings acting without
     the knowledge of the supreme God. Unlike traditional mythology, the resulting offspring
     are mortal humans who do not gain eternal life. In essence, this story results in shortening
     the human lifespan.

5   Similarly, in the Midrash: "And the sons of Elohim saw – what were the judges doing?
     They would take women from the marketplace and make them suffer. If this is what the
     judges were doing, all the more so the common people" (*Sifrei*, Bamidbar 11:6).

awareness of mortality, which became evident in their lives after eating from the Tree of Knowledge. Perhaps at the root of this desire for eternal life lies a quest for identity and existence inherent to manhood.

The masculine seed, with its infinite potential for life, is an expression of masculinity and the perpetual movement of life within it. In contrast, women encounter "small deaths" in their lives through the cycles of menstruation and birth. These experiences allow women to intimately recognize the realm of death more completely. The actions of the sons of Elohim can be interpreted as a manifestation of a certain masculine nature. However, this is not the nature that the Creator intended when He bestowed the breath of life upon humanity. These fundamental elements represent a call for unique consciousness when harnessing masculine life forces – a call to work on the connection between abundant sexuality and conscious intimacy.

The word *good* used to describe the daughters of man may indeed imply their physical beauty. The pursuit of beauty and aesthetics provides a sense of holding onto life, a conscious illusion that distances us from death and fosters a feeling of eternal life. As long as the appreciation of beauty remains a pure value untainted by the possessive urge, it retains its purity and precision. Thus, the appreciation of beauty can be a shared experience among many without the need for ownership and the imposition of a personal stamp.

It is the attempt to capture and possess it that corrupts the sons of Elohim in the eyes of the Divine. This is not how humans are meant to confront desire and the primal fear of death. Surely, in the creation of woman, the Creator did not intend for this kind of relationship.

This pursuit of possession regarding the daughters of man does not truly address the challenge of embracing life and facing the fear of death.

Why? Because this action does not engage the human spirit; it is not connected to the "soul of life," which is the only genuine means of confronting the fear of death with strength, recognizing that the soul is eternal.

The sons of Elohim believed that by satisfying their desire for possession, they could connect to the Tree of Life, gaining the ability to break free from the fear of death. However, through their actions, they became entangled in the thorns of the Tree of Knowledge – and they feared death.

This significant narrative symbolizes the beginning of men using women as objects. The sons of Elohim present a strong and dominant paradigm of the perception of women in our world.

When God said, "It is not good for man to be alone," He meant that a man and a woman would bring about a new kind of "good," with a unique sense indicated by "this time, bone of my bones" (Gen. 2:23). The intention was a special intimacy in which the experience of one flesh could lead a person to the Tree of Life, transcending loneliness and fear.

The inability to see women as subjects rather than objects is a "primeval sin" that exists not only in romantic relationships but has implications beyond gender relations. Any exploitation of power, the objectification of others, siphons its strength from this deep-seated narrative. Consequently, the story of the sons of Elohim and the daughters of men, beyond the realm of relationships between men and women, symbolizes workplaces, power structures, and any place where it is possible to transform a person into an object.

The specific command given to Abraham of *ve'heyeh berachah* was meant to rectify the deep-rooted sin of the sons of Elohim. If sibling relationships are the key to fostering bonds and brotherhood on a societal level, then romantic relationships are the key to seeing the face of the other, often in a more intimate way, as a subject, as a separate living being, with independent will and desires.

The actions of the sons of Elohim tilted the balance against the Creator's plan for His creation.

> And the Lord saw that the wickedness of man was great in the earth, and that every imagination of the thoughts of his heart was only evil continually. And it repented the Lord that He had made man on the earth, and it grieved Him at His heart. And the Lord said: 'I will blot out man whom I have created from the face of the earth; both man, and beast, and creeping thing, and fowl of the air; for it repenteth Me that I have made them.' But Noah found grace in the eyes of the Lord. (Gen. 6:5–8)

Here, we encounter verses that reveal the Creator's deep emotions of heartache and regret. We are confronted with a dimension that touches upon divinity. The expulsion of humanity from the Garden of Eden and the separation from the Tree of Life did not lead to a "good" world in terms of enhanced life, healthy relationships, genuine intimacy, and a sense of unity. The delicate balance between the Creator's "soul of life" and the "dust from the earth," the foundational elements from which humans were created, appears disrupted.

Living in the shadow of the Tree of Knowledge of Good and Evil fails to allow for proper existence. Despite freedom of choice and the ability to distinguish between good and evil, Cain and the sons of Elohim allow themselves to be activated by the fundamental aspects of our spiritual and primal nature that are akin to "dust."

Noah and His Sons after the Flood

The third story deals with parent-child relationships. Immediately after exiting the Ark, with hope for a fresh start, Noah planted a vineyard, got drunk, and exposed himself. Noah cultivated grapes and sought to create wine, an entirely human cultural endeavor, not part of natural creation. Perhaps Noah wanted to relieve himself of some of the responsibility imposed by the "knowledge of good and evil" that was imposed upon him after leaving the Ark.[6] By drinking wine, he may have aimed to return to the innocence and the illusion of lack of responsibility that he experienced in the pre-knowledge Garden of Eden.

> And he drank of the wine, and was drunken; and he was uncovered within his tent. And Ham, the father of Canaan, saw the nakedness of his father, and told his two brethren without. And Shem and Japheth took a garment, and laid it upon both their shoulders, and went backward, and covered the nakedness of their father; and their faces were backward, and they saw not their father's nakedness. And Noah awoke from his wine, and knew what his younger son had done to him. (Gen. 9:21–24)

Noah revealed himself to his sons, reminiscent of the Garden of Eden. Wine can lighten the burden of life and the curse of the land and can even bring

---

6   Noah is responsible for "restarting" creation, focusing on the strict prohibition against murder, permission to eat meat, and the commandment to procreate.

joy to the human heart. It can also reveal inner secrets, touching the soul's core, seeking honesty and personal integrity.[7] For Noah, drinking wine led to physical exposure without revealing any meaningful secret. This embarrassing situation resulted in a lack of boundaries in his son Ham's behavior.

The three sons are the forefathers of post-Flood civilization. "These three were the sons of Noah, and of these was the whole earth overspread" (Gen. 9:18). The verse adds an important note: "And the sons of Noah that went forth from the Ark were Shem, and Ham, and Japheth; and Ham is the father of Canaan" (Gen. 9:18), Canaan representing a wicked society lacking moral boundaries.

Ham observes his father's nakedness and then shares what he saw with his brothers. This act may represent an inappropriate intrusion into Noah's private space. After this intrusion, Ham "sells" it by telling his brothers. The narrative suggests that Ham's actions, whether they involved physical contact (as the Sages determined)[8] or just looking, were problematic due to a lack of respect and the crossing of boundaries. By focusing on the physical aspect of his father, Ham reduces the parent-child relationship to mere biological connection, ignoring the broader and richer aspects of parenting that include education and intergenerational transmission. This incident, starting with Noah's lack of boundaries and exacerbated by Ham's actions, damages the delicate intergenerational dynamics.

This story, the first in the Torah to delve into parent-child relationships bordering on physical or emotional impropriety, presents Noah, the righteous man who preserved life in the Ark, as failing to provide an educational model for his descendants on how to continue the world order. This third narrative highlights the complexity of the value of "honoring one's parents" and the challenges in intergenerational communication. Like the previous failure stories, this foundational story is not just about Noah and his sons; it symbolizes humanity's struggle to transmit traditions and life quality from one generation to the next.

---

7   On the Jewish holiday of Purim, we celebrate by drinking wine to the point of intoxication.

8   Some say that he castrated his father, and others say that he sexually assaulted him (*Sanhedrin* 70a).

Similar trends are evident in the Western world and postmodernist principles. Intergenerational transfer capabilities are dwindling. Blending tradition with innovation, a great life skill, emerges as a highly complex art, often accompanied by pessimism and a sense of failure. The concept of boundaries between children and parents is undergoing significant changes today. On one hand, in Western society, we see an increasing disconnect as children leave home post–high school to start life as adults, weakening ties with their parents and sometimes limiting interactions to shared meals during holidays. The concept of honoring parents is fading in the modern world, as children seek to discover their separate identities, somewhat detached from past generations.

On the other hand, we often see an opposite scenario where parents seek to be their children's best friends, sometimes reliving their own painful childhood through them. These parents strive to be ever-present, not allowing the healthy detachment necessary for their children's growth. They fail to realize that our children are entrusted to us, not owned by us. Parenthood, too, should connect with being a conduit of abundance.

Balancing the release of children to live their lives and build their families, with the commandment of honoring parents, is key to creating a blessed family. This correction of Noah's story and his sons is manifested in a proper understanding of the parental role and children's ability to respect their parents, representing a healthy intergenerational transfer. This rectification, beginning with Abraham and his family, continues to this day.

Upon exiting the Garden of Eden, we encountered three family-related stories: the first about sibling relationships, followed by the essence of the couple relationship between man and woman, and the last dealing with parent-child dynamics. It appears that almost everyone experiences pain in at least one of these family areas.

The ability to be responsible among siblings, to regard a woman as an independent being and subject, and to master the art of intergenerational transfer, will form the foundation of a blessed family, which is key to a blessed society.

The Tower of Babel

The Tower of Babel story, the fourth and final one before Abraham's historical entrance, differs from its predecessors. It is a human story about collaboration.

Unlike the previous narratives, it lacks violence and rather embodies a shared human desire for creativity. This tale steps beyond the familial sphere, delving into societal constructs.

The Divine expresses concern: "And now nothing will be restrained from them, which they have imagined to do" (Gen. 11:6). This apprehension seems contrary to the earlier hope in the creation narrative, where human creativity, as an extension of the divine image, was seen as a positive force. Here, the narrative necessitates a reflection on the Eden story from chapter 2 of Genesis.

The story of the Tower of Babel is a stark contrast to the Garden of Eden narrative. In Eden, humanity understood its place in the world, maintaining a balance between cultivating and preserving it. This equilibrium, stemming from a sense of abundance, is missing from construction of the first city in the world by the exiled Cain. It is the product of a worker of the land who is unaware of the balance and goal of his work. Later in the exile, the Tower of Babel represents the ultimate creative and dominating structure that humanity aspires to build.

Lacking the horizontal expanse of Eden, the people turn to a vertical ambition. They say, "Come, let us build ourselves a city and a tower with its top in the heavens, and let us make a name for ourselves, lest we be dispersed over the face of the whole earth" (Gen. 11:4).

What is the "name" sought by the builders of the Tower of Babel? A name has great significance – in the creation story, Adam names the animals, each name signifying a unique essence. Similarly, Eve names her son, and the descendants of Shem (which literally means "name") begin to invoke the name of the Lord. Cain names a city after his son. The builders of Babel, representing unified humanity, seek to bestow a new essence upon human identity by making a "name" for themselves. Their city and tower symbolize humanity's total creative power, challenging even the heavens. This aspiration to reach the heavens and supplant God's place signifies a hubristic desire for exclusive control, disregarding any accountability to a higher entity.

The difficulty with the Tower of Babel lies in the totality of human unity and creation. The builders' dialogue was entirely instrumental, focused on language, strategy, and aspiration. This process, centered on objectives and methods, left no room for mysteries or existential inquiries. It did not allow for personal growth or consideration of others. The emphasis was on the goal and the strategy to achieve it:

> The tower had seven levels on the east and seven on the west. Bricks were carried up on one side and descended on the other. If a worker fell down and died, he was ignored, but if a single brick fell, they would sit and weep, lamenting, "Woe to us! When will another come in its place?" (*Midrash Pirkei d'Rabbi Eliezer*)

The Midrash highlights the devaluation of human life when goals sanctify means. Interestingly, God doesn't destroy the Tower of Babel as He did with the Flood or as He would later with Sodom. The issue is not human creativity itself, but preventing its unbounded harmful effects. God confuses Babel's languages, introducing the experience of being misunderstood. This frustration could lead to fertile ground for new communication, later reflected in Judaism's emphasis on the power of words and the centrality of healthy, blessed communication. The tower's instrumental use of language is replaced by the hope for personal speech, creating new interpersonal realities.

The story of the Flood teaches us the consequences for a civilization focused solely on individuals, lacking a collective perspective. In contrast, the Tower of Babel demonstrates the pitfalls of a collective overshadowing the individual's uniqueness and significance. The generation of the Flood sinned by harming the Tree of Knowledge of Good and Evil, choosing evil: "And the Lord saw that the wickedness of man was great in the earth, and that every imagination of the thoughts of his heart was only evil continually" (Gen. 6:5). Consequently, their end was justified, as such a life should not be allowed to persist.

The generation of the Tower of Babel, unlike that of the Flood, did not sin with the Tree of Knowledge. They might have even been as moral as Noah in his time. However, they erred in their relationship with the Tree of Life. They did not strive for meaningful lives or face-to-face encounters, nor did they create tools for better human relationships. They enjoyed their creative abilities but lacked the pleasure in creation. This generation ignored the development of quality personal and familial language; their start-up lacked the emotional intelligence essential for building individuals, families, and a decent society.

The confusion of their language was an opportunity to create a new language and consciousness. Our generation is not like that of the Flood; humans today, by and large, can discern between good and evil (although since October 7, some people appear to suffer from moral confusion over which party is the aggressor).

We are more akin to the generation of the Dispersion – the builders of the Tower of Babel, who did not understand the secret of the Tree of Life and the quality of a blessed life. Capitalist life trains its participants to measure relationships by the question "What do I get out of it?" – sometimes gauging relationships for their "market value." This thought pattern hinders the formation of relationships not as the means to an end but as the purpose of life itself.

Thus, alongside the immense blessing of Western progress in many fields, there is a great fear of increasing earthly alienation. Utilitarianism is at the forefront. Israel, as a "start-up nation," sometimes resembles the builders of the Tower of Babel. The utilitarian aspect of technology often overshadows its blessing. The discourse about the future of artificial intelligence adds a significant layer to the question of the blessing of technology. Can we imagine creativity and start-ups primarily concerned with the human aspect, improving the sense of visibility and alleviating loneliness?

God's decision to turn to Abraham was influenced by the background of four universal human stories that embodied failure. In the absence of a healthy family structure, a person may seek redemption outside the home and turn to "building towers." A tower can take the form of a city aspiring to the heavens; a boundless pursuit of wealth, ego, and honor; or it could be in the form of grand spiritual theories and beliefs lacking integrity and honesty at their core.

God's statement to Abraham, beginning with *lech lecha* and continuing with the mission of *ve'heyeh berachah* or blessing consciousness, seeks to rectify the stories of humanity that preceded this call. In the continuation of the book, we will examine these foundations and how the Jewish people's mission indeed seeks to heal this broken world.

Chapter 4

"You Shall Be a Blessing" – A New Hope

From the moment of exile from the Garden of Eden until the end of the Tower of Babel story, the world is unbalanced and far from its purpose. The world in its many parts fails to create a life of health and growth. The earth is filled with violence, familial relationships are broken, and human exploitation is rampant. The story of the tower expresses the failure of human unity in understanding the purpose of growth and creativity.

The reader's impression at the end of these chapters is that the Creator has not succeeded in producing a world that justifies itself, especially regarding the creation of humans. This is not what the Creator hoped for when forming humans in His image, as told in the creation story in chapter 1 of Genesis. The behavior of humans in these chapters does not give a sense of balance between the breath of life in humans and the element of dust in them, as described in the creation story of chapter 2 of Genesis.

The Uniqueness of Abraham

Despite humanity's imbalances, the Creator of the world, Whose entire concern is with life and not death and Who believes in repair, does not completely destroy His world. He also does not withdraw from the world He created, leaving it to manage on its own until its loss. Instead, He turns to Abraham, to one family that will expand into one nation, in the hope that it will succeed in touching the essence of creation as a place of unique, quality life. Within it lies the hope for partnership between the Creator and man:

> And the Lord said to Abram, "Go forth from your country, and from your kin, and from your father's house, to a land that I will show you. And I will make of you a great nation, and I will bless you, and make your name great; and you shall be a blessing. And I will bless them that bless you, and him that curses you will I curse; and in you will all the families of the earth be blessed." (Gen. 12:1–3)

Contrary to the aspirations of the Tower of Babel generation, who sought fulfillment by reaching the heavens, Abraham is called to a different destiny. Being a blessing is linked to the understanding that we possess life forces – powers of abundance, giving, and creativity. The central question of life is how we live with these forces and bring them precisely into the world, so that creations feel meaningfulness and joy of life.

There is a new structure in the world. The human foundation does not consist of a collective with one language, but rather geographically and culturally separate nations with different languages. From this separateness, Abraham's family is called to fulfill a destiny and to serve as a model for humanity.

The *lech lecha* command to Abraham is first and foremost personal. Abraham is asked to embark on a new journey, to disconnect from parts of his past and to connect with the blessing within him. This personal introspective process of blessing consciousness to which Abraham and his descendants are called is crucial before embarking on their broader mission.

The mandate of blessing consciousness involves sibling relationships, an understanding of responsibility and admitting mistakes, fundamental issues of mutual responsibility and brotherhood, hope for healthy couple relationships and parent-child relationships, and the ability to transmit life across generations. It offers a new paradigm for creativity and human economy.

What was Abraham's uniqueness that led him to be chosen as the first Hebrew, the father of the nation?

The traditional belief is that God's choice of Abraham as the first Hebrew, the first Jew, was due to his proclamation of faith in one God. This view is reinforced by the famous Midrash of Abraham smashing the idols,[1] though this theological direction is absent in the plain reading of the verses.

---

1   *Midrash Genesis Rabbah* 38:13.

I suggest a different perspective: God's choice of Abraham was due to his unique attitude toward wealth and abundance. Abraham was the first to understand that the source of all human prosperity is God. This fundamental understanding is at the root of God's reason for choosing him. God chooses and blesses Abraham because Abraham sees God as the source of blessing. For the first time since the creation of the world, there is a kind of intimacy between them.

This personality of blessing consciousness, endowed with substantial material wealth, attracts others precisely because of its approach to power and abundance. The observer senses a unique yearning for closeness in this connected use of wealth. The understanding that God is the source of blessing allows the wealthy person to feel akin to a fruit-bearing tree full of life, drawing its waters from a source higher than itself. In this tree metaphor, there is no duality. Receiving from God, being enjoyably self-fulfilled, and giving to others are all nourished from the same root.

Indeed, Abraham traveled through the length and breadth of the Promised Land, recognizing the source of his blessings.[2] He did not attribute his success to himself – this was his innovation. Moreover, the consciousness of blessing and its source helped him cope with famine in the Promised Land, his wife's infertility, and many other challenges. In moments of crisis, he found meaning, understanding there was a Creator inviting him to confront these issues. There is a source for abundance and also for difficulties; it's the same awareness. This approach of God as the source of life's scenarios helped him in dividing the land with Lot, refusing spoils in the kings' war. Perhaps this consciousness of blessing was also integral to his handling of the commandment of the Binding of Isaac.

Abraham is the patriarch of the consciousness of blessing. Every trial and crisis he faced contributed to the development of this consciousness. In this respect, the phrase *ve'heyeh berachah*, "and be a blessing," especially the command form of the verb "to be," has great significance. The word is a permutation of the divine name Y-H-W-H and represents God as "was, is, and

---

2 He does this by building an altar. "For he proclaimed the name of the Lord loudly before the altar, making known His existence and divinity to mankind" (Nachmanides, Gen. 12:8). "To call upon the name of the Lord" is an act that points out the source of blessing and life.

will be," a God evolving in parallel with His creations. The consciousness of blessing is part of and perhaps enables this evolution. In this light, "to be a blessing" is to fulfill the human purpose, to reach one's full potential.

The partnership in the development of blessing between God and Abraham leads God to share with Abraham the decision to destroy Sodom. Given these considerations, there is a clear distinction between Abraham and Lot. They need to part ways, not only due to the lack of grazing land for their flocks, but also because they represent different ideological views on the role of wealth.

> And Lot lifted up his eyes, and beheld all the plain of the Jordan, that it was well watered everywhere, before the Lord destroyed Sodom and Gomorrah, like the garden of the Lord, like the land of Egypt, as you go to Zoar. So Lot chose him all the plain of the Jordan; and Lot journeyed east; and they separated themselves the one from the other. (Gen. 13:10–11)

Lot sought to increase his wealth without limit. He chose to go to Sodom, described as "like the garden of the Lord, like the land of Egypt" – a place of seemingly endless possibilities, where the abundant Nile was deified. This choice reflected his desire to return to a Garden of Eden–like abundance. However, as we have learned, a return to Eden is not possible and can lead to great danger. Not uncoincidentally, the verse appearing after Lot's choice of Sodom is "Now the men of Sodom were wicked and sinners against the Lord exceedingly" (Gen. 10:13).

Life without the awareness of the divine source as the foundation of success can lead to moral decline. This is exemplified by Egypt, which benefited from the Nile, yet became the greatest house of bondage in the ancient world. By choosing Sodom, Lot shows he does not live with the consciousness of blessing, and therefore, separation from Abraham is necessary.

Lot moved to Sodom while Abraham remained on the mountain. Despite having been promised the land, Abraham allowed Lot to choose first, demonstrating his trust in the power of restraint and contentment with his lot, a reflection of his consciousness of blessing. After their separation, God blessed Abraham:

> And the Lord said to Abram, after Lot was separated from him, "Lift up now your eyes, and look from the place where you are northward, and southward, and eastward, and westward: For all the land that you see, to you will I give it, and to your seed forever." (Gen. 13:14–15)

Lot gained the wealth of Sodom but lacked divine blessing. In contrast, Abraham, dwelling in a rain-dependent area, was filled with blessing. Abraham's actions rectified the emphasis on possession that characterized Cain's perspective.

Maintaining family unity is challenging when members have fundamentally different ideologies. Abraham's separation from Lot did not diminish his responsibility toward him. This separation was temporarily set aside during a regional conflict in the ancient Near East, where Abraham waged war to rescue his captured nephew, Lot. This act significantly rectified the concept of brotherhood, especially given their ideological differences. Through his actions toward the captive Lot, Abraham corrected Cain's sin, effectively declaring, "I am my brother's keeper!"

This war and its outcomes represent a significant test of the victor's greed for wealth. Abraham, who won immense riches from the peoples of the region, proclaims,

> "I have lifted up my hand to the Lord, the Most High God, the possessor of heaven and earth, that I will not take a thread even to a shoe latchet, and that I will not take anything that is yours, lest you say, I have made Abram rich." (Gen. 14:22–23)

Abraham does not see a problem with wealth itself. He opposes the notion that success is solely a human achievement, believing instead in a divine source for prosperity. This belief, rooted in a sensory and experiential understanding rather than a theological or philosophical one, leads to his faith in one God. As stated in Job 19:26, "Yet within my flesh will I see God." This perception of divine blessing as the source of success forms the basis of Abraham's household: recognizing the origin of wealth as a blessing from God and passing it on to others.

The understanding that success originates from divine blessing shapes the life philosophy in Abraham's household. This view emphasizes receiving abundance from God and sharing it with others:

> For I have known him, to the end that he may command his children and his household after him, that they keep the way of the Lord, to do justice and judgment. (Gen. 18:19)

This contrasts with Noah and his sons under the shadow of the vineyard he planted. In Abraham's family, the intergenerational transmission of values will focus on righteousness and justice. This aspect of intergenerational transfer will be explored further in the lives of Abraham, Ishmael, and Isaac.[3]

In Abraham's journey, the promise of "I will make your name great" is fulfilled. There is a link between our name and our growth. As seen in Genesis, a name signifies essence, and in these opening verses, there is a connection between name, greatness, and blessing. For Abram and Sarai, changing their names involves adding or altering a letter, signifying their entry into their blessing. The addition of the letter *heh* represents the presence of God in their names and consciousness. Similarly, every person has a significant name that expresses their potential for blessing.

Quality of Blessing

Before Abraham, the concept of blessing is seen as an action through which the Creator endows His creations with His power – such as the blessing of fertility to all creations and dominion over fish and animals (Gen. 1:28). Additionally, God blesses the dimension of time – "And God blessed the seventh day, and sanctified it" (Gen. 2:3).

The call to Abraham ending with *ve'heyeh berachah* differs from the earlier instances of blessings in the creation narrative. This moment marks a pivotal shift in which the Sovereign of the Universe transfers the focus of blessing from Himself to man. Rashi, in his commentary on the words *ve'heyeh berachah*, says: "The blessings are given into your hand. Until now, the blessings

---

3   I expand on this topic in chapter 16, on trials and blessing.

were in My hand, I blessed Adam and Noah, but from now on, you will bless whomever you wish."

The passage is not just about transferring the ability of fertility and dominion, but it's an invitation to a new consciousness and a radically new approach to life. From this point, a person who is aware of inner strengths and abundance can also bless others with this prosperity. The word *ve'heyeh* (and be) comprises the same letters as the Ineffable Name of God (which means "being"), and from this understanding of mutual connection, a person can bless others.

"Being a blessing" involves three stages. The first is knowing how to receive. This means understanding that it's okay to receive and that one is worthy of the infinite abundance of life forces and creativity. This realization isn't simple. Many people feel unworthy of being recipients and conduits of abundance and blessing, a topic often explored in psychotherapy.

The second stage is internalizing this abundance. It's about the ability to fill oneself, to experience oneself as a vessel of blessing, and to be aware of the fullness of life forces within us. It means giving space to this experience, to the feelings it evokes within us and in our bodies.

This middle stage, centered around the experience of "dwelling," is crucial in the process. Similar to the act of breathing, in which retaining air in the lungs symbolizes balance and patience, so too is the stage of internalizing abundance in a person, without the immediate need to express it externally. Here, one learns about the quality present in restraint and containment.

The final stage is the transfer of blessing and abundance to others. The precision in giving is an essential part of human blessing. Excessive distribution of abundance can lead to dominance or even aggression, while weak distribution fails to maximize the potency of life. Therefore, the precise delivery of abundance is a pivotal moment in the manifestation of blessing consciousness in the world.[4]

All stages of blessing – the ability to receive, internalize the blessing within us, and the skill of accurately passing it on – are crucial steps on the path

---

4   In Parashat Mishpatim, the Beit Ya'akov (Rabbi Ya'akov Lainer of Izhbitz) compares the fulfillment of the commandments to a cow's teat. Just as in nursing, there is an abundance of milk, which is released in balance and precision through the teat, so too the purpose of the commandments is to assist a person in regulating abundance to balanced giving.

to blessing consciousness. A person who blesses another aims to elevate the recipient from the consciousness of the Tree of Knowledge to that of the Tree of Life; this type of giving enables one to become a vessel of blessing, allowing abundance to flow in.

In an ancient Jewish custom, parents bless their children before the Friday night Kiddush. Typically, the person bestowing the blessing wishes for the recipient to have health, academic success, social relationships, and more. However, the essence of blessing seeks a slightly different understanding. A blessing is not just a wish; it emanates from a sense of fulfillment. The person blessing is aware of the abundance within, connected to the Tree of Life, experiencing existence as a vibrant river of vitality, eager to pass this on to his or her loved ones. The recipient, too, must open the gates of consciousness to receive the blessing, akin to an egg awaiting the seed in the act of fertilization.

The blessing is in the moment of gentle contact, in the quality of transferring abundance to loved ones. Blessing the children is essentially a call for parents, at the end of six days of work, to bless their children with a consciousness of abundance, with the unique gift they have to give to their children.

When I shared this idea with my children about blessing their own kids on Friday nights, they reacted with some indifference. They reminded me of the great fatigue at the end of the week and the difficulty of being in such a state of mind: "You haven't been a parent to young children in a long time," they said. Despite their point, the question remains: How can parents of children be enabled to have moments of awareness of the abundance within them in order to bless from this conscious place? Perhaps focused couples work could assist in realizing this important insight during the complex years of raising children.

Blessing as Conduit

The Admor of Izbica said, "With the blessed God, the conduit that sends life must itself be of life."[5] The human body, the conduit through which influence is transmitted, is itself alive. All aspects of being a blessing are present in the conduit before the arrival of the influence. The conduit is connected

---

5   *Mei Hashiloach*, part 1, Parashat Vayeshev, s.v. "and Judah went out from his brothers."

to the vitality of life in the garden.[6] This point is important, indicating that our body and consciousness are a source that has its own life, even before the arrival of influence from above. From here comes another insight into the importance of maintaining our body's health.

In language, we find interesting concepts related to blessing. The knee is the part of the leg that connects the foot to the rest of the body. The knee's movement is two-way, circulating blood back and forth and allowing mutual impulses from the foot to the body and vice versa, enabling human movement. The Hebrew word *berech* (knee) is from the same root as the word *berachah* (blessing). As we saw with Abraham, blessing symbolizes a two-way movement. It allows one to walk from the house of the father to the unknown while maintaining a careful connection to the family of origin.

Another example exists in agricultural language: *havracha*, known as layering, is a method to propagate vines in a vineyard. (The Hebrew shares the same root as *berachah*, "blessing.") The worker uses long branches still connected to the vine, embeds them partially in the ground, and once they root and begin to flourish as independent vines, they are detached from the original source. This branch then becomes an independent vine, thereby adding an additional vine to the vineyard.

Similar to the concept of layering in agriculture, blessing consciousness involves a connection to the source of abundance. Like the second vine, which outwardly appears independent, it internally acknowledges its origin from the first vine, receiving its vitality from it. Abraham's task was to create new roots in this manner of *havracha*, to connect the world to the source of life, allowing human life to create and act freely within this consciousness.

In the state of blessing consciousness, there is also an element of surprise in the circular movement. There are situations in which the reality of the blessing works in the opposite direction: the parent needs the child, for the joy of life of the elderly is nourished by their connection to the young. Sometimes there is a blurring between male and female in unique moments of connection. Sometimes, even the wealthy need the poor. The one who blesses is also blessed.

---

6   In Hebrew, "conduit" is *tzinor*; transposing the letters produces the word *ratzon* (will, as in volition). Our will is itself an elevated divine source.

These rare moments are an expression of a unique state of delight that comes from a deep release of a constrained identity.

Slavery in Egypt on the Way to Blessing

Until the establishment of the blessing as a destiny for the descendants of Abraham, the Israelites will experience difficult historical chapters. The path to a future Garden of Eden will pass through the slavery in Egypt, and this was explicitly stated to Abraham in the Covenant of the Pieces as part of a divine "master plan" concerning his offspring:

> And when the sun was going down, a deep sleep fell upon Abram; and, lo, a dread, even a great darkness, fell upon him. And He said to Abram: "Know of a surety that thy seed will be a stranger in a land that is not theirs, and will serve them; and they will afflict them four hundred years; And also that nation, whom they will serve, will I judge; and afterward will they come out with great substance." (Gen. 15:12–14)

What was the reasoning of this fearsome God in planning such difficult labor for His beloved children? What did Abraham think of God after this ceremony, which foretold the harsh bondage of his children?

Only someone who has experienced the essence of alienation inherent in being a stranger, the experience of slavery embedded in the DNA of their consciousness, can aspire to a transformative shift in awareness. The slavery in Egypt represents the complete antithesis of the Garden of Eden.

Slavery is a deconstruction of all that is human. The slave is merely a tool for the product of his labor. He himself is irrelevant and has no value as a person. In the state of slavery, you are unseen, unheard, and gradually become utterly devoid of any human worth. It is difficult for a slave to develop a new consciousness, a different perspective on reality. Slavery, in all its forms, is the complete opposite of blessing and stands far from the Tree of Life.

The slave mentality within us is also a foundation for the deeper quest for meaning and freedom in our souls. Once a year on Passover, we are commanded to return to Egypt, to eat the bread our ancestors ate there, and to reexperience the essence of slavery. We recite from the Passover Haggadah,

"In every generation, one must see oneself as having personally left Egypt." We are commanded to feel the tears of the oppressed through the bitter herbs and to tell the story in the most relevant way possible.

Touching the collective childhood wound that we experienced in Egypt is essential to creating a purposeful life. It starts with the personal experience, "seeing oneself," and only then moves to the collective, formative experience.

Human history oscillates between the poles of Egyptian slavery and the freedom of the Garden of Eden. The people of Israel are commanded to live a life of blessing, not to fall into the pole of slavery, and not to allow others to be there. Many commandments in the Torah are a reminder of the Exodus from Egypt: the Sabbath, treatment of strangers, gifts of leftover produce in the field to the needy, employer-employee relations, and more. Slavery can manifest through tyrannical rule, a coercive employer, enslaving technology, oppressive relationships, and in other areas of life. What's common to all these commandments is the attempt to connect their root to the essence of the Tree of Life and being a blessing.

Ruth and Boaz – An Archetype of Blessing

In the workshops of the Ve'heyeh Berachah project, we invite participants to enter the Garden of Eden consciousness, to meet the qualities of the different trees in our lives and the essence of the river, and to ask: When do we walk in the consciousness of the Tree of Life, and when in the consciousness of the Tree of Knowledge? When do we feel flow and clarity? We touch on questions of leaving our parents' home on life's journey, and, like Abraham, we ask: What do we take from our parents' home and what do we leave behind, as a necessary step for identifying and understanding our blessing?

The continuation of the workshop emerges from a reading of the Book of Ruth, focusing on the encounter between Boaz and his servants, his consciousness of abundance, and his perception of Ruth. In this workshop, we try to discover the foundations of blessing in our lives.

The Book of Ruth is historically situated in the days of the Judges, about which it is said, "Every man did that which was right in his own eyes" (Judg. 17:6). This situation somewhat recalls the days before God's historic calling to Abraham, which also had a sense of human existence without purpose, without God, where every man did what was right in his own eyes.

During these times, an extraordinary story unfolds.

The background: Elimelech and Naomi from Bethlehem went down to Moab due to a famine in the land. During their extended stay in Moab, their sons married Moabite women. During these years, all the men in the family died: Elimelech, Mahlon, and Chilion.

Naomi, the widow, returned to the fields of Bethlehem accompanied by Ruth, her daughter-in-law, after hearing that "the Lord had visited His people" (Ruth 1:6) and prosperity had returned to the fields of Bethlehem. Ruth insisted on her desire to go with Naomi and not to remain in her father's house, her land, and her birthplace:

> And Ruth said, "Entreat me not to leave you, or to return from following after you; for whither you go, I will go; and where you lodge, I will lodge; your people will be my people, and your God my God; where you die, will I die, and there will I be buried; the Lord do so to me, and more also, if nothing but death part you and me." (Ruth 1:16–17).

We cannot know what drove Ruth to such devotion. Was it Naomi's personality that won her over, to the point of embarking on an unknown journey? Was it marriage into the family of Elimelech? What causes a woman to leave everything behind and devote herself entirely to a new path? What triggers such movements in us?

Naomi's return to Bethlehem with Ruth is accompanied by a strong sense of spiritual emptiness.

> And they two went until they came to Bethlehem. And it came to pass, when they were come to Bethlehem, that all the city was moved about them, and they said: "Is this Naomi?" And she said to them: "Call me not Naomi, call me Mara ["bitter"]; for the Almighty hath dealt very bitterly with me. I went out full, and the Lord hath brought me back home again empty; why call ye me Naomi, seeing the Lord hath testified against me, and the Almighty hath afflicted me?" (Ruth 1:19–21).

Naomi left her community during a crisis, and upon her return, she was greeted with shock. Naomi's self-awareness, both as a person and especially as a woman, is extremely low. She requests that the local women not call her Naomi. Again, we find that the name is essential. However, this time the movement is reversed, from greatness to smallness, from a feeling of fullness to a sense of emptiness. Naomi asks to be called Mara, "bitter," because "the Almighty hath dealt very bitterly with me." This name reflects her feeling that the image of God as "El Shaddai," the God of abundance, is not the God she experiences. Furthermore, she undergoes a feminine physical experience of depletion of her own nourishing sources. By her side is Ruth, her daughter-in-law. Two hungry women, but more importantly, lacking lively, feminine, and joyful faces. One woman is diminished yet familiar, and the other is a foreigner, a stranger, committed to a journey.

Naomi's feeling upon entering the city is the complete opposite of the experience of blessing. At the end of Ruth chapter 1, Naomi describes herself as a cursed woman.

Chapter 2 opens with a new spirit:

> And Naomi had a kinsman of her husband's, a mighty man of wealth, of the family of Elimelech; and his name was Boaz. And Ruth the Moabitess said to Naomi: "Let me now go to the field, and glean ears of corn after him in whose sight I will find grace." And she said to her: "Go, my daughter." (Ruth 2:1–2)

Ruth initiates a bold move by going out to the field, an action that was not customary, especially in ancient times. As a foreign woman coming to a male-dominated field, she takes a risk, hoping to "find favor" in someone's eyes. As we will see, "finding favor in the eyes" is an important element in our story and in the language of blessing.

> And she went, and came, and gleaned in the field after the reapers; and she happened to light on the portion of the field belonging to Boaz, who was of the family of Elimelech. (Ruth 2:3)

The field in the Torah is a space in which many events occur. It's an area of hunting and labor and represents male dominion, though women may be present in its surroundings. It has an instinctual element, being a place for expressing hopes of creativity and abundance. On one hand, it can represent an aggressive-sexual area, as an expression of human achievement and power, and on the other hand, it can be a place of blessing, as a field.

> And, behold, Boaz came from Bethlehem, and said to the reapers: "The Lord be with you." And they answered him: "The Lord bless you." (Ruth 2:4)

Boaz is the owner of the field. During the wheat harvest, he visits his field and observes the great abundance of the yield. His statement to the reapers, usually translated as "The Lord be with you," can be translated literally as "The Lord is with you" – God is present here with you, amidst the abundance of the grain. In the fields of Bethlehem, God is revealed through this material bounty. He is not "our Father in heaven," but a deity manifested in the field's yield. This is reminiscent of the Garden of Eden, where there's a feeling of divine presence amid the plentiful trees and rivers.

Naomi returns to the land "because she had heard in the fields of Moab that the Lord had visited His people by giving them bread."[7] The term "visited" (*pakad*) signifies a real presence. God's return to the fields of Bethlehem is experienced through the presence of abundance. The Creator is present in the field, and Boaz captures this awe-inspiring presence in the simple yet powerful words "The Lord is with you."

The reapers immediately reply: "The Lord bless you." In simpler terms, this means: *We wish that the blessing you find in this abundance will continue to be with you. As we experience this abundance now, we hope for its continuity in the future.* Both the owner and the workers sense a higher source in their work in the field. This goes beyond mere output, the "annual report," and the dynamics between manager and workers driven mainly by profit margins.

---

7   Ruth 2:8. This is reminiscent of when God "visits" (*poked*) Sarah and enables her to give birth (Gen. 21:1). For more on the experience of God as "living in earthly realms," see "The Purpose of Creation" in chapter 5, "The Search for *Oneg*."

Here, there's a profound experience of shared prosperity, transcending the economic gap between Boaz and his workers.

This scenario depicts the receipt of bounty from the source, its retention within the blessed person and his surroundings, and its outward distribution. Such a complete cycle is perceived as *oneg* by all involved.

Similar to the ancient garden, this story expresses a sense of fulfillment and security. Boaz is truly blessed, and he receives blessings from his workers in a circular movement where everyone present feels a balance between giving and receiving.

Where does this language of blessing, as used by a field owner like Boaz, originate? What brings companies or factory owners to feel such a sense of divine presence when witnessing the yield of their enterprise? Boaz's identity as a blessed man lies in the understanding that the source of wealth is not his own. He is merely a conduit for reception, a vessel in which abundance is entrusted. The ample bounty in his fields does not dull his senses, nor does it define his human and masculine identity. Boaz continues in Abraham's path, experiencing wealth and abundance as waters flowing into him from a source higher than himself, passing through him onwards.

His workers feel this, and Boaz draws them along in his wake. This presents a unique proposal for creating a blessed work environment, where all employees feel a part of the flow of abundance, regardless of their status in the company.

And here we arrive at the immediate translation of the experience of blessing:

> Boaz said to his servant who was in charge of the reapers, "Whose young woman is this?" (Ruth 2:5)

Boaz's state of being a blessing enables him to notice Ruth. One who experiences his blessing in such a way keeps his eyes open to welfare. "Welfare" has a dual meaning here. Alert and observant eyes are a deep expression of the blessed individual's desire to extend his blessing further. It is clear to him that her presence in his field is not coincidental. Boaz sees Ruth as an inseparable part of his blessing.

The servant in charge of the reapers answers:

"She is a Moabite young woman who returned with Naomi from the country of Moab. And she said, 'Please let me glean and gather among the sheaves after the reapers.' She came and has been on her feet from early morning until now, except for a short rest in the house." (Ruth 2:6–7)

Ruth is part of the realm of abundance, and her presence creates a curiosity that leads to responsibility.

And Boaz said to Ruth, "Listen, my daughter, do not go to glean in another field or leave this one, but keep close to my young women. Let your eyes be on the field that they are reaping, and go after them. Have I not charged the young men not to touch you? And when you are thirsty, go to the vessels and drink what the young men have drawn." (Ruth 2:8–9)

From a place of alienation and vulnerability, Ruth begins to experience fulfillment and security. Her journey starts with meeting a basic need for food and progresses to a sense of safety in which the primary experience is being seen and present. Whereas she arrived as a foreign worker, clinging to the fringes of her mother-in-law Naomi, now, for the first time in a long time, she feels that she is being noticed. "Let your eyes be on the field" signifies a gesture of laying one's head on a shoulder. She has something to rely on. There is a man present – the beginning of intimacy.

One of the most touching verses in the entire book is this:

She fell on her face, bowing to the ground, and said to him, "Why have I found favor in your eyes that you should take notice of me [*l'hakireni*], when I am a foreigner [*nachriah*]?" (Ruth 2:10)

Ruth asks: "Why have I found favor in your eyes?" *How did I transform from a stranger to someone recognizable?* The Hebrew words for "stranger" and "recognizable" share the same root. What enables a person to shift from being unknown to known?

The concept of "finding favor in someone's eyes" works in both directions, symbolizing a reciprocal, face-to-face engagement. The charm of one who "finds favor" intersects with the look of the observer. The favor is now seen through the eyes of the one who recognized the charm in another. The person who "has found favor" perceives this change. This exchange of favor exists in the relational space between the two individuals.

Here we have a meaningful description of a broad and circular blessing, beginning with a unique encounter in the bountiful field. From this blessing of abundance, Boaz sees Ruth as an integral part of the blessing. Ruth feels seen, and this visibility is reciprocated by Boaz.

> And Boaz answered and said to her, "All that you have done for your mother-in-law since the death of your husband has been fully told to me, how you left your father and mother and your native land and came to a people that you did not know before." (Ruth 2:11)

By leaving her father's house, her native land, and venturing into the unknown, Ruth echoes the original *lech lecha*, which also involved leaving one's parents and journeying into the unknown. Ruth is the feminine paradigm of "go forth...and be a blessing." Her courage to move from the fields of Moab to the Land of Israel, her audacity to enter Boaz's field, creating a mutual finding of favor in each other's eyes, earns her the status of being a source of blessing for herself, Naomi, and Boaz.

> [And Boaz said,] "May the Lord recompense your work, and may your reward be complete from the Lord, the God of Israel, under Whose wings you have come to take refuge." Then she said, "Let me find favor in your sight, my lord; for you have comforted me." (Ruth 2:12–13)

In the story of Boaz and Ruth, the foundational elements of the entire approach are interwoven. The blessed wealthy man experiences the pleasure of abundance passing through him and understands that his role in the world is to extend his blessing to those less fortunate. This is not philanthropy, which typically comes as a second stage of great wealth accumulation. The acts of receiving and giving are part of a unified consciousness.

In the workshop on Boaz and Ruth as archetypes of blessing, we touch upon four main areas.

1. **The experience of emptiness** – following Naomi's return home. When do we feel a sense of emptiness in life, a feeling of being drained? A sense of distance from our "personal name," our gender identity, and our body? Is the process of emptiness, as characterized by Naomi, necessary for receiving blessing in our lives?

Typically, this is a personal exercise, without group sharing. For many, this is a surprising stage that turns out to be very significant, emphasizing space and emptiness as tools for receiving abundance.[8]

2. **The experience of blessing** – the visit to the field and Boaz's encounter with the young men. When do we feel as if we possess abundance and blessing? Is this experience connected to the presence of others (i.e., field workers), or can it exist without human interaction? What are the characteristics of this experience? Is it possible to describe such an experience in the workplace, where both manager and employees feel "The Lord be with you"?

At this stage, we hear stories about moments of blessing. Sometimes these occur within the family structure, and other times in the spheres of work and volunteering. We try to collect characteristics of these scenarios. We pay attention to whether the blessing comes from a conscious effort or arrives unexpectedly. We attempt to delve into the depth of the experience of "the rich man who is happy with his lot." In what part of our lives, when we are in it, do we feel abundance?

3. **Seeing the other** – following Boaz's example ("Whose young woman is this?"), who sees the commitment to the "other" as an integral part of his blessing. We ask: When do we direct our gaze toward the other? What enables a direct look at a person who is not part of our immediate family or social network?

Participants in the workshop often struggle to recall this unique kind of gaze. It's easier for them to describe giving charity donations through recurring bank payments. However, when people do remember an individual,

---

8   See chapter 15 on recognizing lack and the Tree of Life.

personal moment of giving, very special moments emerge. The fear and difficulty sometimes transform into an experience of significance.

4. **Finding favor in each other's eyes** – based on the paradigm of the encounter between Ruth and Boaz. We explore the transition from being a stranger to becoming known. When do we experience a mutual sensation of finding favor? In practice, we ask – when am I able to look directly into the eyes of someone who is also gazing into mine? What quality emerges in this mutual gaze?

Later, we ask people to go out of the room or into the street for thirty minutes and try to find favor in any way they see fit.

In summary, Boaz's field is a vital symbol both in the Torah and in life, embodying the essence of life as a blessing. It is a haven akin to sheltering under the Tree of Life. The workers are more than faceless laborers; they feel part of something greater, transcending the mere outcomes of their toil. This field is a space where humans are recognized. Ruth's nourishment extends beyond physical sustenance; her soul, too, is fulfilled.

We can envision the transformation in Ruth's expression as she evolves from an unknown, foreign girl to a recognized woman. Suddenly, her previous words to Naomi – "your people will be my people, and your God my God" – crystallize into a tangible, unified truth. Boaz, who approached her from among "the people," and God, as manifest in the plentiful harvest, converge into a single reality. This amalgamation of society, economy, and the Divine paves the way for a unique start to Ruth and Boaz's relationship, setting the stage for a lasting future, as they lay the groundwork for the lineage of King David, their great-grandson.

Indeed, Boaz's field seems akin to the Garden of Eden, yet it possesses a quality of renewed innocence. The story of Boaz and Ruth, set in the era of the Judges, illustrates how swiftly salvation can come and is indeed within us. Boaz's field is a field of life, rising from years of struggle, despair, and suffering. It's a place where the dynamics between employer and employee or man and woman and the awareness of power, sight, and perception all intertwine to form a tapestry of blessing.

When Ruth returns to Naomi, she recounts the events of her day in Boaz's field. Naomi notices a change in Ruth's demeanor. Responding to Naomi's question about her day, Ruth says, "The man's name with whom I wrought today is Boaz." One can only speculate about the tone in which she spoke these words.

The Sages commented on this: "Rabbi Joshua taught: More than what the homeowner does for the poor, the poor does for the homeowner. As Ruth said to Naomi, 'The man's name with whom I wrought today' and did not say, 'who wrought with me'" (*Midrash Ruth Rabbah*). In Boaz's field, there is a clear depiction of rich and poor, a blessed individual versus a foreign worker. However, there exists a relationship between them. Contrary to the initial impression that only Boaz seems to be the giver in a one-way act of charity, the Midrash invites us to see a dynamic in which Ruth is the significant and central "doer." It's a moment when the identity of the less fortunate fills the "giver." When the poor person steps out of the role of the receiver, even temporarily, a mutual and meaningful movement begins. The rich man's understanding that he is merely a conduit for passing on the blessing can lead to a unique sense of pleasure. In giving, he is actually fulfilled. Thus, it is specifically Ruth "who wrought with him." According to this perspective, it is Boaz who is actually the recipient.

A similar principle appears in the *Zohar*:

> The rich are represented by the male aspect, and the poor by the female. Just as they are united, supporting and giving to each other, and showing kindness, so too should humans be. The rich and poor should form a single union, exchanging charity and acts of kindness, supporting one another. (*Zohar*, Introduction, 13b)

One of the most profound experiences of being a blessing is when the roles of giver and receiver interchange, creating a pure, unadorned, and surprising encounter, free from external identities.

The story of Ruth and Boaz is significant for its enhancement of the concept of being a blessing with the imagery of a field, representing the social dimension. It portrays healthy power dynamics between a landowner and his workers and a unique meeting between man and woman – a special bond between the Jewish man and Moabite woman, later foundational for national leadership. Boaz's field serves as a metaphor for a society in tune with the Tree of Life consciousness.

The establishment of a blessed society is key to connecting with the wider world. Blessing is attractive, in that it draws attention and finds favor. The role of the people of Israel – and at its heart, the State of Israel – is to be a blessing in all areas of individual and societal life. On a social level, this blessing manifests in good human communication, healthy family life, a proper approach to property and wealth, and the ability to forgive and enable personal rectification. It may create a new understanding of the role of communication and media and influence how a leader perceives the limits of power and our ability to cope with brokenness and pain. These abilities create, on a personal level, a person who attracts blessing and a society that shines with a unique light.

"And in you will all the families of the earth be blessed" (Gen. 12:3).

PART TWO

Oneg versus Joy

"The world was lacking rest, pleasure, longing, and yearning, which are the essence of the world's existence and vitality." (Menachem Mendel of Kotsk, *Sefer Ahavat Shalom*)

Chapter 5

The Search for *Oneg*

During the period leading up to writing this book, I sought to ask fresh questions about Jewish existence in our era. I wanted to slow down the race after the Jewish values I had engaged in for most of my life – which emerge from the Tree of Knowledge – and to seek within Judaism an explanation for the root of our human existence, which emerges from the Tree of Life.

I asked various spiritual leaders, educators, and rabbis about Judaism's contribution to contemporary human existential questions – not about Judaism's unique role in the past, but about its contribution to the present and, more importantly, to the future of both Jewish and human existence. Some people did not understand the question. They asserted that the mere fact that we have reached this point, after such difficult years of exile, is proof of the success of the Jewish story. I heard many people lamenting, "If only we could recreate the wisdom of preservation of our heritage, we could step confidently into the future." Some pointed out Judaism's contribution to the world: they mentioned Shabbat and the concept of a day of rest; others added the notions of justice and repair. Some brought up the limitations of a king's power and the healthy leadership it inspires, as a Jewish innovation we have brought to the world. These are indeed very important values, and if indeed it was Judaism that contributed these values, we could say that we have contributed to human existence.

However, I wanted to sharpen the focus on the Jewish message, specifically in the current era. In a world in which social justice, power limitations, and a weekly day of rest are integral parts of the hopes and aspirations of most of the world, could it be that our historical role has ended?

Be a Blessing

Being a Jew Today

Among some of the religious people I consulted, I heard spiritual concepts such as "serving God," "living a life of holiness," and "devotion to the Creator." These are powerful words, but for me, they describe tools more than purpose.

The feeling of irrelevance intensified when I asked rabbis whom I respect about the interpretation of the foundational verse spoken to Abraham at the start of his journey – "And in you will all the families of the earth be blessed" – and whether they align their lifestyle with this vision. I encountered silence or significant hesitation. Most are deeply engaged in internal Jewish, typically religious questions that do not seek to engage in existential dialogue or to serve as a model for humanity.

Of course, many highlight the centrality of Jews in the world of technology and the number of Jews who have received Nobel Prizes as an expression of a unique Jewish talent in the modern world. I do not underestimate these facts. The question is, are talent and creativity sufficient foundations for the existence of the Jewish people? Is this what God hoped for us when He called upon Abraham to create a different model for humanity?

Liberal Jews hold onto the concept of *tikkun olam* (repairing the world).[1] This concept has long lost its Jewish uniqueness, as our world has many "world repairers" who are not Jewish.

Many religious Jews are focused on preserving the Jewish people. Indeed, the quest for survival is a profound existential foundation, deeply ingrained in the Jewish DNA. The Dalai Lama, whom I met during the intermediate days of Sukkot in 5780 (2019), was fascinated by the Jewish people's survival ability. He admires the figure of Rabban Yochanan ben Zakkai, who enacted regulations for a people exiled due to the destruction of their Second Temple. We take pride in this survival capability, and rightfully so.

The perception of Judaism as primarily focused on survival is deeply entrenched, even among secular liberal circles. To many, Judaism is a tradition with appealing elements worth preserving: the Passover Seder, Chanukah, Purim, and rest on Shabbat. Yet even they often view Judaism's main strength

---

1   This concept is originally found in the Aleinu prayer, which mentions "repairing the world in the Kingdom of God," indicating a direct connection between the act of repair and divine kingship.

as its conservative nature, more fitting for a bygone era of exile. This perspective leads many to distance themselves from such Judaism. People seeking life, creativity, and love do not usually realize that these issues are fundamental to Judaism, rooted in Abraham's journey.

As Diaspora Jewry has addressed identity issues, questioning the connection to the State of Israel amid a rise in interfaith marriages, significant programs like Birthright and MASA have emerged. These initiatives strengthen ties with Israel and cultivate a sense of belonging among Jews. To enhance unity among the Jewish people, a new Hebrew term was created: *amiyut* or "peoplehood." The success of a program like Birthright, which has brought over 850,000 young Diaspora Jews to Israel, lies in the hope that participants will forge a bond with the Jewish people and Judaism through their connection to the land and Israelis.

I met many leaders of these programs that focus on Jewish continuity and the concept of peoplehood. I asked them all one common question: *Peoplehood for what purpose? What is the vision, the future picture? Fundamentally, what is the essence of Jewish life that you so ardently want people to connect with, to the extent of seeking love and marriage only within their community?* Many acknowledged this as an important – perhaps the most important – question. However, most of them do not actively engage with it.

A significant portion of Jews, both in Israel and around the world, do not see Judaism, in all its forms, as a central life resource. To the majority, Judaism is a religion/culture with emotional and historical significance and interesting holidays, but it does not touch upon the fundamental questions of human existence. There is a danger that such Judaism might not endure for long. As mentioned, the problem is inherent in the most basic message of Judaism in this era.

Therefore, we need to envision a future that draws from Judaism and provides strength for today. This vision should enrich our lives in Israel and worldwide with the unique life quality that Judaism offers, impacting every aspect of our daily secular lives. This envisioned future, in its full ideological grandeur and practical elaboration, should shape the strategies of Jewish leaders and institutions and foster dialogue with the wider world.

This led a valued group of collaborators and myself to realize that we must revisit the concept of the Tree of Life as a central tenet for modern Judaism.

Linking this fundamental awareness to the practical mission of being a blessing, highlighted in this book, infuses our everyday lives as twenty-first-century Jews with deep significance.

Abraham the Ivri (Hebrew) was selected for this destiny. The Midrash elucidates the meaning of *ivri*, which is based on the root meaning "across": "The entire world was on one side, and he was on the other" (*Midrash Genesis Rabbah* 42:8). This concise phrase holds immense significance: Abraham was the man who swam against the tide. He understood that the normal functioning of the world he lived in was not obligatory and could lead to a meaningless existence, as in the generations before him. He was ready to battle this.

Before we became the Jewish nation, we were the descendants of Abraham the Hebrew. Our patriarch teaches us that with determination, one can forge a unique path, pave a new way, and possibly create a personal current. Abraham's legacy is a significant challenge for us and sets a high bar. It also offers solace. When overwhelmed by the currents surrounding us, we know we can resist them if we choose to act against these overwhelming forces. While we may not reach the level of an Abraham who established a new nation, our efforts against the prevailing environment can nevertheless be empowered.

Warren Bennis, a renowned researcher of leadership, wrote:

> By the time we reach puberty, the world has shaped us to a greater extent than we realize. Our family, friends, school, and society in general have told us – by word and example – how to be. But people begin to become leaders at that moment when they decide for themselves how to be.[2]

This embodies the essence of Abraham: the courage to reinvent life, to believe in the possibility of a different path.

Being an Ivri invites us to bravely explore both the external and internal worlds, to ask questions, and not to shy away from initiating change. The critical and important morality of the Tree of Knowledge shouldn't suppress our inherent courage to seek the beyond. This pursuit is from the Tree of Life.

---

2   Warren Bennis, *On Becoming a Leader* (New York: Basic Books, 1989), 49.

These principles are relevant to personal life but are equally applicable to our collective existence. Just as an individual dares to inquire about his or her life and its foundational purpose, a society, too, can ask similar questions: *What motivates us and what are we aiming for?*

The late Rabbi Jonathan Sacks explains that being on the other side of the surrounding culture has a purpose:

> I want you, says God to Abraham, to be different. Not for the sake of being different, but for the sake of starting something new: a religion that will not worship power and the symbols of power – for that is what idols really were and are.... To be a Jew is to be willing to challenge the prevailing consensus....[3]

Well-Being

A dramatic change is taking place in our era. For the first time in human history, there's a broad focus on the essence of well-being. New metrics of quality of life and happiness are being created worldwide,[4] and it seems we're on the cusp of a new era, seeking an additional dimension to life beyond mere existence. While elements and questions of survival still persist in human existence, particularly in the State of Israel, these don't seem to fully capture the foundational experience of our world. Today's reality feels closely the resources of abundance and seeks a new meaning for human existence and purpose. This is certainly true for the younger generation – the millennials, a group seeking to address deeper questions alongside their growth. Every person should nurture his or her own "millennial," a youthful voice eager to ask new questions about life.

The increasing focus on technology in this generation might amplify the need for questions of meaning. Often, when we shut down our computers or disconnect from a WhatsApp group or Facebook, a sense of emptiness,

---

3   Rabbi Jonathan Sacks, *Covenant and Conversation,* "The Courage Not to Conform," Parashat Lech Lecha, 5774, 5781, https://rabbisacks.org/covenant-conversation/lech-lecha/the-courage-not-to-conform/.

4   See more on this in chapter 7 on the Western conception of the good life as discussed by Professor Martin Seligman.

bordering on loneliness, surfaces. Moreover, Facebook's algorithm is designed to reinforce our opinions, not to challenge our fundamental assumptions. The culture of "likes" sometimes comes at the expense of a culture of fruitful and life-giving debate. The ubiquitous and effortless "selfie" is also an expression of the difficulty in reaching out to others.[5]

There's a renewed place for questions of purpose and meaning, especially in a postmodern world where this very concept is unravelling. The consciousness of blessing that calls for an awareness of the power of our inner life forces can find blessing in technology, while also managing its influence in our lives. We should control it, not be controlled by it.

Many thinkers have viewed the transformations of the modern era, including the renewal of Jewish existence in the Land of Israel, as a significant and dramatic psychological turning point toward the rejuvenation of Jewish life. Alongside these thinkers, I sought to add another dimension – or perhaps to dig into the foundation of the house – and touch upon a fundamental question. What is the purpose, the destiny, the life movement that will renew our personal, conjugal, community, and social lives as Jews? What is the real meaning of "And in you will all the families of the earth be blessed"?

As my dear sister Chava, who chose a lifestyle based on Eastern teachings, said: Buddhism contributed mindfulness to the Western world in the twentieth century, a significant contribution whose value cannot be understated. What is Judaism's contribution to the world in the twenty-first century?[6]

The Purpose of Creation

In the biblical creation story, the Creator is the source of life and the architect of the world. In the first description of the creation of man, we are made in

---

5   The internet preserves systematic documentation of everything we write and store there, including details about our medical condition. This raises a question about the nature of human beings as entities capable of change. The most basic human hope, that what was yesterday does not have to dictate our actions tomorrow, is not recognized by the internet and other virtual documentation spaces. When we enter this mindset that seeks to document ourselves, we constrain the potential for movement and change in life.

6   My sister Chava's late husband Bernie Glassman, of blessed memory, founded a movement that connects Buddhism with social responsibility. They exposed me to some Eastern philosophy and its connections to my Jewish world.

His image, while in the second, the Creator breathes into us the breath of life, making us a "living soul."

In both descriptions, there is a direct connection between humans and the Creator Who formed them. The concepts of "image" and "the breath of life" are essential descriptions that connect the created with their Creator. In these narratives, human creation and purpose are not vague or meaningless. "Life" is not just a period between birth and death. It holds a connection to the force of being, growth, development, touching the numinous, and seeking refined emotion.

In various writings, especially in kabbalistic texts, we find direct references to the reason for creation, related to the question of the meaning of life. One of the most important is that God desired to have a dwelling in the lower worlds. This statement, originating from the Midrash,[7] speaks of the Creator's "desire." The word *desire* in the context of God is an expression of primal and powerful vitality. The "dwelling in the lower worlds" is to be a vessel that contains this presence. This "dwelling" begins with our relationship to our bodies, extends to our loving relationships, and encompasses all earthly aspects of our lives.

The concept of "a dwelling in the lower realms" provided the foundation for the following ideas:

> The purpose of creation is to bring *oneg* to the created beings, and there is no inherent pleasure for the created being while being separated from the Creator. Furthermore, as we learn, God desires to dwell in the lower realms. (Introduction to the *Zohar*)

There is a direct connection between our pleasures as human beings and the divine desire to dwell in the lower realms. God wishes us to link our enjoyment with His desire to dwell within us. This connection between God and man creates a remarkable picture of life that requires explanation and precision.

This key principle – that God desires to give *oneg* to His created beings and dwell in the lower realms – is central in kabbalistic circles and to members of

---

7   *Midrash Tanchuma*, Parashat Naso 17.

the Chasidic world.[8] The purpose of creating the world, especially humanity, was to serve as a vessel, body, and home for the infinite divine light. God, as the source of life, asks us to live on this earth with an awareness of this profound force, reflected in a proper quality of life. Man may originate and end in dust, but between birth and death, he is meant to live with his entire body and soul imbued with vitality from the life source.

This is not an endorsement of hedonism or the pursuit of bodily pleasures. Rather, it's a hopeful vision at the foundation of creation, through which humans learn to integrate their divine essence, representing a soul with a deep yearning for life paired with an earthly aspect that embodies temporality and life on earth.

This forms the essence of life's challenge and the central imagery of the Garden of Eden.

Rabbi Baruch Ashlag, who lived in Tel Aviv in the early twentieth century, developed a complete life philosophy around the principle of "dwelling in the lower realms." According to his approach:

> It is known that the purpose of creation is to benefit the created beings. This means that as long as a person has not reached a state in which he feels good in this world, he should know that he has not yet attained the goal for which humans were created.[9]

These passages and many others discuss the purpose of creation as an invitation to a life that embodies our duty to be an earthly dwelling for God, for the Creator sought the experience of "to do good and delight His creations." He sought to manifest the "good" – meaning the powerful vitality of divinity – particularly through the creation of a material world, with an emphasis on human creation. "Good" and "pleasure" are central to this purpose. Dwelling alongside the source of life can bring a person to the most balanced state of

---

8   In Chabad literature, particularly the *Tanya*, this principle represents the essence of creation. The last Admor of Chabad, Rabbi Menachem Mendel Schneerson, listed this as one of ten foundational sentences that Chabad children should recite each day.

9   Rabbi Ashlag, *Igrot*, letter 69.

senses and desires. This proximity to the divine shapes the consciousness of blessing, adding an experiential value to enjoyment, known as *oneg*.

The concept of *oneg* is unique and difficult to explain. It is often translated as "pleasure" or "delight." I would like to distinguish between these two. *Oneg* is an experience that is rare and unique, an expression of deep physical experience. The difference between pleasure and *oneg* is that pleasure reflects the self's desire to be filled up, addressing a basic and primal void that drives us. In contrast, *oneg* connects to the fullness of creation, expressed as a desire to give further.

The Ba'al Shem Tov is quoted as saying, "Constant *oneg* is not pleasure."[10] According to this, *oneg* involves elements of temporariness and possibly surprise, enabling new self-discovery. It's a revelation from a hidden layer of life, akin to a blessing. Hence, the pursuit is not of continuous delight but rather an awareness that there are everyday aspects of life filled with pleasure, and then unique moments and situations in which *oneg* can be experienced. Recognizing the mundane, our basic needs, our natural hunger, and our dependencies in human relationships allows for authenticity and a yearning for a different state in which the experience of *oneg* holds a unique place.

In contrast to *oneg*, pleasure has a potent and short-lived impact, often followed by a quick decline. Maintaining pleasure over time often requires increasing amounts of the same basic source of pleasure. This is true for food, sexuality, money, the use of words and communication, and in other areas of life. Moreover, there can be difficulty or negative feelings, even sadness, when the pleasure ends. Of course, there's nothing wrong with pleasure; in fact, pleasure contributes to states of personal happiness. But the quality of pleasure is measured and even dependent on what remains within us after the pleasure ends.

The drive for pleasure and *oneg* comes from filling a sense of deficiency deep within our identity.[11] This deficiency exists in every person. However, in filling this void, there's a significant difference between pleasure and *oneg*. Often, pleasure can lead to loneliness, as it doesn't take a person out of his or herself but temporarily satisfies a basic need without our awareness of the

---

10   *Keter Shem Tov* 1:121.

11   See chapter 15 on lack and the Tree of Life.

connection between this deficiency in our existential foundation and our present lives. People can move from one pleasure to another, as something fundamental in their inner world is not satisfied – and not just in extreme cases of addiction.

Such pleasure provides much temporary satisfaction. However, unlike pleasure, *oneg* touches the inner soul. It's linked to a fundamental essence in a person that awakens slowly and grows delicately. Therefore, those who experience *oneg* don't rush to teach, publish, or share. *Oneg* calls for things to settle, often remaining hidden from sight, as the Talmud says: "Blessing is not found except in an object that is hidden from the eye" (*Ta'anit* 8a). Describing *oneg* isn't easy; words often fall short, perhaps because *oneg* is a state usually accompanied by silence.

Oneg also involves a kind of negation of the ego amidst surprising life situations.

While pleasure touches the temporal, delight touches the eternal. Pleasure can bring satisfaction, but delight brings fulfillment, as in the verse "You anoint my head with oil; my cup overflows" (Ps. 23:5). Pleasure has an element of depletion and death, whereas delight has an element of life, expressed in alertness and a desire for precise giving.

In the context of this book's foundational language about the dialogue of trees in the primal Garden of Eden, delight is the sensual expression of a person connected to the essence of the Tree of Life within.

These are rare moments amidst a life of duality and choice when there is a sudden meaningful identification – moments of deep sensory experience when one encounters the mystical, a connection reminiscent of "this time, bone of my bones" (Gen. 2:23). These are moments when we might say to ourselves, "This is worth living for."

In such instances, our existential loneliness can uncover a surprising and additional dimension within us or others, offering a new view of ourselves. This is similar to the thrill sometimes experienced when reconnecting with someone.

Oneg/delight should not be driven by an obsessive impulse and must not be forceful. There's a mutual connection between delight (*oneg*) and Eden (*eden*), symbolizing refinement and pleasure. In the *Zohar*, the letters *ayin*, *nun*, *gimmel* in the word *oneg* form an acronym for "A river flows out of

Eden to water the garden" – Eden-river-garden. Thus, delight links to the primordial Eden, where the flow nurtures and brings abundance, present in the original Garden of Eden under the Tree of Life.[12]

Given this, it can be cautiously stated that life's meaning involves navigating between the Tree of Knowledge, which activates us, and the Tree of Life, which brings us *oneg*. It's about feeling how in areas such as speech, listening, food, sexuality, power, leadership, and material wealth, there's a potential for delightful experiences. In these moments, something of the essence of existence is revealed to us. "And in my flesh will I see God" (Job 19:26) implies that the Creator indeed resides in this earthly dwelling and is even pleased to "return home."

A biblical example illustrating the difference between pleasure and delight is found in the story of Esau returning exhausted from the field:

> And Esau said to Jacob: "Let me swallow, I pray you, some of this red, red pottage; for I am faint." (Gen. 25:30)

Esau rejected the blessing of the birthright because of his craving for a lentil stew. His desire for the here and now, for immediate gratification, does not align with the language of blessing and delight, leading to his loss of the birthright and blessing.

A person who is aware of inner deficiencies, of an inner hunger, might follow Esau's path. Esau represents the immediate need for satisfaction. This approach at best leads to pleasure that does not impact the soul internally. The demand for pleasure is expressed in exhaustion – "for I am faint" – characteristic of Esau. Each of us has an element of Esau within us, whether in obsessive eating, a desperate need for touch, for receiving love, and sometimes even in the overwhelming need to teach and influence.

In contrast to Esau, Jacob worked for many years before achieving the companionship he sought. The ability to delay gratification, to calmly observe one's deficiencies from a distance, can lead to an experience of *oneg* due to the capacity to live with a perception of eternity, accompanied by longing and great desire.

---

12   See also the piyut *Kah Echsof* by the Admor of Karlin: "Shabbat is the pleasure of the souls, and the seventh day is the pleasure of spirits, an Eden for souls to delight in love and awe for You."

Be a Blessing

Blessing and *oneg* belong to the same family. Blessing operates at the level of consciousness and influence, while *oneg* resides in the quality of the experience. Common to both is the desire for interaction with others. On this point, there is a distinct difference between significant aspects of Eastern culture – meditation and the mindfulness that evolved from it – and the concept of delight in Jewish sources.[13] *Oneg* is inherently connected to engagement with others. It seeks dialogue while acknowledging separateness. *Oneg* is fundamentally linked to the concept of human intimacy. Eastern cultures emphasize the enlightenment of the individual, marking an important cultural dialogue and significant difference.

The approach to pleasure in Jewish sources has been complex throughout the ages. Many Jewish philosophers saw the body and its pleasures as distractions from a person's spiritual work and as obstacles in connecting with God. These thinkers, following Maimonides (Rambam), considered the pursuit of intellect and the quest for divinity as the essence of human nature, the reflection of God's image in us. This work requires a healthy body (Maimonides was a physician) but views the body itself not as a part of the divine service. On the contrary, it is seen as a hindrance to the functioning of our active intellect. According to this view, a healthy body allows the intellect to operate without bodily distractions, but it is merely a tool, not a separate essence. Pleasures have no spiritual value.

This view is clearly expressed in the following passage:

> Eating, drinking, sexual relations, and generally the sense of touch, are pleasures which Aristotle explained in *Ethics*, saying that this sense is a disgrace to us. And how beautiful is his statement! And it is indeed correct that it is a disgrace! For it pertains to us insofar as we are animals and nothing more, like all other beasts. There is nothing in it of interest to humanity. (Maimonides, *Guide for the Perplexed* 3:8)

The concept is straightforward: Many of the body's pleasures, especially the most basic ones, are akin to our animalistic side. "There is nothing in

---

13   See also chapter 8 below on my encounter with the Dalai Lama.

it of interest to humanity." According to Maimonides, the distinctiveness of humans compared to other animals is not expressed in the nature and quality of bodily pleasures; rather, this aspect is exactly what they have in common! Aristotle's significant influence in this perspective is clear and acknowledged.

Elsewhere, Maimonides discusses the sexual drive:

> Similarly, when engaging in sexual relations, it should not be out of mere desire, but rather for the purpose of physical health or procreation. Therefore, one should not have sexual relations whenever he feels the desire, but rather when he knows there is a need to release semen, similar to a medical procedure, or to fulfill the commandment of procreation. (*Mishneh Torah*, Hilchot De'ot 3:2)

Sexuality is seen as a biological necessity (an impulse) or a tool for procreation (pregnancy). It is not considered an expression of intimacy!

Maimonides had a dramatic influence on the face of Jewish education from the Middle Ages to modern times. His monumental personality and the significance of his Torah commentaries were central to the Jewish existential field from the medieval era to our times. However, alongside his immensely positive influence on shaping halachah (Jewish law) and Jewish thought across generations, he also had a complex attitude toward the body, food, sexuality, and consequently, the whole concept of *oneg*. The impact of this influence was far-reaching, and its implications for Jewish education, which still grapples with its relationship to the body and pleasure, are significant. Furthermore, the centrality of Maimonides' approach in the Jewish world greatly affects perceptions of what Judaism is fundamentally about, the role of humans in the world, and the overall question of creation's purpose and destiny.

A second perspective within Jewish sources views the body, its senses, and its pleasures as vital components of spiritual work. This view, rooted in the Torah, became central in the literature of the Sages, influenced medieval thinkers who contributed significantly to Kabbalah, and subsequently shaped the emergence of Chasidism and its modern-day expressions.[14]

---

14 For an extensive exploration of this issue, see Yair Lorberboim, *Tzelem Elohim* [in Hebrew] (Tel Aviv: Schocken, 2004).

The Torah is filled with narratives involving desire, the downfall of significant figures, and their attempts at rectification. It acknowledges the physical beauty of Rachel, Joseph, David, Esther, and others. Throughout these biblical texts, the enjoyment of food, sexuality, and general human needs is seen as stemming from a life-affirming place, integral to our existence and aligning with God's intentions for us. While acknowledging the inherent health and vitality of desire and the love of life, the Torah also emphasizes refining and directing these desires appropriately.

In the teachings of the Sages, various stories address the body, such as the well-known story of Hillel the Elder:

> All your actions should be for the sake of heaven, like Hillel. When Hillel would go somewhere, they asked him: "Where are you going?" He replied, "I am going to perform a mitzvah." "What mitzvah, Hillel?" "I am going to the bathhouse." "Is that a mitzvah?" He said to them, "Yes. It is for cleansing the body." You should know that this is so; just as [Roman] caretakers who are responsible for cleaning and polishing the statues in royal palaces are paid a salary and are elevated in the king's court, how much more so we, who were created in God's image and likeness, as it is written, "For in the image of God made He man" (Gen. 9:6). Therefore, caring for this body is all the more important. (*Avot d'Rabbi Natan*, version B, chapter 30)

Hillel innovatively teaches that caring for the body is part of an act with sacred purpose. The religious act is inherently connected to the body, fulfilling the Creator's desire to dwell in the lower realms. This act, in Hillel's words, is performing a mitzvah.

While Maimonides views the image of God in us as an intellectual foundation,[15] Hillel sees the body and its care as part of this foundation. It appears

---

15   "As man's distinction consists in a property which no other creature on earth possesses, viz., intellectual perception, in the exercise of which he does not employ his senses, nor move his hand or his foot...on this account, i.e., on account of the divine intellect with which man has been endowed, he is said to have been made in the form and likeness of the Almighty" (Maimonides, *Guide for the Perplexed* 1:1).

that Maimonides follows the approach of Shammai, who views the body as a burden compared to the essence.

Explicit teachings on the body as an image are found in the following source:

> God created man in His image.... The physical body of man is suitable for God and fits a divine purpose. Thus, the Torah teaches us to recognize and appreciate the divine honor of the body. Indeed, the Torah came not only to sanctify the spirit but primarily to sanctify the body. This is the foundation of all human morality: the human body, with all its inclinations and forces, was created in the image of God; it is incumbent upon man to sanctify his body appropriately to its divine purpose. (Rabbi Samson Raphael Hirsch, Gen. 1:27)

This approach views the body – and its pleasures – as an important element in serving the Creator. It seeks to refine the type of pleasure, to sanctify it, and to give it a unique flavor.[16] Furthermore, it urges a person to touch the layer of *oneg* in all aspects of life and calls for a conscious effort to crown the consciousness of the Tree of Life over the consciousness of the Tree of Knowledge.

The development of this idea to a radical stage is found in the teachings of Rabbi Shalom Dovber Schneerson, the fifth Rebbe of Chabad. According to his approach, in the future, the dynamics will reverse: "The soul will receive light and vitality from the body."[17] While in our world, the soul imparts light and vitality to the body, in the future, the body will be the source nourishing the soul! Creation and history will evolve to a state in which the physical matter of creation is essentially divine. This represents another stage in the Creator's desire for a dwelling in the lower realms. The returning light from the body impacts the soul and creates a special connection and union between God and man.

---

16 "Man was created for no other purpose than to rejoice in God and to derive pleasure from the splendor of His Presence" (Rabbi Moshe Chaim Luzzatto, *Mesilat Yesharim*, chapter 1).

17 "*B'sha'ah she'hikdimu*," 5672, part 3.

We circle back to the tale of the trees in the Garden of Eden. When the focus is on the Tree of Knowledge of Good and Evil, the essence of human endeavor is knowledge and understanding, discerning between good and evil, and applying this discernment in our actions. In this context, material reality – including the body – might become a hindrance to the primacy of knowledge.

In contrast, the Tree of Life symbolizes a belief in life and humanity. Positioning the consciousness of the Tree of Life at the forefront of our lives allows the experience of delight to have a place in our existence. This aspiration, though perhaps infrequent, is immensely significant, fostering a profound yearning for transcendence in our existential experiences.

According to this approach, the function of the Tree of Knowledge, encompassing laws and commandments, is to refine and direct *shefa* (abundance). Without such precision, the abundance might interact with the world or others in a potentially harmful way. Uncontrolled power and abundance can be damaging or exploitative, despite good intentions. Conversely, too little abundance can limit potential and giving. The role of laws and commandments is to allow the vitality of the Tree of Life to manifest appropriately, in a way that the recipient can absorb. Precision in merging abundance with reality is a key indicator of the consciousness of blessing and the experience of *oneg*.

Beyond the model focusing on the uniqueness of the *oneg* experience, there are realms in which the experience of *oneg* might be particularly concentrated. Just as a gym emphasizes the physical body, various areas provide opportunities to practice and focus on the experience of *oneg*, drawing essential meaning and tools from these spaces to enrich other aspects of life.

In the next chapter, we will explore the Sabbath as a day when the experience of *oneg* holds a central place. We'll focus on the development of the concept of *oneg* on this day and emphasize significant ways that we receive a unique touch of *oneg* specifically on this day.

Chapter 6

The *Oneg* Experience of Shabbat

As we observed in the introductory chapters of this book, the concept of *oneg* is not explicitly mentioned in the description of the Garden of Eden – yet its expression there is evident. A distinctive portrayal of human experience in the garden can be found in the following commentary, which we discussed earlier:

> He was placed there to indulge and frolic as he wished. His suste-
> nance came from the garden's trees, his drink from the streams of
> Eden, and his garments were clouds of glory. His time there was
> spent in immense, unabated delight. (Rabbeinu Bachya, Gen. 2:15)

We find here a set of elements that combine to form a full picture. In Eden, Adam and Eve could enjoy themselves and frolic freely, evoking a childlike joy devoid of worries. Sustenance was obtained with ease by picking the fruits of the garden's trees. Water – the source of life – flowed from the river of Eden. The clouds of glory provided clothing, offering security for their physical bareness. These aspects created an experience of the highest level of pleasure.

The manner of eating and drinking in the Garden of Eden represent direct nourishment from God. The knowledge that God takes care of and nourishes the individual as the source of their existence fosters a deep sense of security. When we are in a state of *oneg*, it is as if we "recall" the experience of the Garden of Eden.

Chapter 58 of the Book of Isaiah is pivotal in understanding this concept of *oneg* as it evolves through our daily lives. This remarkable chapter is read in Jewish communities on Yom Kippur (the Day of Atonement) as the haftarah[1] of the morning service. In this chapter, the prophet speaks to the Jewish people, detailing their transgressions and sins. Surprisingly, he addresses a people actively seeking God, adhering to righteousness and justice, and longing for proximity to God (v. 2). The community is left wondering why their actions do not yield a response, based on the established belief in the doctrine of retribution. Their initial expectation was that good deeds would ensure a favorable response (v. 3).

Upon studying the verses, we find that the required correction goes beyond merely adhering to the commandments through acts such as fasting on Yom Kippur or even ordinary level of care for the vulnerable. Here, additional principles borrowed from the language of the Tree of Life come into play, working together in the subsequent verses to cultivate a consciousness of *oneg*.

The first is the demand for freedom for all oppressed people. "And let the oppressed go free, and remove every yoke" (v. 6). Freedom is a fundamental value for a people who knew the slavery of Egypt. We cannot accept freedom for only one part of the community.

The second is the creation of an encounter of human closeness, a face-to-face meeting between the giver and the weak. "When you see the naked, clothe him, and do not ignore your own flesh" (v. 7). When we see a naked person, we must cover him. Seeing the naked takes us back to the Garden of Eden, an existential situation that is simultaneously both unique and vulnerable. This situation leads us to share our personal bread – "You shall share your bread with the hungry, and bring the homeless poor into your house" (ibid.) – and then to the act of bringing the poor into your house, creating a sense of visibility and belonging, beyond physical satiety.[2] "And satisfy the afflicted soul" (v. 10) – opening your soul to the weak creates a deep human closeness that can uplift the downtrodden soul.[3] It is a meeting of one soul with another.

---

1 The haftarah (literally, "parting") is a series of selections from the books of Prophets of the Hebrew Bible that is publicly read in synagogue as part of Jewish religious practice.

2 In the Talmud, we find stories that illustrate the tension between the principle of "anonymous giving," where there is no interaction between the giver and the recipient, and the needy individual's desire for recognition, warmth, and affection. See the tale of Peleimu and the devil (*Kiddushin* 81a), and the account of Mar Ukva's wife (*Ketubot* 67b).

3 "Rabbi Yitzhak said: One who gives a coin to a poor person is blessed with six blessings, but one who appeases him with words is blessed with eleven blessings" (*Baba Batra* 9b).

"Then your light will break forth like the dawn, and your healing will spring up quickly" (v. 8) – this depicts a relationship rooted in seeing the impoverished and oppressed not for their outward circumstances, but for their inherent humanity. When we embrace such depth of connection, it functions as a transformative blessing, catalyzing a dawn of new understanding and empathy. When we offer warmth and bring the other into our home, creating a nurturing environment and sharing freely, we abolish the dichotomies of rich and poor, good and evil – distinctions that arose from the knowledge gleaned from the Tree of Knowledge. Instead, we herald a unified shared reality, reminiscent of the Tree of Life. In a world often fragmented and polarized, this approach creates moments of Eden. This call to action transcends moral obligation; it is a call to forge a quality of life filled with blessings, in which everyone is seen and secure.

"Then you will call, and the Lord will answer; you will cry, and he will say: *Hineni* [Here I am]" (v. 9) – the word *hineni*, spoken by Abraham at the Binding of Isaac and by Moses at the Burning Bush becomes a remarkable expression of God's presence in our lives, in which He says to us: *Here I am.*

The prophet invites us to awaken a unique consciousness toward the other. This is not the usual work of moral sensitivity, but rather an encounter that comes from a blessed consciousness. It integrates eye contact and the experience of togetherness, like when Boaz sees Ruth.

"You will be like a well-watered garden, like a spring whose waters never fail" (v. 11). In this state, all individuals are nurtured by the river that flows from Eden, sustaining our lives. Reading this chapter specifically on Yom Kippur points to the special quality of this day – the ability to grant a person a fresh start through embracing the principles embodied in the Tree of Life.

Now, the prophet remarkably steps up a notch, shifting from discussing the unique form of societal repair through behavior that creates blessing, to Shabbat: "if you call Shabbat *oneg*" (v. 13). While the fast day indeed serves to open one's eyes and heart, the normative routine of life compellingly steers us toward Shabbat.

Shabbat as a Day of *Oneg*

If you restrain your foot because of Shabbat, from conducting your own affairs on my holy day; if you call Shabbat a delight [*oneg*] and the holy day of the Lord honorable; if you honor it by not going your own ways, seeking your own interests, or pursuing your own affairs; then you will take delight in the Lord, and I will cause you to ride upon the heights of the land; I will nourish you with the heritage of your forefather Jacob; for the mouth of the Lord has spoken. (Is. 58:13–14)

"If you restrain your foot [*raglecha*] because of Shabbat" – this verse describes Shabbat as a day when we cease our usual survival routines. In Hebrew, *hergelecha* or "routines" comes from the same root as "your foot." In doing so, we enter a different state of consciousness in which we can momentarily return to the Garden of Eden.

"Conducting your own affairs [*heftzecha*]" – on this day, our view of life is not centered around "objects" [*hefetz*] and the drive for possession, but shifts toward seeing ourselves as subjects, intrinsically linked to the surrounding reality. Freeing ourselves from the perspective of life as an object allows us to view life with "desire," which is another meaning of the word *hefetz*, referring to heartfelt desire, an expression of genuine will. This transition converts our materialistic desires into living with a clarified will.

"If you call Shabbat *oneg*" – the depiction of Shabbat in this chapter diverges from other descriptions in the Torah, which often emphasize cessation from work. Here, the emphasis is on Shabbat as a day of *oneg*, a day offering a different, more sensual quality of experience.

The description of Shabbat in the book of Exodus (20:10) states, "and He rested on the seventh day." What is the relationship between the principle of rest and the experience of delight? Resting on Shabbat is more than just the passive act of retreating from weekday work. The particular rest of Shabbat invites us to reach a unique place of consciousness. Its purpose is to understand Shabbat as a weekly event that serves as a platform for conscious and physical pleasure. In *Sefer Ahavat Shalom*, a Chasidic work, Menachem Mendel of Kosov writes: "'What was the world lacking – rest.' This means that the world was lacking rest, pleasure, longing, and yearning, which represents the main foundation and vitality of the world."

This rest is not just a break, but a conscious, physical state in which longing and yearning play a central place in the feeling of being alive.

The Ari (Rabbi Isaac Luria) says that if only Adam had waited for Shabbat to begin, he could have eaten from the Tree of Knowledge.[4] Fundamentally, Adam was right to eat from that tree, only he did it too soon. Had he waited to eat until Shabbat began, he would have connected to the experience of *oneg* and to the consciousness of the Tree of Life. This would have given a new meaning to eating from the Tree of Knowledge.

Here we encounter a renewed understanding of Shabbat. The essence of Shabbat is to touch the very foundation of delight and experience the meaning of earthly life at a unique level of consciousness.

Holiness and *Oneg*

> And the heaven and the earth were finished, and all the host of them. And on the seventh day, God finished His work which He had made; and He rested on the seventh day from all His work which He had made. And God blessed the seventh day, and hallowed it; because in it He rested from all His work which God in creating had made. (Gen. 2:1–3)

The concept of "holiness" entered our world with the start of the first Shabbat.

Much has been articulated and written about the term *holiness*. In the general realm of philosophy, and particularly in the Christian tradition, holiness is predominantly associated with the notion of estrangement from the body and materiality. The German-Christian philosopher Rudolf Otto regards holiness as the unique attribute of religion when compared to secularism. He perceives the sensation of holiness as a dichotomy between awe and yearning, a lifestyle tethered to a celestial deity as opposed to the needs of the earthly human. In this definition as well, the emphasis is on the distinction between the holy and the mundane. According to Otto, the feeling of holiness is a mental and spiritual property, which we understand as a fundamental given. He characterizes this feeling as "the numinous," representing a divine concept that transcends sensory perception.[5]

---

4   *Sha'ar Hakavanot*, Rosh Hashanah Discourses, discourse 1.

5   William James offers a similar explanation: "The collective name for the ripe fruits of religion in a character is Saintliness. The saintly character is the character for which

Within the Jewish world too, we find a critical principle of separation and withdrawal associated with holiness. Fundamentally, this separation pertains to abstaining from "sin," not necessarily from the material and mundane. However, we may find the foundations of a disagreement regarding the essence of holiness within the Jewish world in the ancient debate between Hillel and Shammai:

> It has been taught: It was said of Shammai the Elder: all his days he ate in honor of the Shabbat. If he found a fine animal, he would say, "This is for Shabbat." If he found another better than it, he would set aside the second one and eat the first. However, Hillel the Elder had a different approach; all his actions were for the sake of heaven, as it is said, "Blessed be the Lord, day by day" (Ps. 68:20). (*Beitzah* 16a)

Shammai is wholly focused on Shabbat, seeing it as a day embodying holiness. He sets aside the finest animal he can find in the market during the weekdays, so that he can eat it on Shabbat. In contrast, Hillel interprets the phrase "Blessed be the Lord day by day" to express the belief that even the ordinary days carry God's blessing. He opts to eat the animal he finds in the market on that same day, even if it falls in the middle of the week.

Here we witness different perceptions of sanctity. Both viewpoints hold value in eating as an expression of pleasurable experience. In Shammai's approach, this enjoyable experience is exclusively reserved for Shabbat, sanctifying time. As for Hillel, the concept of "residing in the lower realms," or the sanctity found in ordinary daily life, is not confined to a specific time. His citation of the verse from Psalms "Blessed be the Lord day by day" signifies that God's blessing permeates human existence inherently, extending even into the quotidian.

I would like to give several definitions of the concept of holiness, which I learned from three individuals of our time.[6] Professor Rachel Elior writes:

---

spiritual emotions are the habitual centre of the personal energy" (*The Varieties of Religious Experience: A Study in Human Nature* [New York: Modern Library, 1902], 271).

6   This study took place within the framework of Tehuda, a unique project that took place at Kolot. We invited three speakers to discuss the concept of sanctity, and I will present

Holiness is linked to the cessation of the world of action, manifested in a fixed "seven-day" cycle that delineates the boundary between the sacred and the profane, which is a realm overseen by humans. This pause is orchestrated through a mandated relinquishment of human dominion and its enslaving force, because the holy represents time and space, or a concept or entity that is uncontrollable. Holiness suspends the earthly concerns associated with the mundane world, characterized by labor and servitude, all emanating from a shared root. It involves halting the dominating and controlling activities of humans in the controlled domain. This ensures a realm of rest, holiness, freedom, and liberation, unburdened from the enslaving rigidity of the mundane. It is facilitated through a sanctified regime of cycles of seven, embodying freedom.[7]

According to Elior, holiness is tied to a profound freedom that requires a person to detach from their possessive, enslaving identity in order to touch upon an inner sanctity that opposes control. This freedom takes place in a cyclical seven-day rhythm in the dimension of time. According to this view, holiness is associated with detachment from the principle of ownership.

Professor Moshe Halbertal writes:

The holy is not just a source of deterrence or restriction; it also serves as a focal point of desire, because we crave a non-instrumental relationship in which we are released from our specific role as dominators. In this sense, there is a deep connection between holiness and love, since love itself is a hope for a non-instrumental relationship, a relationship in which one does not see the other as a tool, but as a person with intrinsic and independent value.[8]

---

their ideas below. I would like to thank my colleague Shay Zarchi, who played a central role in formulating the topic and inviting the speakers.

7   Rachel Elior, "On the Sanctity of Time and Place," in *Limits of Holiness: In Society, Philosophy, and Art* [in Hebrew], ed. Emily Bilsky and Avigdor Shinan (Jerusalem: Keter, 2003).

8   Moshe Halbertal, "On the Sanctity and Boundaries of Artistic and Linguistic Representation," in Bilsky and Shinan, *Limits of Holiness*.

Revisiting Elior's perspective, we may argue that the more an individual constructs an identity devoid of the underpinnings of dominating power – be it toward others or against them – and the greater their detachment from a dependency on ownership, the more they embody their "pure self." From this viewpoint, holiness is anchored in a profound connection to oneself, unshackled from restrictive external identities.

On the other hand, according to Halbertal, it is specifically the engagement with the "other" that facilitates refining the quality of a relationship. Central to this refining process is a quest for a pure connection, untainted by utilitarian objectives. It is a connection in which the other is not seen as a means to an end, but is appreciated for his or her intrinsic value.

There is a resonance between these two approaches in the shared aspiration to liberate individuals from the coercive elements intrinsic to personality. For Rachel Elior, this manifests in the realm of time, whereas Moshe Halbertal emphasizes the sphere of human relationships and specifically the role of love.

I heard a third interpretation from Rabbi Shimon Gershon Rosenberg (commonly known by his Hebrew initials Sh.G.R., or Rabbi Shagar).[9] He posits that the interpretation of "holiness" should be sought in the concept of *oneg Shabbat* (delight in Shabbat). This approach perceives a deep connection between the experience of holiness and the notion of enjoyment, essentially incorporating the previously mentioned views while adding a sensuous dimension of *oneg*. Holiness, according to this view, is not about detachment from the world in favor of something higher and sublime, but rather a terrestrial, sensual, and experiential phenomenon centered around the realms of Shabbat enjoyment. In a certain respect, Halbertal is on the same wavelength as Rabbi Shagar. The concept of holiness is not fundamentally tied to separation but rather involves a specific kind of expansion of the soul.

In Halbertal's case, this would be turned toward the other, while emphasizing the precision of love and communication; for Rabbi Shagar, it relates to the overarching notion of enjoying the Shabbat, which extends to various aspects of life that come to the fore during the Shabbat, as we will see below.

---

9   From a class given by Rabbi Shagar, of blessed memory, to the students of the Tehuda program of Kolot and the Midrasha at Oranim in 2006.

The Oneg Experience of Shabbat

The corpus of halachah (Jewish law) regarding Shabbat emphasizes the thirty-nine categories of labor prohibited on that day. In a simple reading, these laws emphasize what is permitted and what is forbidden – like the Tree of Knowledge of Good and Evil. However, if Shabbat is a pronounced expression of the experience of *oneg*, how does the Tree of Life, embodying the joy of Shabbat, give forth the world of permitted and forbidden?

Indeed, one can avoid various labor activities on Shabbat to intensify the peace and rest from the external world that drives us during the weekdays. In the secular world, we encounter a similar principle – avoiding work in favor of engaging in family gatherings, going outside to experience nature, and other similar recreational activities. These experiences, halachic, traditional, and secular, reflect the desire to take a step back from the mundane aspects of life.

Exploring further, we may view detachment from the mundane as a necessary condition and stage for creating a different consciousness of blessing, in which weekday creation and labor are replaced with a consciousness of rest, tinged with a shade of earthly life. This rest reflects consciousness of a deep connection to the essence of the Tree of Life and to the experience of *oneg* in the Garden of Eden.

In other words, the entire purpose of the prohibition to engage in labor on Shabbat (represented by the Tree of Knowledge) is to serve as the first stage toward the main goal: reaching a consciousness of blessing (represented by the Tree of Life).[10] This presents us with a new proposal for observing Shabbat. Shabbat is the weekly day of *oneg*. It represents the pinnacle of existence, because its observance is a particularly special experience characterized by experiencing delight in many facets of life. Shabbat is the dimension in time where we make a "dwelling in the lower realms" for the Creator.

---

10   The Sages expressed this eloquently: "Rabbi Yochanan said in the name of Rabbi Yosi: Anyone who delights [*mit'aneg*, from the root *oneg*] in the Sabbath is given a heritage without boundaries, as it is said (Is. 58:14), 'Then you shall delight yourself [*tit'anag*] in the Lord; and I will make you ride upon the high places of the earth, and I will feed you with the heritage of Jacob your father.' Rav Judah said that Rav said: Anyone who delights in the Sabbath is given the desires of his heart, as it is said (Ps. 37:4), 'Delight yourself also in the Lord; and He shall give you the desires of your heart.' I do not know what this *oneg* is, but when it says 'And call the Sabbath *oneg*,' it must be referring to Sabbath *oneg*" (*Shabbat* 118a–b).

This *oneg* Shabbat is mainly expressed in five central domains, which we will explore below.[11]

1. Lighting Candles

Lighting candles is more than just a ceremony that marks the transition from Friday to Shabbat. At its core, lighting candles is an expression of the day in the week when we are commanded to add light to the home.[12] In ancient times, the entire home of the Jews was illuminated on Shabbat, and this was one of the prominent characteristics of the home. However, beyond the increase in physical light, we are commanded to use the lighting of candles to foster a different quality of vision. "Lighting candles on Shabbat is a requirement according to the Sages, because it is the foundation of all *oneg*, as there is no *oneg* without light.... One who enhances pleasure, cleanliness, and cherishes the commandments of Shabbat is indeed praiseworthy" (Hameiri, *Beit Habechirah*, *Shabbat* 25b).

What does the lighting of a candle symbolize that encompasses the *oneg* of Shabbat? The light enables additional reflection and awareness of what is happening in the home. This light allows for a different perspective on others, with a focus on family members. This inner vision is a part of building *oneg*, as it creates an experience of connection. The external light in the home and the inner light inside the individual both enable and seek a face-to-face experience, encouraging us to examine and sense the welfare of our family and loved ones, in all their aspects.[13]

---

11 To this list, we may add sleeping on Shabbat as a delight (*Shulchan Aruch*, Orach Chaim 290), as well as studying Torah as a Shabbat delight (*Peirush Hameiri* by Rabbi Menachem ben Solomon Meiri, citing the Jerusalem Talmud, *Shabbat* 118). Both sleeping and studying Torah on Shabbat aim for a different quality of experience compared to weekdays, but we will not expand on this here.

12 "Lighting a candle on Shabbat...is a duty. Both men and women are required to have a lit candle in their homes on Shabbat. Even if one has nothing to eat, one should beg at the doors and purchase oil to light the candle, as this falls under the category of enjoying Shabbat" (*Mishneh Torah*, Hilchot Shabbat 5:1).

13 The concept of domestic peace is also tied to Shabbat candles. The Talmud discusses someone who has money for only some of the Shabbat commandments: "Rava said: It is obvious to me that if [one has to choose between] the candle of his home and the Hanukkah candle – the candle of his home is preferable because of domestic peace;

Lighting the candle is an invitation to open one's eyes and to ask "how are you," not as a technical question, but as a bid for connection and meaningful contact with our loved ones, to touch their souls. Disconnecting from the technological world for a few hours (with emphasis on the smartphone) can aid in this vision.

2. Shabbat Meals

In ancient times, it was customary to have two meals daily: one in the morning and another in the evening. The obligation to partake in three meals on Shabbat arises from the desire to both savor the delight of Shabbat and to honor it more than we would on a regular day, incorporating the addition of meat and wine.

> With what does one experience *oneg* on Shabbat? ...With a dish of beets, and large fish, and heads of garlic. Rav Hiyya bar Ashi said in the name of Rav: Even if one prepares a small item in honor of Shabbat – this is *oneg*. (*Shabbat* 118b)

The difference between a "meal" and a "feast" mirrors the distinction we drew earlier between enjoyment and true *oneg*. Eating is a fundamental need for humans as for other creatures. Food serves a functional role, as we find enjoyment in a meal. In contrast, a feast provides a deeper level of *oneg*, touching our souls. Eating then becomes an expression of heartful joy and a celebration of the soul. Moreover, the wine and its impact on individuals play a role in the transformation of consciousness during the feast, facilitating this elevated experience. By reciting the Kiddush over the wine, we articulate a heartfelt yearning to reach this state of *oneg*, a state potentially facilitated by the effects of wine.

The dining experience on Shabbat transports us back to the Garden of Eden, to an engagement with a type of sensual nourishment rooted in the

---

[between] the candle of his home and sanctifying the day – the candle of his home is preferable because of domestic peace" (*Shabbat* 23b). In the absence of money, there will always be a preference for the aspiration of "domestic peace." This peace is tied to a different quality of encounter enabled on Shabbat that is more complete, due to the hope for a renewed perception.

initial creation of the world and the quality of life that existed in the garden. Here, food transcends being a mere "necessity" and becomes a kind of profound spiritual journey.[14]

3. Speech on Shabbat

From the verse in Isaiah cited earlier, "…to seek your own pleasure and speak your own words," our Sages learned: "One's speech on Shabbat should not be like one's speech on a weekday" (*Shabbat* 113a). Therefore, discussing or planning for weekday concerns is forbidden.

While on weekdays, speech mainly serves as a tool for communication and a means to an end, on Shabbat we seek a different quality of speech. The goal is to strip the instrumental element from speech, reaching toward a discourse whose words foster meeting and connection.[15] The increasingly common practice in some circles of the liberal Jewish world to refrain from using smartphones on Shabbat is not just about abstention – primarily, it is an invitation to a different kind of listening, to the heart and the words that emanate from it. Technology accustoms us to efficient technical communication, yet it might reduce the ability for genuine conversation. Shabbat can serve as a day on which we engage in a different kind of speaking and listening, and a different, more precise use of the power of words.[16]

---

14 For a discussion on delightful eating as a rectification for eating from the Tree of Knowledge, see chapter 12 on food and the Tree of Life.

15 Rashi interprets the type of speech that is prohibited, "such as in buying and selling and accounting." There is a debate among the halachic authorities regarding which speech is forbidden. The Ba'alei Tosafot and many others make a general statement that on Shabbat, one should speak much less than on weekdays. The Terumat Hadeshen (1:61, 2:155) wrote that it is permissible to engage in extensive conversation if it brings *oneg*. Although walking like on a weekday is prohibited, the Sages permitted running for pleasure, and they ruled similarly regarding excessive talk. In our interpretation, the kind of speech one should avoid on Shabbat is instrumental. Therefore, engaging in work-related matters and discussing purchases is a return to viewing people as functionaries. Such speech is forbidden on Shabbat, whereas speech that creates connection, encounter, and bonding is desirable. Again, we find the hope for a different, clean speech, as a foundation for *oneg* and as a general call for proper speech.

16 See chapter 11 on the speech of the Tree of Life.

4. Sexuality on Shabbat

The connection between sexuality and Shabbat appears in many sources.[17] "'He will yield his fruit in its time' (Ps. 1:3) – this refers to a Torah scholar, who is physically intimate with his wife on Friday evenings" (*Ketubot* 62b).

One can see the connection of sexuality to Shabbat as an act of seeking a time of intimacy, given that Shabbat is a day of rest from work and everyone is at home. However, in light of our discussion on the *oneg* of Shabbat, one can see interpersonal relationships on Shabbat as an invitation to a different kind of connection between man and woman, one that does not arise only from a place of need, but rather from a place of soul mating. The term "Torah scholar" expresses this aspect of connecting to a higher consciousness, a consciousness we seek to bring into the couple's relationship.

5. Weeping on Shabbat

The foundations of *oneg*, change of consciousness, and the quest for intimacy on Shabbat may invite the elements of sensitivity and vulnerability within us to surface and be present. Surprisingly, weeping has a place on Shabbat. The Midrash relates:

> Rabbi Akiva would sit and weep on Shabbat. His students said to him: "Master, you taught us 'and you will call Shabbat *oneg*' (Isaiah 58:13)!" He said to them: "This is my *oneg*." (*Shibbolei Haleket*, "Shabbat" 93)

Often, weeping is a result of the gap between dreams and reality. On Shabbat, the soul might long for another world. Sometimes we actually feel as if we are in another world on Shabbat. Shabbat seeks to accommodate this space in our lives. "Similarly, one who finds pleasure in crying to remove sorrow from his heart is permitted to cry on Shabbat" (Rema, *Shulchan Aruch*, Orach Chaim 288).

---

17   Regarding the nature of Shabbat eve, Rashi says that it is a night of pleasure, rest, and bodily enjoyment (*Ketubot* 62b). Regarding marital relations on Shabbat, Maimonides says: "Marital relations are part of the delight of Shabbat" (*Mishneh Torah*, Hilchot Shabbat 30:14).

Conclusion

To summarize our discussion, the face-to-face gaze inspired by the lighting of the candles, the dining experience in the form of a feast, the personal conversation that opens the heart, and the physical connection in intimate relationships are all expressions of the concept of *oneg* on Shabbat. All require the individual to adopt a different consciousness, creating an experience that differs from weekdays. The open invitation to weep adds another dimension to this experience.

Shabbat is an invitation to experience life on a different frequency. There is a hidden element of ego in the weekday act of survival. When Shabbat arrives, we remind ourselves that we can also live on a different frequency, recalling that we need not remain slaves to our habits. We do not wish to enslave anyone – not even ourselves.

Understanding Shabbat as a day that enables a special quality of life has the potential to generate a fascinating conversation in Jewish society about the role of Shabbat in our lives. In Israel, such a conversation might replace the political discourse on coercion and freedom with a new discourse that facilitates connection and perhaps even unity. In the Jewish world, a meaningful conversation about Shabbat as a day when the individual and the family touch the level of life's significance can be initiated. It is also an opportunity to discuss the meaning of the weekly day of rest observed by many of the world's religions and nations.

Shabbat is a day when we enjoy "an extra soul," a weekly visit to the Garden of Eden.

Questions for Reflection

- Do you identify states of *oneg* in life? What characterizes this experience?
- Imagine your Sabbath day. Is the Sabbath primarily a time for needed rest, or does this day have a connection to a different consciousness, at the center of which is the experience of *oneg*?

Chapter 7

The Good Life, Western Style – Prof. Martin Seligman

As I delved into the language of the Tree of Life, blessing, and expressions of our life quality from a Jewish perspective, I realized that a parallel conversation is happening in the general world. One of the defining features of our era is that a large part of humanity no longer experiences life as a battle for survival. Employment opportunities are broad, and there is more free time and greater freedom of choice than in any previous generation.

The modern era has highlighted the experience of connecting to oneself. People attend workshops urging them to "feel yourself" and "be in touch with yourself." People are discovering themselves, their bodies, and investing time in caring for their bodies and souls. However, alongside the very positive aspects of these revelations, self-engagement can be excessive. One of the factors contributing to depression, a quiet yet painful epidemic also rampant in our world, is excessive self-focus. It happens that depressed people primarily think about themselves and attribute exaggerated importance to their feelings.

Investing in trends that emphasize light and enjoyment can sometimes lead to spiritual decline. When such engagement isn't balanced with long-term and fulfilling processes, it can quickly turn into an existential pit. Light is replaced by darkness. A desire for change that is not supported by stable tools for training and spiritual work will not endure.

In recent years, there has been extensive research on the concept of well-being. This is not just a powerful human experience, but a perspective that has grown in the academic world. The modern model of well-being converses with fundamental trends in psychology, addresses existential questions on a philosophical level, and even attempts to measure quality of life. Quality of life is not an expression of spiritual elevation or thrilling moments, but an expression of a lifestyle with many aspects that together create a measurable quality.

In this chapter, I will explore the connection between the discourse of quality of life in the Western world and the goal of being a blessing that is articulated in this book.

Quality of Life Metrics

My initial steps in the field of quality of life were guided by Dr. Anat Itay. Anat is a graduate of Kolot, specializing in measuring quality of life. She worked with the Joint Distribution Committee in collaboration with the Israeli government on quality of life in Israel, as part of the country's involvement with the Organization for Economic Cooperation and Development (OECD) in measuring quality of life across the world.

The various areas typically measured include employment quality, personal security, health, housing and infrastructure, education, skills development, personal and social well-being, environment, civic engagement and governance, material living standards, leisure, culture, community, and information technology.

According to the OECD, quality of life is a combination of the availability of functions required to satisfy various human needs, integrated with the ability, opportunity, and freedom of individuals to pursue personal goals, to thrive, and to feel satisfied.

Quality of life measurement is not just for gathering information about citizens of countries in the twenty-first century. It serves as a significant factor in determining governmental budget priorities. Thus, the growing focus on quality-of-life metrics is gaining a prominent place globally as well as in Israel.

Comparing Israel's quality of life metrics with other OECD countries reveals interesting data. Israel excels in some areas – especially in health, social care, and education levels. However, it lags in income levels (too low), cost of living (too high), housing (expensive and in short supply), and public satisfaction with governance. There are also complex areas, such as education, where high attainment in advanced degrees contrasts with low student performance.

The Good Life, Western Style – Prof. Martin Seligman

To evaluate a country's quality of life, it's crucial to consider differences among various populations. Israel, a highly diverse society, shows significant disparities between the Jewish and Arab populations and within those groups. Interestingly, while the ultra-Orthodox and Arab populations share low standings in many measured dimensions such as poverty, workforce participation, and education, their satisfaction levels differ. Most Israeli Arabs aspire to the quality of life of the secular Jewish society, whereas the ultra-Orthodox have internal values driving their lives, unrelated to the external world, challenging the logic of government-defined quality-of-life metrics.[1] This fact is vital for our ongoing discussion.

The following example illustrates the complexity of quality-of-life metrics. The OECD uses a measure asking individuals whether they have someone to contact in times of trouble. Canada's version goes a step further, asking whom they would contact. However, these questions, intended to assess one's support system in difficult times, do not fully address issues of loneliness or despair, offering only a partial picture of a person's mental state in daily life. They fall short in measuring the capacity for intimate connections and dialogue, crucial components of personal happiness.

This realization led many, including myself, to conclude that these broad and intelligent metrics, while useful, cannot encompass foundational questions about what brings happiness and a sense of meaningful existence. I understood that the global discourse on these metrics misses a critical step concerning the essence and purpose of being human. Perhaps global metrics simply cannot touch on the foundational questions of human existence. Our quality of life is tied to a variety of philosophical and spiritual questions, making it challenging to create clear human metrics. Yet the very effort to measure life quality signifies the uniqueness of the era in which we live.

Positive Psychology and Happiness

During the time that I was studying quality-of-life metrics, I first heard about Professor Martin Seligman,[2] a leading figure in the discourse and vision of

---

1   Statistics Department, OECD Paris, January 2016.

2   I wish to thank the Lippman Kanfer Foundation in the US, who brought me into the conversation on quality of life from a Jewish perspective. Special thanks to Joe Kanfer,

life quality in the Western world. I was invited to teach at a conference of senior educators in the USA that focused on the question "Why be Jewish in the twenty-first century?" The conference engaged in a sincere and authentic search for the meaning of existence in general and the contribution of Judaism to these questions in particular. I was in the early stages of exploring the language of blessing, which forms the basis of this book. Ahead of the conference, we were sent Seligman's book *Flourish*, which opened my eyes to the contemporary discourse on life quality.

Seligman is one of the founders and designers of positive psychology, a field that developed in the late twentieth century. Its main innovation is the emphasis on meaning, defining purpose, and the ability to change. One of Seligman's colleagues defined it as "a scientific field of study on what makes life most worth living."[3] To elaborate, the approach of positive psychology seeks to engage with the whole human being, focusing on strengths rather than weaknesses, building on the good instead of fixing the bad, and aiming to take the lives of average individuals to a higher level of meaning and satisfaction, rather than just achieving normalcy.

Much of the research in classical psychology has historically focused on human pathology. Questions of happiness and meaning were not given significant attention. Many people, through their experiences in psychotherapy, are intimately familiar with these views. I deeply appreciate their importance in personal growth. Every person has a foundational pain, and recognizing this pain is part of self-discovery, fundamentally touching upon one's longing in the world.

Publicly, the experience of slavery in Egypt, a formative trauma for the Jewish people, is a highly significant Jewish cultural memory. Many commandments are derived from it. However, a Judaism that only reacts to the slavery in Egypt, or derives its meaning solely from our historical hardships, risks losing something essential from its original identity and purpose.

This understanding of the need to touch upon the foundational purpose of humanity aligns with the principles of positive psychology. It does not negate

---

founder and former director of the foundation, and Professor John Woocher, of blessed memory, for their trust and partnership on the very questions this book addresses.

3   Chris Peterson, Seligman's partner in his first studies in 1998.

personal memory and dealing with the past, but seeks to draw strength from a positive future. The person thirsty in the desert can only drink from the half-full part of the glass, even if the heart aches for the half that is empty. This analogy is probably true for other moments of distress in life – coping with a crisis draws strength from a person's positive qualities and abilities, not just from understanding the sources of the crisis. In the life of a nation too, it is important to identify the source of vitality and future vision, beyond the consciousness of past memories.

One of the first to address this aspect of human beings was Viktor Frankl in *Man's Search for Meaning*, which introduced existential therapy. In his book, Frankl, a survivor of Auschwitz, describes his personal experience of maintaining his sanity amidst chaos and hell. His therapeutic approach, developed in subsequent years, suggests that modern humanity has lost the meaning of life and suffers from an "existential vacuum," leading to the boredom, depression, aggression, and addiction prevalent in modern times. To escape this inner void and its mental illnesses, Frankl believed that one must find meaning in life. He often quoted Nietzsche's saying: "He who has a 'why' to live for can bear almost any 'how.'" These principles are crucial in relation to the massive crisis that began in Israel in October 2023, with many hoping that at the end of the tunnel, a light of meaning and hope will shine through a vision.

Although Frankl's books gained widespread recognition, a relatively small number of therapists adopted his therapeutic approach.

Indeed, humanistic psychology serves as a prelude and gateway to positive psychology. It focuses on the human dimension of psychology and its context in the development of psychological theory, emerging in response to behaviorism on one hand and psychoanalysis on the other.

Alongside Viktor Frankl, we find researcher Mihaly Csikszentmihalyi, who introduced the concept of "flow," which is directly linked to Martin Seligman and the language of well-being. Csikszentmihalyi, a Hungarian psychologist and professor of business who was a prisoner during World War II, developed the theory of flow after studying the phenomenon for about twenty-five years. Flow occurs when people are so immersed in what they are doing that they lose their sense of time and space. It is characterized as a holistic sensation people feel when they are fully engaged and internally satisfied with their activity.

The merger of consciousness with action, which characterizes the experience of flow, is the main difference between it and other states in everyday life where consciousness is divided. Instead of observing the action from the outside, in the experience of flow, the person becomes part of the performed action, as if the doer and the deed have become one. This is a state in which different levels of awareness are in complete harmony. Csikszentmihalyi found that this phenomenon exists in various life domains and activities, where people described their experience as a kind of flowing with nature – hence the name.

In his research, Csikszentmihalyi describes this state as time standing still, like in a meaningful conversation where time flies. According to him, satisfaction is not necessarily derived from an experience that is considered valuable. Rather, it can be from any experience in which the individual is immersed to the point of forgetting oneself for a while. This is, of course, a completely opposite experience to mere pleasure, a sensation that involves a high level of focus on oneself and one's sensory experience. One of the educational challenges in child education is to teach children what causes them a flow experience and to redirect time resources from pleasure-focused activities to satisfaction-focused activities.[4]

In the state of flow, there is a delicate and precise balance between challenge and skill. If the challenge is too great, we become frustrated. Conversely, if our skills are too advanced relative to the challenge, we become bored and are not sufficiently engaged.

As Csikszentmihalyi puts it:

> The best moments in our lives are not the passive, receptive, relaxing times.... The best moments usually occur if a person's body or mind is stretched to its limits in a voluntary effort to accomplish something difficult and worthwhile.[5]

---

4   Mihaly Csikszentmihalyi, *Flow: The Psychology of Optimal Experience* (New York: Harper and Row, 1990).

5   Csikszentmihalyi, *Flow*, 3.

The Good Life, Western Style – Prof. Martin Seligman

In the late twentieth century, Martin Seligman, who worked with Csikszentmihalyi and even described him as "the greatest researcher in positive psychology," took this approach a step further by becoming the official founder of positive psychology. According to Seligman, to promote happiness, one should choose strategies that are suitable and comfortable for long-term practice. To experience a minimal sense of psychological well-being, there should be at least three times more positive than negative emotions.

Barbara Fredrickson, a researcher in positive psychology, argues that a ratio higher than 11:1 in favor of positive affect does not promote a person's development and may even have the opposite effect, causing one to lose touch with reality. Negative affect can sometimes be a suitable and vital component for mental health. Grieving over a loved one or anger when injustice is done are reality-congruent responses indicating mental health.

A group of psychologists led by Martin Seligman found that before the development of classical psychology, the average rate of depression was 1 to 4 percent. However, the current rate of depression that affects functionality stands at 20 percent. Children born today have a 20 percent chance of suffering from a severe syndrome of depression or anxiety before finishing high school. A century ago, during Freud's time, this rate was only 4 percent over the entire lifespan. Freud, therefore, targeted his psychological treatment only to a small population of "sick" people who came to the clinic with various syndromes. The cautious conclusion is that classical psychology, which mainly focuses on developmental disorders, mental disorders, psychological disorders, etc., has not succeeded in achieving its purpose. The study of these disorders has not produced significant results in preventing or reducing them.

The World Health Organization predicts that by 2030, depression will be the most severe disease affecting human life expectancy and quality of life. Depression significantly affects our immune system and is considered more life-shortening than any other disease.

At the beginning of his career in positive psychology, Seligman wrote *Authentic Happiness*, a foundational book on positive psychology that deals entirely with the fundamental components of expressing happiness in our lives. In this book, he builds an important level on top of the preexisting theory of flow and lays out the principles of his theory. Published in 2002, it became a bestseller because it presented all the basic assumptions of positive psychology and added a method of measuring happiness. He wrote:

> Positive psychology takes you through the countryside of pleasure and gratification, up into the high country of strength and virtue, and finally to the peaks of lasting fulfillment, meaning and purpose.[6]

Below are the foundations of happiness as described in Martin Seligman's book *Authentic Happiness*:

1. Positive emotions: The ability to approach life from a positive perspective. This is not just about having a cheerful disposition, but an optimistic approach that seeks life advancement. In this state, a person accepts different aspects of life with understanding and self-acceptance. This acceptance can create positive emotions, vital for a sense of accomplishment and satisfaction. Internalizing positive emotions can help in relationships, our approach to work, our ability to be creative, and more.

2. Engagement: Similar to the concept of flow, engagement involves total commitment. It's about connecting our entire personality to our involvement in life. It's the sensation of time passing due to intense focus on a unique experience. This experience requires letting go of the centrality of reasoning in life – a challenging task for the modern individual – and requires more effort than just experiencing positive emotions.

3. Meaning: A sense of purpose and meaning is a crucial element in a fulfilling life. This state is not about asking "What am I doing?" but rather "What do I want to be?" According to Seligman, especially in the current era, it's essential to consider the question "Why do I get up in the morning?" Given that the question of survival is less central nowadays, finding meaning in our times is a vital component of well-being.

In the years following his initial work, Martin Seligman expanded upon his theories. Recognizing the limitations of his earlier perspective, he sought to add another dimension to the understanding of life's meaning, moving

---

6   Martin Seligman, *Authentic Happiness: Using the New Positive Psychology to Realize Your Potential for Lasting Fulfillment* (New York: Simon and Schuster, 2002), 134.

beyond just authentic happiness to a broader consciousness of life quality. In his 2011 book *Flourish*,[7] he introduced two additional elements to the description of a fulfilling life, beyond authentic happiness:

4. Relationships: This area represents one of Seligman's significant innovations compared to his understanding just a few years earlier. He contends that a person can be happy without meaningful relationships, but "well-being" is possible only for those who have significant relationships with parents, siblings, friends, and, above all, a romantic partner. Seligman even refers to medical research showing that people who "disconnect" from relationships activate pain areas in the brain, which can harm our immune system. This principle includes the ability to create intimacy and live within it over time.

5. Accomplishment: Setting reasonable goals and achieving them gives a person a sense of joy and fulfillment. This is not just about flow and awareness of life, but the understanding that one needs to set a goal and allow space for the satisfaction of achieving that goal, serving as fuel for continuing life.

These additions by Seligman reflect a more comprehensive approach to understanding the components of a fulfilling and meaningful life.

Martin Seligman summarized the five key elements of well-being with the acronym PERMA: Positive emotions, Engagement, Relationships, Meaning, and Achievement. These components collectively form a framework for understanding and measuring well-being in a comprehensive manner.

Continuing to evolve and add depth to his theories, in 2018, Seligman published another book, *The Hope Circuit*. This work is a somewhat autobiographical account that reflects his personal journey and insights. In this book, Seligman emphasizes the necessity for individuals to live according to a purpose and vision. This perspective speaks volumes about the importance of having a future-directed outlook that can provide strength and motivation in the present.

We identify a notable parallel between positive psychology and the Tree of Life in the Garden of Eden, as well as between the concept of flow and the river flowing out of Eden.

---

7   Martin Seligman, *Flourish: A Visionary New Understanding of Happiness and Well-Being* (New York: Simon and Schuster, 2011).

My Meeting with Seligman

I contemplated Seligman's five principles and their connection to the concept of being a blessing and saw a direct and comprehensive intersection. The chapters of this book engage with these principles, expand upon them, and explore what Judaism can contribute to the meaning and quality of life.

As I delved deeper into the teachings of this esteemed individual, I felt an internal challenge – to see the connection to the language of blessing and the Tree of Life consciousness. I was eager to meet him, to tell him about my book and project. I sent him an email before my trip to the USA in the summer of 2018, hoping it would lead to a meeting. In his response, he asked me to elaborate a bit on the concept of the language of blessing before agreeing to meet. After I briefly wrote to him the essence of the idea of the Tree of Life consciousness, he replied: "I am not clear how this is related to Judaism, but let's meet."

Thus, on the last day of my visit to the USA, I rented a car from New York to reach his office at the University of Pennsylvania in Philadelphia, intending to drive back to Kennedy Airport and catch the flight to Israel at seven in the evening.

I entered the Positive Psychology Center at the university and made my way to Seligman's office – he was the head of the center. An hour was allocated for the meeting. I thought that after it, I would have ample time for a relaxed meal and a two-and-a-half-hour drive to the airport.

I met a man with a radiant face and a sense of humor. Humor, particularly a willingness to laugh at oneself, plays a significant part in opening the mind to meaningful conversations.

Within a few minutes, we found ourselves in a personal discussion. We talked about what excites us in life, the role of childhood images in positive psychology, whether he completely dismisses classical psychology, and we even touched on love and relationships. I learned about the courses on life quality he offers to senior command of the U.S. Army, about his student who was appointed Minister for Quality of Life in one of the Emirates with a substantial budget, and the guidance he provides her.

During our conversation, Seligman shared that he is Jewish. He hadn't visited Israel for over forty-two years and spoke of his minimal involvement with the Jewish community and Judaism in general. I mentioned Woody Allen's quote from one of his early movies about nostalgia not being what it used to be. He smiled and nodded in agreement, then thoughtfully asked whether Judaism had completed its historical role. His question was respectful, not confrontational or cynical. He wondered if Israel's existence and focus on the physical aspects of life might detract from exploring deeper existential and spiritual questions of being Jewish. He also questioned whether Israel's success as a start-up nation might obscure deeper existential inquiries.

I found our conversation fascinating and began sharing details of my Ve'heyeh Berachah project. I argued that Judaism has a significant role in shaping the future, beyond its contributions in the past. As our discussion deepened, he inquired about my schedule. I enthusiastically replied that I was free, hoping to catch a later El Al flight at eleven. He called his secretary to clear a few hours for us.

We opened a Bible and read the story of the Garden of Eden, discussing the quality of life in Eden, the symbolism of the Tree of Life, and life without the awareness of the Tree of Knowledge.

We went out to eat together, continuing our discussion of being a blessing. We explored the connection between individual blessings and the destiny of the Jewish people, clarifying concepts and engaging in lively debate.

During a poignant moment in our conversation, Seligman looked into my eyes and asked me to share insights about mysticism and the spiritual sources that had been driving me in recent years. He was curious about the connection between his work in developing the concept of "well-being" and the limitations of rationality and the academic world he was part of. He expressed an interest in exploring the world of Kabbalah and Chasidut and discussed the role of faith in God in contemporary times. He shared his engaging conversations with his Christian theologian friends on the relevance of faith in God today.

I felt that something valuable was happening. I shared that being a Zionist for me means believing that we can create a life of blessing in Israel, a model for the world, reflecting the verse "and in you will all families of the earth be blessed." Seligman was intrigued and shared details about his new book, *The Hope Circuit*, which focuses on the need to create a vision for the future that can energize our present lives. This resonated with me, reminding me of Rabbi Soloveitchik's concept of a "covenant of destiny."

Seligman then asked how I reconcile a culture so focused on memory with a vision for the future. I asked him to ponder this question: How does a culture connect a powerful and often traumatic past with an inspiring vision for the future? This question became a precious parting gift for me, a query that stays with me to this day.

Before we parted, he gave me a copy of his new book, inscribed, "For Mordechai – with admiration, Mordechai." He smiled, hugged me, and mentioned that he hadn't used his Hebrew name, given to him at his brit, since his bar mitzvah. This was the first time I ever felt compelled to take a selfie with someone.

Returning to my car, which had earned two parking tickets, I managed to catch the late El Al flight. On the flight, I reflected on the connection and differences between my world and Seligman's. I pondered particularly his critique of capitalism, a significant point of convergence between us.

> Positive psychology is a politics that advocates no particular means but rather another end. That end is not wealth or conquest but well-being. Material prosperity matters to positive psychology, but only insofar as it increases well-being.... What is wealth for? I believe it should be in the service of well-being. But in the eyes of economists, wealth is for producing more wealth....[8]

He dedicates an entire chapter to the subject of economy driven by well-being. I felt that the vision of being a blessing resonated with this perspective, with the ideal of a blessed economy.[9] Similarly, the emphasis on relationships as a core component of life quality according to Seligman's approach aligns with the Ve'heyeh Berachah vision, focusing on repairing familial relationships – sibling dynamics, parenthood, and especially the rectification of intimate relationships as a repair for the story of the sons of Elohim and the daughters of men.

---

8   Seligman, *Flourish*, 221.

9   See chapter 9 on money and the Tree of Life.

The Good Life, Western Style – Prof. Martin Seligman

When I discussed with Seligman the concept of blessed speech and a different kind of media, I noticed his strong identification with these ideas. The parallels are indeed numerous and profound.

Several weeks later, I wrote him an email:

Dear Professor Seligman,

I have been reflecting on the many similarities between the world of blessing and your vision of flourishing. However, I would like to delve deeper into a few questions to clarify our discussion:

You are pioneering a new consciousness and practical approach in the world. Is there a structured pathway for individuals to practice the changes you propose? What learning tools do you offer for internalization?

For instance, one of the innovations of the PERMA model is the emphasis on healthy relationships as a measure of well-being. This seems to be one of the most innovative metrics. Yet you do not offer tools for constructive communication essential for building a steady and fulfilling relationship. Nor do you address the quality of intimacy sought.

I am keen to understand more about this from you. How can such dramatic change, which you are leading and advocating for, occur without a conscious effort that requires work and practice? Are you addressing the necessary tools?

The Torah delves into details, some of which are burdensome. Many Jews indeed shy away from the intricacies of halachah. However, it believes that without applying these principles to daily life, real change in the world is unattainable. The Torah engages in employer-employee relationships, establishes interpersonal communication rules, delves into marital life, commands respect for parents, and through the Sabbath and holidays, it demands a pause from routine to engage in the fundamentals of pleasure and meaning in life. The laws of Shemittah (the sabbatical year), both in land and monetary realms, challenge the foundational assumptions of Western economics. The examples are numerous.

Furthermore, in the realm of mystical teachings, the inner meaning of many commandments is expanded, attempting to understand their deeper wisdom. This domain also offers new spiritual tools that touch on the soul, the heart, and various aspects of our being, beyond mere intellect. And there is still much work ahead.

The main thing is, your voice refreshes my Judaism.

I would love for you to visit Israel. I will try to find funding. I believe we can create a meaningful dialogue with many of your students and my colleagues in Israel. Perhaps you will be convinced that there is potential here to create a blessing model for the world, especially as a small nation? In short, I look forward to continuing our conversation. Thank you very much.

Several days later, I received his response:

Mordechai –

I enjoyed meeting you as well. I wish you success in connecting these worlds.

Let's be in touch.
Yours,
Martin

At first, I was disappointed by his brief response, and at first, I thought I'd been more excited about him than he was about me. Then I realized that this was his way of virtual communication. I understood how valuable this person was. Essentially, he was telling me that he has opened a gateway to a language, to a different psychological emphasis, a tangible vision of quality of life, the need for a future vision. But he does not claim to provide all the tools and the entire methodology. There's a humility in that. He understands that different people will engage with his innovation, share, expand, and propose new practices. The world needs practice.

What makes this man special, beyond his pleasant, attentive, and dynamic personality, is his ability to create metrics. Perhaps these metrics are a kind of halachah, a way to examine the desired change through actions. Many of us struggle with the language of metrics. I must admit, after meeting him, I became a proponent of metrics that demand from us a tangible expression of the practical difference in our lives.

Influenced by him, I thought that together with my friends and colleagues, we need to create "blessing metrics."[10] How do we measure the blessing of abundance, blessed speech, blessed family and relationships? How do we measure the ability to forgive and trust in processes of repair? What constitutes a blessed process of emotional healing, and how do we cope with life's trials with this consciousness?

I believe we need to engage with people like Martin, Jews and non-Jews alike, to discuss the meaning of being created in the image of God that every person embodies, and to foster new hope for the world and a vision for the future. I imagine a broad human dialogue on the simple question: Why do we wake up in the morning?

From this dialogue, we return to the universal quality of life metrics we began with, to take part in shaping the fundamental premises of the OECD, and to create metrics for a blessed world. To start auspiciously, touching the human hope embedded in the words said to Abraham: "And in you will all the families of the earth be blessed."

Being a Blessing and Positive Psychology

Beyond the conversation I had with Martin, I think it will be useful to conclude this chapter with a comparison between the well-being movement and being a blessing.[11] A central foundation of this book is the understanding that being a blessing seeks to connect to the consciousness of the Tree of Life and to the quality of life in the Garden of Eden.

---

10 In chapter 19, on the vision of *ve'heyeh berachah*, I have attempted to propose metrics for blessing.

11 This is not a thorough academic comparison, which would be appropriate to perform in another context.

Be a Blessing

The river flowing out of Eden, one of the life forces in the garden, is not just for quenching thirst. It represents a type of flow, conversing with Csikszentmihalyi's world, and a feeling of life beyond time.

Another characterization of the world in flow is the loss of awareness of time. The lack of awareness in a world before eating from the Tree of Knowledge is similar to this state – consciousness in the Garden of Eden was a natural state of flow. But now that we ate from the Tree of Knowledge and gained awareness of the world outside that state of flow, we can only touch flow by becoming conscious of being a blessing, to the exclusion of awareness of all other states. This is perhaps the essence of the Shabbat. The river also represents a type of enlightenment – clarity of the heart, the ability to connect different parts of life.

Seligman's quest for meaning converses with the hope of touching *oneg* in all areas of our lives and receives a broad design and meaning in the words "be a blessing." The essence of Tree of Life consciousness is to give a vital request to our lives, which matches Seligman's principle regarding positive emotions.

The understanding that "it is not good for man to be alone," which opens the second part of the garden story, matches Seligman's innovation regarding the centrality of a healthy relationship in our lives as a characteristic of well-being; a life of quality is essentially linked to the ability to be in a meaningful relationship.

A significant difference relates to the attitude toward one's deficiencies and life's trials. According to our *ve'heyeh berachah* philosophy, Tree of Life consciousness directly touches our life's wounds. Tree of Life consciousness was present in all of Abraham's trials, precisely because he was a blessing. I did not find in positive psychology a significant engagement with the areas of difficulty, the trials of our lives, that characterize us as human beings. Moreover, positive psychology sometimes shows an aversion to engaging with underlying pain.

In this regard, there is a place to connect to some extent with classical psychology, which predates positive psychology. Classical psychology views the created world – and humanity – as something fundamentally broken.

However, there is a place for engagement with pain precisely from the perspective of being a blessing, from an understanding that our wounds and trials – and all of life's difficulties – are intrinsically linked to human growth and the quest for meaningful life alongside healing. Particularly, the existence of a future vision can help heal the past. As mentioned, Seligman strongly emphasizes this need for creating a vision of the future that gives strength to the present.

Being a blessing is a Jewish societal message that begins internally within the Jewish world and ends as a model for the entire world. According to our way, we should not expect societal change without a change in individual consciousness. However, the change needed is to repair the individual with a focus on society and the world. These words make a statement about the place of nationalism, the particular basis in dialogue with the global village's universal context.

As mentioned earlier, the quest for meaningful quality of life requires work. It cannot be achieved merely through breathing techniques, fitness training, and positive thinking – despite the importance of these activities. Conscious change is one of the most revolutionary areas in a person's life and therefore requires significant practice. It is, in fact, a way of life.

Tree of Life consciousness, alongside the vision of being a blessing, touches many areas of life, essentially all aspects of our existence. Sometimes we may encounter the need to confront old paradigms, when being a blessing seeks to diverge from existing paradigms. Often, we may ask: What is the overarching purpose of an economic, social, or psychological perspective? In the following chapters, we will clarify the underlying assumptions that form these perspectives. We will touch on a wide range of areas in which the blessing consciousness offers a reinterpretation of these perspectives.

Questions for Reflection

* Imagine images of quality of life in your own daily existence. Are they related to Judaism? Does it matter?

Chapter 8

Meeting the Dalai Lama

There is something in India that touches me deeply – a certain humility and quietude in the air. For me, and apparently for many others, there is something healing in it. A revered guru in Rishikesh, who has met hundreds of Israelis, once told me, "Jews don't know how to breathe."

I thought a lot about this statement. The Jewish alertness, creativity, and many questions about reality come with a cost.

India is a wondrous land. It's no coincidence that many Israelis find their way there after their military service. India and Eastern philosophies are connected to my family story. My older sister, Chava, left Israel at the age of twenty-one and eventually delved into the world of Zen and Buddhism, marrying a remarkable man, a leader and a great teacher in this realm. To my parents' relief, he was a Jewish boy from Brooklyn – Bernie Glassman was his name. Like my sister, he rebelled against his upbringing and found himself in Japan, deeply studying Zen until he received advanced certification and began ordaining other students, including his wife, my sister.

Bernie established a new movement called Socially Engaged Buddhism. He was known for founding Greyston, conducting "Street Retreats," where participants live on the street for a week with only a dollar in their pocket, learning to survive in life's other spectrum. He founded an annual seminar in Auschwitz, comprised of second-generation Nazis and Jews, seeking dialogue and compassion. He went to remote villages in Mexico with a clown (Moshe Cohen) to entertain tens of thousands of children gathered from the region, among many other eye-opening and heart-opening initiatives that contrasted with the Torah v'Avodah movement (a religious Zionist orientation with a focus on integrating Torah observance and love of Israel with the values of the modern world) in which I was raised.

Some of his teachers from the East opposed this approach, arguing that there's no need to add a social action element to Buddhism, and it even contradicts the core teachings. Bernie of blessed memory once told me that the principle of *tikkun* (repair) is the central concept that remained in his philosophy from his Jewish identity, influenced by his close connections with Rabbis Shlomo Carlebach and Rabbi Zalman Schachter-Shalomi, both of blessed memory.

A "Chance" Encounter

I spent most of the Jewish High Holidays of 2019 in Bhagsu, Dharamshala, working on my book. Where else would I be leading the Yom Kippur Shacharit and Musaf prayers, acting as the "responsible adult" to dozens of bright-eyed young Israelis?

Later, as I sat alone in a café in McLeod Ganj, the Dalai Lama's residence, a group of crimson-robed monks walked in – not an unusual event in this village. They seemed more serious than usual. As the other tables were all full, they asked to join me. Noticing my kippah, they inquired about my work, leading to a discussion on the Tree of Life, abundance, blessing, and Israel. One monk was particularly close to their leader, the Dalai Lama. I recalled that the Dalai Lama was intrigued by Rabbi Yochanan ben Zakkai, who had crucially shaped Jewish life in exile after the Second Temple's destruction. This rabbi had famously asked the Roman conqueror of Judea, "Give me Yavneh[1] and its sages." The Dalai Lama, facing his own challenges of leading the Tibetan people in exile, was deeply interested in Jewish survival strategies in Diaspora.

Half-jokingly, I requested a meeting with the Dalai Lama, positioning myself as "an expert on Rabbi Yochanan ben Zakkai." To my surprise, a monk informed me that the Dalai Lama, having just canceled a trip to Germany due to illness, might be available to meet.

---

1   A city about thirty miles west of Jerusalem, which became the very first center of Jewish learning and leadership after the destruction of the Second Temple.

Meeting the Dalai Lama

The next afternoon, I received a WhatsApp message inviting me for a session with the Dalai Lama to discuss Rabbi ben Zakkai. Frantically, I managed to photocopy Talmudic sources in English within two hours, not an easy task under the conditions of that place. At the Dalai Lama's residence, after a security check, I entered his room with the monk from the café. We exchanged greetings and bows, and then the Dalai Lama requested a Jewish joke. I obliged with a story about an Italian driving a Lamborghini and a Jew with sideburns who keeps overtaking him. I was charmed by the Dalai Lama's hearty laugh and sense of humor.

We commenced our learning session together, delving into several texts. There were moments of profound emotion throughout our study. As we neared the conclusion of our session, we explored a particularly impactful excerpt:

> When Rabbi Yochanan ben Zakkai became ill, his students visited him. Upon their arrival, he began to cry. His students, puzzled, asked, "O Candle of Israel, pillar of the righteous, mighty strength of a hammer – why do you weep?" He replied, "If I were to stand before a mortal king, who is here today but in the grave tomorrow, whose anger isn't eternal, whose imprisonment isn't everlasting, and even if he sentenced me to death, I could still appeal to him with words or bribe him with money. Yet I would still weep. But now, I am to stand before the King of Kings, the Holy One, blessed be He, eternal in His reign. If He is angry, His wrath is everlasting; His imprisonment is infinite; and if He decrees death, it is eternal. I cannot persuade Him with words nor bribe Him with riches. With only two paths before me – one leading to Paradise and the other to Hell – and not knowing which I will be led upon, should I not weep?" (*Berachot* 28b)

As we studied this passage, the Dalai Lama repeated the word "beautiful" and seemed deeply moved by Rabbi Yochanan's integrity and humility. His face glowed with admiration.

Curious, he inquired, "Why does Rabbi Yochanan doubt his ascent to Paradise?"

I suggested that Rabbi Yochanan's uncertainty might stem from his own introspection regarding his negotiations with the Romans and his decision to see exile as a new opportunity for the Jewish people. I explained that Rabbi Akiva, a significant leader from the subsequent generation, had opposed Rabbi Yochanan's initiative to relocate the center of rabbinic learning away from Jerusalem. At the moment of his death, Rabbi Yochanan could not have known if his radical paradigm shift in Jewish history and its exile from Jerusalem would be favorably viewed in heaven.

Upon hearing this, the Dalai Lama began to cry.

Seeing his emotional response, I asked him gently, "Why do you cry?"

He looked into my eyes, a silence enveloping us. After a pause, he shared, "The Tibetan people endure immense suffering. I am uncertain how history will judge my role."

I felt an overwhelming urge to comfort him with an embrace, but out of deep respect and awe, I refrained.

After a few moments of silence, our conversation continued as a modest dinner was served. The Dalai Lama, displaying his characteristic kindness, asked if there was anything he could do to assist me. I took this opportunity to discuss the concept of blessing, and thus we delved into a dialogue about abundance, power, and their interplay with spirituality, particularly contrasting the notion of power in Israel with his belief in nonviolence.

His presence was a harmonious blend of inner greatness, leadership, presence, humor, and humility. Joy seemed to radiate from him, making the atmosphere light yet profound.

I found it challenging to convey the principle of *oneg* (delight) to him. I attempted to differentiate between simple pleasure and the deeper concept of *oneg*, especially in the context of Shabbat versus weekdays. Each time I explained, he looked at me with a kind of warm, inquisitive surprise, saying, "So that is how you feel. Interesting." His response was free of cynicism, criticism, or pretense. It reminded me of my late brother-in-law, Bernie Glassman, who would often respond to differing opinions with a straightforward "So that is your opinion," without any bitterness. I admit, at times it drove me nuts.

In the Dalai Lama, I saw a fusion of a humble monk and an enlightened being – one who listens and observes with depth and simplicity. The nuances of our disagreements became apparent, touching on subjects such as family, sexuality, passionate work, will, and even the media.

As the night progressed, it was nearing 10:30 p.m., and I sensed that he was growing tired. His assistant entered the room, signaling that it was time for me to depart.

On One Foot

Before I left, the Dalai Lama posed a thought-provoking question: "Could you please summarize the essence of the Torah for me on one foot, and don't use Hillel's answer."[2]

I was momentarily caught off guard, surprised by his sharp inquiry and awareness of Jewish tradition. To add to the challenge, he stood up, playfully balancing on one foot at the age of eighty-four, demonstrating what he expected of me.

I couldn't match his balance. I leaned against the nearest wall, His Holiness laughing gently at my attempt. Then, in that moment of quiet and with my heart racing, I responded while balanced awkwardly on one leg: "It's all about relationships."

There was a profound sense of connection between us in that moment. The Dalai Lama approached, expressing a gentle but significant difference in our perspectives: "Here we differ, and now we will also part." That simple statement was followed by a warm embrace. He bid me "Shalom," and I responded with a deep, respectful bow: "*Shalom u'vrachah*" (peace and blessing).

Exiting his room, I stepped into the crisp autumn air of McLeod Ganj. I walked the streets, deeply contemplating the extraordinary encounter that had just transpired during Chol Hamoed of Sukkot, under the inspiration of the day when we invite Moses, our greatest spiritual leader, into the sukkah as our *ushpizin* guest (symbolic biblical guests traditionally invited into the sukkah on each of the nights of the festival).

---

2   This refers to a well-known story of a convert who asked Rav Hillel to explain the Torah to him while standing on one foot. Rav Hillel said: "What is hateful to you, do not do to your fellow man. This is the whole Torah; the rest is commentary."

My mind drifted back thirty years to my first encounter with His Holiness in Israel. I was part of a large audience that had gathered to hear him speak. I remembered a question from the audience that had created a palpable tension: "What do you think about the Jewish nation believing it is the Chosen People?" The Dalai Lama's response, marked by his signature smile, was both profound and disarming: "I wish every nation would think it is the chosen one. The world would look better. Only let's not forget humility and humor." Those words had left a lasting impression on me.

Now, reflecting on our recent meeting, I pondered the uniqueness of this remarkable man, a pioneer among the "Tibetan Tannaim,"[3] grappling with his yearning for Tibet and his reality of exile in India. I admired his steadfast belief in his people and their place in the global community. It made me question why his brand of nationalism felt more palatable than the often-contentious national discourse in Israel.

As I continued my walk back to Bhagsu, several *tuk-tuk* drivers offered rides, but I chose to walk, seeking solace in the quiet forest. The lively chatter of monkeys was my only company as I mulled over our discussion. Maybe what I had shared about the importance of relationships was indeed a point of departure.

Long before Martin Buber's philosophy of dialogue, there was an intrinsic element in Judaism deeply connected to communication, intimacy, the meeting of eyes, disagreements, and touch. I recalled telling the Dalai Lama that a moment of blessing is not just an internal, subjective feeling of abundance but also involves how that moment and feeling are conveyed to others. This is the essence of blessing on one foot.

---

3   The Jewish Sages during the Mishnaic period, after the destruction of the Second Temple.

PART THREE

Blessing in the Twenty-First Century

"In all your ways acknowledge Him, and He will make your paths smooth." (Proverbs 3:6)

Chapter 9

Money in Blessing Consciousness

Tevye the Milkman's plea to the Creator in *Fiddler on the Roof* – "Would it spoil some vast eternal plan/If I were a wealthy man?" – has always touched me. What is it about money that affects us so deeply? What impact does money and wealth leave on our hearts and souls? Undoubtedly, money drives the world, certainly our external world – we work for it, buy with it, save it, and meticulously track its growth. Yet money sometimes also defines our internal world, as an expression of self-worth and social status; at times, it compensates for emotional voids within us.

Economic and public policies directly affect our financial situation. We are all tied to the trade relations between the United States and China, questions of additional taxation on the wealthy, and the economic philosophies of countries and their leaders. The relationship between economic perspective and social responsibility is direct. Classic capitalism typically strengthens the immense wealth of a minority and the gap between the rich and poor. Many of the world's wealthiest are involved in solutions for vulnerable populations, both through charity and by creating rehabilitation programs for weakened populations in their immediate surroundings and the wider world. However, in countries that adhere to classic capitalist ideologies, the gaps between social classes are still very large. The United States and Israel are among the leading countries in this disparity. As Jews, this fact should concern us, or at least provoke thought. The number of Jews leading Wall Street, one of the capitals of capitalism, is quite large relative to their proportion in the population. And in Israel, there is still a strong correlation between wealth and power.

Be a Blessing

Money and Longing

What is the role of money in forming individual identity? What can the consciousness of blessing contribute to the healthy, natural desire for abundance and security, for inner calm, and the ability to enjoy our portion in this world? Rabbi Nachman offers a deep contemplation on the desire for money:

> All souls long and desire for money, and not only do they desire and love money, but they even love the person who has money.... This is because the soul comes from a high place from which money originates and derives, for certainly the beginning of the place from which money originates is of a holy aspect. (*Likutei Moharan* 68:1)

The connection of the soul and the desire for money thus come from the same place. We use money to express the soul's longing to return to its place. Hence the deep connection between money and longing. Yet how do we connect to this place without the enslavement that often accompanies this desire? Over the years, I have contemplated this often. The fundamental assumption of this chapter is that wealth is one of the signs of blessing, with which Abraham our father was blessed. Indeed, Abraham enjoyed material abundance. The desire for abundance is part of the language of blessing in our world. However, as we see, not every wealthy person is indeed blessed.

On the evening of Sukkot in the year 2008, I received an email from a significant donor to Kolot whom I knew well. The subject of the email read: "Sitting shivah over my money – come and comfort me." In the body of the email, he described how the economic crisis at that time had significantly impacted his finances and how his world had essentially crumbled. He managed a hedge fund in which several US universities had invested, and they too suffered similar losses. The crisis affected his family, his professional world, and consequently, his reputation. Thus, I found myself traveling to the US during Chol Hamoed Sukkot to comfort this dear man. I had never before traveled during the holidays. I found him pale and broken. He shared how his basic identity had disintegrated – first and foremost, his masculine identity. With a shattered spirit, he described how his personal stature was tied to the power and strength that money gave him. In the midst of the holiday, I found myself as if shaking a broken lulav, trying to help this man regain his backbone.

Through this man, I understood how deeply money touches the core of our identity. He was also a mirror for myself. Despite the vast economic differences between us, I saw how money touched some existential void within me. I had always identified with Tevye's statement – I would have been ready for the "trial" of being a rich man. My encounter with this dear man lasted about three days. While engaging in a partnership with him, I found myself touching fundamental places of identity and money, as well as the lack within me.[1]

At the end of my impactful visit during Sukkot 2008, I went to visit my important teacher in New York, Rabbi Yitzhak (Yitz) Greenberg, may he live a long life. I asked him: How is it that in the midst of this economic crisis, we do not see our role as Jews, scholars, and teachers of Judaism in creating a new paradigm against the boundless capitalism of Wall Street? Doesn't Judaism have something to say in the face of this broken reality before us? Is it possible that the primary Jewish voice heard is the mournful one of the infamous scammer Bernie Madoff, who was arrested during that time?

He closed his eyes and said to me: "The reason we are not conducting a Jewish soul-searching on economics to lead to a new proposal is twofold. Firstly, to my regret, we do not see Judaism as relevant to the big questions of life, including economic paradigms and the like. We are accustomed to dealing with personal, familial, and community issues. However, we have not succeeded here in the US and in Israel in discussing broad policy issues as befits a strong community in the Diaspora or a sovereign Jewish state."

I nodded my head like a student before his teacher. "Secondly," he continued, "the infrastructure of the institutions and organizations we run is largely funded by the very system we are questioning. It is difficult to conduct a soul-searching investigation that might shake our world to its foundation."

I was moved by the self-awareness in his answer. The two reasons he cited shook me profoundly, as someone who had been part of the world of Jewish learning for so many years. The inability of the world of the *beit midrash*

---

1   See also chapter 15 on lack and the Tree of Life.

(Jewish study center) to ask foundational questions about trends in our world is akin to a deep cultural bankruptcy. A healthy Judaism knows its purpose, including engaging with fundamental paradigms in the world that need reexamination. As for the second reason, I acknowledged that I, too, lacked the courage to challenge the foundational assumptions of some of the donors, who ensured that the organizations I managed thrived. These donors showered me with love, trust, and a lot of money.

This visit to the US during Sukkot 2008 had a profound impact on me. I saw how difficult it was for the people around me to pause and ask foundational questions that could affect their inner security and life perspectives. As a Jew, I felt we were not fulfilling our mission in the world. If we had among us figures like Rabbi Akiva and his contemporaries, I thought, we would be engaged in some of the fundamental questions of economics, the impact of the Western world, and other areas that call for a new perspective.

Fifteen years later, that man and his family returned to their previous level of wealth and beyond, not because of the hours I spent with him, but due to the American market's ability to overcome crises. Indeed, the Wall Street paradigm still dominates the global economy. Yet many economists around the world are writing on the wall, saying that this paradigm will not last forever.

I add cautiously: it's hard to shake off the feeling that Jews have had a certain part in creating this situation in the world, and therefore have an important role in its repair. The Jewish people, with Israel at its center, have a duty to propose a new socioeconomic model in this era.

The following passage strengthens this claim. Rabbi Yitzchak Arama, one of the prominent rabbis of Spain before the expulsion, wrote the following about the desire for money in his time, the fifteenth century. Regarding the second of the Ten Commandments, "You will have no other gods before Me" (Ex. 20:2), he wrote:

> This includes the great idolatry that exists in the world today, a strong reality. It is: the intention of all thoughts and businesses toward the accumulation of money and the success of assets, which are to them the mighty gods, and on which they rely. In their faith, they count on this and deny God above.... This is the essence of idolatry. (*Akeidat Yitzchak*, Ex. 20:2)

This is a fascinating definition of idolatry: an overwhelming desire for accumulating wealth and success in property. He observed this among parts of the Jewish community in Spain before their expulsion. For him, the core issue wasn't about the overt worship of God through commandments, but rather the relentless pursuit of wealth, which he equated with idolatry. One wonders what he might think about the situation in today's Jewish world...

Excessive greed for money can undermine a person's inner freedom to develop an identity and personality without external influence. This concept of freedom is intertwined with Tree of Life consciousness. It fosters a state of being in which one finds satisfaction in one's portion in life, independent of material cravings.

My journey exploring money, including candid discussions with wealthy individuals, led me to a profound realization. As a Jew living in Israel, where I believe the State of Israel should be both a blessing to itself and a model for the world, I recognize the need to propose a new approach to understanding money and prosperity, both on the personal and social levels.

Be a Blessing – A New Economic Model

We begin by examining the ideological foundation of Western economics, which has had the most significant impact on our world.[2] Most Western economic models view the purpose of economics as increasing societal wealth through moral agreements and seeking transparency. Some focus on the state's responsibility to enhance economic equality, while others emphasize free-market dynamics and individual responsibility. Both perspectives aim to increase economic resources for human beings, assuming that people primarily derive benefit from consumption. In these models, human interaction is not necessarily considered of central value. Moreover, the other person is often seen as an instrumental means to achieve the goal of resource maximization. The market is a mechanism intended for the efficient and wise creation and distribution of scarce resources, with maximum transparency and without exploitation.

Regarding the Jewish context and the Jewish people's connection to this economy, Milton Friedman, a Nobel Prize laureate who specialized in

---

2   I wish to thank my friend Rabbi Aharon Ariel Lavi, who had a profound influence on my thoughts on this matter.

developing the concept of the "invisible hand" in economics (a theory proposed by eighteenth-century Scottish economist Adam Smith) and was an unequivocal supporter of free-market economics, said:

> Two propositions can be readily demonstrated: first, the Jews owe an enormous debt to free enterprise and competitive capitalism; second, for at least the past century the Jews have been consistently opposed to capitalism and have done much on an ideological level to undermine it.[3]

Friedman concludes that we should firmly support the former and reject the latter. This approach characterizes many Jewish leaders, including religious politicians who rejoice in the direct connection between Israel and the USA in economic matters.

My dear friend Yoel Cheshin, a major Israeli businessman and a leader in impact investments, recently wrote:

> The myth of "maximizing profit" was born as a mirror image to the less successful parts of the socialist worldview, a feedback to attempts to prevent the growth of corporations and the realization of their purpose. At those times, terms such as purpose, vision, and realization in the business world were not yet common. Therefore, the way to move away from the principle of maximizing profit is to replace it with a new principle – realizing purpose.
>
> The ideal of Israel as the "impact nation," as Sir Ronald Cohen defines it, does not, in my opinion, fully realize our historical purpose. I would prefer to call Israel the "purpose nation." It not only harbors the opportunity for a better future for us and the world, it also offers us the chance to fulfill our purpose as a people.[4]

---

3   Milton D. Friedman, "Capitalism and the Jews," October 1, 1988, Foundation for Economic Education, https://fee.org/articles/capitalism-and-the-jews/.

4   Yoel is the founder and chairman of 2B.VC and BR Israel. From an article on Sir Leonard Cohen's concept of the impact nation, "Time for a Revolution" [in Hebrew], *Globes*, June 20, 2022.

This image, which connects economics and meaning, sees the motivation of financial resources in the world as visibility and human blessing. The experience of abundance seeks to touch the roots of the soul and questions of meaning and joy.[5] This means that the economy is fundamentally tied to questions about individual quality of life and the society we live in.

For example, in our world, the gross domestic product (GDP) still dominates in determining a country's level of development. However, the problem with this measure is that part of the GDP increases when there are road accidents, cigarettes are sold, and antidepressants are consumed. Each of these areas represents huge amounts of money. In the USA, the GDP tripled over fifty years, while life satisfaction levels dropped! Recent studies reflect an increasing level of loneliness and anxiety, even in countries with the highest GDPs. Part of the GDP is linked to economic sources that harm a person's quality of life.

As we saw in the chapter on quality of life, perhaps it's time to create a more complex economic measure and concept, one that examines the ability to have honest and open communication, to engage in constructive disagreements, to play a balanced and beneficial family role as an integral part of the desire to increase personal abundance.

In the description of the world's creation in Genesis chapter 2, we can see the beginnings of this concept:

> These are the generations of the heavens and the earth when they were created, in the day that the Lord God made the earth and the heavens. No plant of the field was yet in the earth and no herb of the field had yet sprung up; for the Lord God had not caused it to rain upon the earth, and there was no man to till the ground; but there went up a mist from the earth and watered the whole face of the ground. And the Lord God formed man of the dust of the ground, and breathed into his nostrils the breath of life; and man became a living soul. (Gen. 2:4–7)

---

5   See Seligman, *Flourish*, chapter 8, on a similar principle in understanding well-being.

These verses describe the beginning of the relationship between Adam as a consumer and the source of resources – the earth. According to these verses, creation cannot grow without the combination of the earth, rain, and human labor. The elements that the earth needs – water and man – are created from it: the mist rises from the earth, and man is created from the earth. There are no resources and consumers here, but a system of relationships and dependencies, involving giving and receiving from all participants. The earth alone is barren, and so are the water and even man; growth is created only when each creation steps out of its boundaries toward another creation. Moreover, the purpose of all parts of creation is to create a foundation for the creation of man, and for him to be a living soul. In the words of my friend Rabbi Dov Berkovitz:

> Each creation must turn outward to give something of itself to another creation, and it can only fully realize its unique blessing when it receives the life-giving blessing of another being.[6]

Here begins the formation of a new consciousness. In this consciousness, the abundance in the world is fundamentally a product of the relationships between its parts. The existence of resources and consumers is not just to create profit, distribution, and consumption, but to create reciprocal relationships among people who build a society.

After the verses cited above, in which the reciprocal relationships between the parts of creation are described, the Creator makes man, trees, adds rivers, and places man in the Garden of Eden. The river nourishes both the earth and man. In the names of the rivers in the story of the Garden of Eden, we find expressions of many resources: gold, bdellium, and more. The river is in motion, and so is the movement of money. The ancient Hebrew term for money, *zuzim*, comes from a root that means movement. Money that remains in one place is like stagnant water. As the *Zohar* says:

> It is said: "Drink waters out of thine own cistern, and running waters out of thine own well" (Prov. 5:15). Why does it first say

6   Rabbi Dov Berkovitz, *Mikdash Hachayim* (Jerusalem: Maggid, 5770), 46.

"thine own cistern" and then "thine own well"? A cistern is called so only when it is empty and does not flow, while in a well, the water flows. Rather, the intention is the same place: at first, it is called a cistern, when it has nothing of its own and there is only what is put into it, and later it becomes a well. (*Zohar*, Parashat Noach 60)

A person who enriches himself for the sake of enhancing his personal identity is like a cistern in which the water stands still, and over time it loses its quality as it accumulates. The well, on the other hand, can signify the flow of material abundance. The expression of this flow in the Torah comes through lending to those in need. The Written Torah does not speak of charity as it appears in the world of the Sages and throughout history. A loan is not a free gift, but rather a creation of a relationship and dialogue: a reality that involves flow, albeit slow, requiring trust, at the end of which the loan is to be returned.

The "cistern" person, even if very wealthy and even generous in charitable giving, will not feel abundance. Money that defines internal identity stops the flow of abundance, even with philanthropy alongside it. Abundance is connected to a fundamental understanding of the role of money as flowing to me and from me. This principle is true also in other non-economic realms, linked to the various dimensions that create the experience of abundance and satisfaction.

"Well" people, by contrast, feel how the river of life, flowing out of Eden, visits them often. They indeed experience abundance. Psychologically, this river contains elements beyond economic security. It includes the ability to create relationships, love, a sense of security, a life of meaning, to see and be seen.

The emerging socioeconomic picture is that the purpose of the economy is to ensure that every person feels equipped with the tools for livelihood, for meaningful relationships, and for a basic experience of a secure home. This quality arises primarily from understanding the mutual dependency of human beings at the most basic level of their existence, even before discussing human moral rights and obligations. In this conscious world, humanity lives in a united realm of connection and visibility. In such an ideal world, there would be no need for charities and philanthropy, at least not as they are expressed today. The nonprofit sector as we know it is a product of a consciousness in which, at first, I enrich myself without limit, and only in the second stage do I give back to society and contribute. In contrast, in a blessed economy, there are no stages or divisions.

This point is clarified in the first economic story after the expulsion from the Garden of Eden, that of Cain and Abel. Why didn't God favor Cain's offering, a development that ended in death? The beginning of the story mentions:

> And in the process of time, it came to pass that Cain brought of the fruit of the ground an offering to the Lord. (Gen. 4:3)

"In the process of time" seems to refer to a period at the end of the year, meaning he brought end-of-season fruits.[7] Besides the likelihood that these fruits were not the best, bringing fruits at the end of the agricultural year implies that the consciousness of blessing was not integral to Cain's world from the beginning of the season. Cain is connected to the Tree of Knowledge. He is entirely focused on creating resources, and only at the end of the year does he "remember" to bring an offering. This is not the Tree of Life consciousness, in which a person is connected to gratitude and giving from the start of his or her work, creating a cycle of blessing, with ongoing giving and receiving. Cain's murder of Abel represents a split, a consciousness of death in Cain, a result of eating from the Tree of Knowledge and his connection to it.

One of the hopes of the Garden of Eden was to live in an experience of abundance of fruit trees and river waters, feeling the Creator's presence as the source of power and life. Joy in abundance is connected to being a conduit for abundance. Cain, by bringing his offering of the earth at the end of the season, represents a person who sees his creation and enrichment as part of his power and identity without the consciousness of being a conduit. God said

---

7   This is the intention of the Midrash (*Genesis Rabbah* 22:5): "Cain's example is like a servant who ate the first fruits and sent the peels to the king." In the first days of the harvest which are obligated in the mitzvah of first fruits, he consumes his property as much as he can, and sends to the King of the world, blessed be He, the peels, or produce from the end of the season (Kli Yakar, Gen. 4:3).

to Cain before Abel's murder: "If you do well, will it not be lifted up?" (Gen. 4:7) – *connect to the Tree of Life within you.*

Linking all these elements into a societal structure brings us the early foundations of the "fourth sector," a new sector in the world and in Israel.[8] This sector follows a new model that breaks the familiar barriers. Part of the ethos of the fourth sector is that there's no contradiction between profit and social activity and that a company can be economically successful and socially responsible at the same time.[9] This sector is still in its infancy and will undergo many changes.

In the Western world's practice, the existence of one thing comes at the expense of another. Social sciences, rooted in exact sciences of profit and loss relations, teach us something else: existence requires cooperation for survival, and it requires us to look for places where the connection between all parts can lead to more abundance, not only material.[10] The social-human connection between a person and others can create profit where classical economics sees scarcity. Therefore, non-material giving is also an essential part of creating a prosperous society,[11] although it is less measurable than material giving in terms of GDP per capita.

This invites a new contemplation, in which the economic and social worlds share the same perspective and vision.

Receive in Order to Give – Repairing Creation

Rabbi Yehuda Leib Halevi Ashlag was a Jewish scholar of the early twentieth century who did not receive the recognition he deserved. Known as Ba'al Hasulam for his commentary on and translation of the *Zohar* into Hebrew,

---

8   I wish to thank my dear friend Alan Hanoch Barket, founder of Dualis and a leader of this sector in Israel, for sharing honest observations about this concept.

9   Interestingly, in Hebrew, the word *chevrah* has several meanings based on the same root, *chet-bet-resh* (*ch.v.r.*) meaning "connection." In English, the word *company* means a business as well as human society.

10   In game theory, this is known as a "win-win" situation.

11   "Rabbi Yitzhak said: Whoever gives a penny to a poor person is blessed with six blessings, and one who appeases him with words is blessed with eleven blessings" (*Baba Batra* 9b). This statement reveals a truth about the nature of the wealthy person, whose mere possession of resources does not guarantee a wealthier soul. The poor person can give him no less than what he gives to the poor.

Rabbi Ashlag had a distinctive socioeconomic viewpoint. His approach was rooted in kabbalistic ideas and posits that the world's existence hinges on the dynamic between "giver" and "receiver." He begins with the fundamental premise that the key difference between humans and God is that humans need to fill an inherent void. There's an existential emptiness in human beings that drives them to seek fulfillment. Faced with this, one has two options. The first is to constantly strive to fill this void, following the more primitive, earthly aspect of human nature, which is focused on self-satisfaction. This natural tendency leads individuals, and sometimes societies, to a perpetual state of dependence on external sources for fulfillment.

The alternative is to engage in continual giving and receiving, such that receiving is intended for the purpose of giving to others. As Rabbi Ashlag puts it, "a person aligns his form with his Creator." Just as God aims to positively influence the world, people should seek ways to properly channel their inner capacity for influence toward others. Through this perspective, an individual connects with the divine soul, as well as the earthly aspect within, by balancing the act of receiving with giving. Essentially, the need to fill our inner void is a natural part of being human. However, the unique aspect of humanity lies in the ability to fill this void, savor its presence, and then thoughtfully pass it on to others.

In a seminal part of his philosophy, Rabbi Ashlag addresses the meaning of life:

> And now we understand that the purpose of creation is for the created beings to receive goodness and pleasure. Creation's repair is when created beings feel no discomfort when receiving these pleasures.[12]

Rabbi Ashlag discusses two fundamental concepts. The first is the purpose of life, which he says is the Creator's desire to benefit created beings and to give them goodness and pleasure. In this context, "good" is not mere enjoyment and pleasure in its commonly understood sense. Rather, here "good"

12　"*Madua hachayim nechlakim l'shtei bechinot* [Why is life divided into two aspects]," in Rabbi Baruch Shalom Halevi Ashlag (son of Rabbi Yehuda Leib Ashlag), *Kitvei Ravash* 1:581.

embodies an invitation to a life of vitality and unique meaning. *Oneg*, as we have seen, is a unique expression of enjoyment with great inner significance. Within this life purpose lies the very desire and ability to receive this abundance. Not everyone is able to say, "I am worthy of receiving abundance." Many people find it much easier to give. People spend many hours of psychotherapy trying to accept themselves as vessels worthy of receiving. Without this understanding and creation of a suitable inner vessel, abundance cannot enter.

The second concept is the "repair of creation" related to the "discomfort of receiving." When we are only receiving pleasure and enjoyment, we feel a sense of discomfort, both consciously and subconsciously. A person who experiences constant external fulfillment may feel shame related to a basic existential imbalance.[13]

How does a person connect the purpose of creation with the discomfort of receiving, which, according to Rabbi Ashlag, represents creation's repair? Rabbi Ashlag continues, saying: "The receiver should be 'in order to give.'" This means that the receiver's fulfillment should be with the intent of passing on the abundance they received, thus eliminating discomfort. The receiver becomes a giver, creating balance and flow.

This is a quality of the Tree of Life, where there is a flow rather than the duality of cognitive decisions. The act of giving does not come from the realm of knowledge and morality, which calculates a balance. Rather, giving comes from the stream of life that flows through us – the balance of giving is natural and not calculated.

Once, when I was riding the subway in Manhattan, a homeless man boarded and began sharing his poignant and difficult life story with the passengers. This is not an uncommon sight beneath the bustling streets of this unique city, with its towering skyscrapers and status as the world's financial hub. As they exited the train, some passengers put handouts in his hat. The journey from Manhattan to Brooklyn is notably long, and the man took a seat next to me for a rest. We struck up a conversation. He told me about

---

13   In the Talmud and kabbalistic literature, we find the expression *nehama d'kisufa* (bread of shame) – this expresses a central concept of several philosophers that explains the goal of creation.

his background and said he had nowhere to go. I mentioned I was from Israel, talked a little about Kolot, and explained that I was on my way to fundraise for the organization. He reciprocated by sharing more about his life – his father had been killed in Vietnam while his mother was pregnant with him. The interaction was cordial and straightforward. Upon arriving in Brooklyn, he resumed his appeal to the new passengers. When my stop came, I approached him with a few dollar bills, intending to give them to him. Seeing me approach, he pulled back his hand, smiled, and said, "I don't take money from colleagues!"

Beyond the subtle humor of this story lies a deeper message. Most of us are engaged in a kind of perpetual negotiation. In a sense, we are all colleagues, all participants in the extensive and existential fabric of relationships involving giving and receiving – and seeking balance between them. The resilience of society and the economy depends on the nature of the relationships formed between the giver and receiver: Do the parties see each other's humanity, or are these relationships solely focused on the utilitarian value derived from them? Giving to the less fortunate isn't measured just by the size of the donation, but by the person's ability to see those in need and create meaningful encounters with them that can unexpectedly expand and redefine the identity of the giver.

The following story illustrates this point. A group from the first cycle of Kolot that I taught wanted to set up a soup kitchen in South Tel Aviv, called So'adim (Feasters). The idea, initiated by Anat Gov of blessed memory, Dedi Zucker, and Prof. Tzvia Walden, was to create a charity soup kitchen offering quality food that would welcome all, both Jews and non-Jews. We established a nonprofit, secured initial funding, and by the winter of 2000, the establishment was up and running. It lasted about three years before it closed.

During a management meeting, I faced an intriguing question: What distinguishes a soup kitchen emerging from a Jewish study center like ours from one developed from a standard humanistic concept? This query was thought-provoking. Is there a significant difference, or as some suggested, perhaps it does not matter, as long as good is being done in the world? At that time, I was newly acquainted with Rabbi Ashlag's teachings. The next day, I shared the question with my colleagues at the study center. I realized that a soup kitchen born in a study center should operate on the principle of "receiving in order to give."

At the next management meeting, I suggested that the soup kitchen maintain its usual operations, but every day at lunchtime, we'd offer guests who agreed to stay for cake and coffee the chance to join a brief discussion led by a social worker. The focus would be on where they could contribute to others, whether through money, food, or more likely through a kind word, a hug, listening, or a meaningful glance. The primary aim was to nurture a giving mindset in the patrons. The next day, those who participated would share with the group how they gave back and what they experienced when they chose to give.

This is a model of a blessed soup kitchen, as it creates a circular movement within the soul and among its parts. The initiative to bring social workers into the soup kitchen did not last long, nor did the soup kitchen itself. This was due to tensions among the directors, as well as broader questions, such as who should be responsible for the soup kitchen's finances and feeding the hungry – private initiatives or the government? Nevertheless, understanding this model of receiving in order to give is an invitation to a new understanding of our own areas of giving and receiving.

The Torah extensively discusses the character of the giver of charity and his or her relationship with the needy receiver. Many Talmudic stories invite precise understanding of this type of giving. In most giving situations in the world, the poor remain poor, perpetuating the duality of the Tree of Knowledge of Good and Evil. There are rarer situations where the poor and the rich step out of their characters and meet openly and honestly. This can happen in lending, in partnerships, and through personal, human connection – moments from the Tree of Life state.

One of the fundamental principles in the model of the giver and receiver is that it's a dynamic system of mutual and complex relationships. The person seen as a "receiver" for one aspect may become a "giver" for another aspect and at a different time. According to this approach, the disparities and differences among people, despite the inherent pain of life, are essential components in maintaining a healthy society and a functioning economy. Both rich and poor are significant. Without the dynamics of giving and receiving, there is no society and no social process. Perhaps this is what the Torah means in the verse "For the poor will never cease out of the land" (Deut. 15:11). Reality contains inherent disparities. While striving to reduce social disparities is important, it's also crucial to understand that when societal and economic mechanisms aimed at achieving equality are based solely on individual rights and neglect the flow of movement created by differences among people, they risk creating an alienated and empty society. In the words of Rabbi Aharon Ariel Lavi:

> Economics isn't merely a competition for survival resources, but resembles an orchestra where each instrument plays a unique role. While some instruments might be more dominant than others, without the interplay among them, there would be no music. Rabbi Nachman of Breslev elucidates this concept in *Likutei Moharan* (13:1), interpreting "negotiation in faith" as being content with one's portion and not rushing to wealth, for the negotiation itself is the melody.[14]

In a thriving economy, whether personal or communal, there's a pursuit of abundant prosperity. True enjoyment of this prosperity stems from a proper balance between giving and receiving, recognizing those who haven't been as fortunate as an inseparable part of economic activity.

During my initial days at the Elul study center, I had the privilege of meeting an extraordinary philanthropist, Joy Ungerleider-Mayerson, of blessed memory. She was one of the earliest benefactors of pluralistic Israeli study centers, a woman with an exceptional personality. During Elul's fourth year, we faced a financial crisis. Although she had already contributed significantly, I took the initiative to discuss our challenges with her. Responding immediately, she generously added another $75,000 from her private funds, as her foundation had already reached its annual donation limit.

I once asked her about her extraordinary generosity, when I visited her at her home in New York's suburbs. She recounted this story:

---

14   Aharon Ariel Lavi, "Face to Face," chapter 7 in *About Economy and Sustenance: Judaism, Society and Economics* [in Hebrew] (Jerusalem: Reuven Mass, 2009), 81–82.

As my bat mitzvah approached, my grandfather bought me a gold necklace inscribed with my Hebrew name, Judith. I wore it with pride on a subway trip to my parents' house in 1931. Upon disembarking, I realized the necklace was missing. After a fruitless search on the platform and a comforting hot chocolate, I tearfully convinced my grandfather to report it to the police. The next morning, we visited the police station on 42nd Street, a place buzzing with activity. After a wait, I narrated the incident to an officer. He smiled skeptically, saying it was likely stolen and made no promises, but took my grandfather's phone number.

As we dejectedly prepared to leave, another officer entered, prompting the first to beckon us back. He asked for an identifying feature, and I mentioned the Hebrew letters. To my surprise, he produced the necklace from a small bag. My joy was immense. My grandfather, deeply moved, inquired about the finder. The officer identified her as Lucy, who had found it on the subway. My grandfather requested her contact details to personally express gratitude, but the officer declined, respecting Lucy's wish for anonymity. However, as we were about to leave, my perceptive grandfather noted the name and address written in reverse on the officer's paper. Determined, he said we were going to thank her personally and give a small token of appreciation.

The address led us to a starkly poor area of Harlem. We ascended rickety stairs and knocked on her door. A heavy black woman answered, her small children gathered around in curiosity. When my grandfather asked if she was Lucy, she replied cautiously, "Yes, what do you want?" As he began to explain and pointed to the necklace, she stepped back, telling her children to move away from the door. Before closing it, she said firmly, "If I accepted a gift from you, I would betray a core principle of my mere existence and world." Then she shut the door.

"This story," Joy told me, "shaped my life and my mission in the world." The unique woman in Harlem taught Joy a lesson in money, identity, and humility.

Joy is one of those people whose money and possessions do not define their identity. I've seen few wealthy individuals with this quality. Of this small group, most were women.

This unique state of mind is echoed in the words of Nachmanides (Ramban) about the character of a judge, who must despise ill-gotten gain:

> Those who despise ill-gotten gain – they are those who detest their own money in judgment.... Rabbi Elazar Hamodai says: Those who despise ill-gotten gain are those who detest their own money. If they detest their own money, all the more so the money of others. (Nachmanides, Ex. 18:21)

What does Rabbi Elazar Hamodai mean by "those who detest their own money"? I understand it as referring to a person who recognizes that dependence on money hinders freedom and judgment. The journey to becoming someone who despises ill-gotten gain begins with defining one's relationship with money. It's difficult for a person consumed by material desires to detest gain. Only someone whose identity is not defined by wealth can truly be in the position of "to Elohim will the matter of both come" (Ex. 22:8), where the judge is referred to as "Elohim." This concept is particularly powerful in a world in which wealth is often linked to power. Such a person may be blessed and wealthy, but the "blessing" isn't a reflection of their bank balance; it's an expression of the richness in the blessed person's soul.

In counseling young couples at the outset of their journey who face tensions around money in their marriages, I've observed how these financial issues can tangibly impact the quality of the marital relationship, intimacy, and family life.

A well-known source from Ethics of the Fathers offers insight into the interplay between money, identity, and relationships among loved ones:

> There are four types of attitudes in people concerning possessions: The one who says, "What's mine is mine and what's yours is yours" – this is an average attribute; some say it is the attribute of Sodom. "What's mine is yours and what's yours is mine" – an unlearned person. "What's mine is yours and what's yours is

yours" – a pious person. "What's mine is mine and what's yours is mine" – a wicked person. (Ethics of the Fathers 5:10)

Much has been said about this source, particularly regarding the first attribute, "What's mine is mine, and what's yours is yours."[15] However, for our discussion, the third attribute, that of the "pious" person, is the most intriguing. What is the world of the pious person like? In the consciousness of pious individuals, money does not define them, and their primary desire is to give it away. Their fundamental concern is to give selflessly. How tragic it is for such a pious person to live in a world surrounded by average people, not to mention the ignorant and the wicked. The pious person, declaring "What's mine is yours, and what's yours is yours," might be considered a "sucker" in the surrounding world. Their naivete is likely to be shattered quickly.

Imagine a world in which two people, close to each other, say, "What's mine is yours, and what's yours is yours." In this reciprocal movement, a relationship system is created, marked by openness and emotional vulnerability, moments when relationships are purely non-instrumental. The connection is pure, a true encounter. We sometimes recognize this in family dynamics and certainly in healthy love relationships. In such a world, there is intimacy and trust, devoid of power dynamics. These are rare moments of unconditional love.

One of humanity's core aspirations is to reach a place where one's exposed, vulnerable, honest, and naked foundation meets that of another, from a place of security and joy. This is the depth of the experience of "What's mine is yours, and what's yours is yours" when expressed mutually. These are moments when we sense something of the essence of life. An encounter between loving pious individuals offers a chance for trust and the revelation of rare and precious states, where the hope of being a blessing in the relationship with one's wealth and possessions becomes a reality.

Once we discover this profound connection in our lives, we are encouraged to expand these circles beyond the confines of our immediate and familiar family environments. The call to "be a blessing" is a continuous invitation

---

15 Mainly on the gap between understanding this as an average quality and as a characteristic of Sodom.

to engage with and broaden this deep-seated aspect within us. Embracing life with such a mindset provides a wonderful motivation to greet each new day.

The essence of the command to Abraham to "go forth" (*lech lecha*) is to "be a blessing." This blessing granted to Abraham is about living a life that is fully aware of the source of abundance at a conscious level, and maintaining a balance between giving and receiving in our tangible existence. It suggests that money, when it becomes entangled with our identity, turns into a stagnant "pit" of water. In contrast, living as a "well and spring" means allowing the waters of a blessed individual to flow into parts of life that crave that abundance. This dynamic creates a sense of freedom.

According to some economic experts, our world is heading toward a major economic shift, possibly even broader in scope than the crisis of 2008. Some even foresee a paradigmatic change that could challenge the dominance of classical capitalism. Our role is to prepare for this new reality, proposing models derived from the fundamental concepts of the garden's trees and the consciousness of blessing.

Questions for Reflection

- What is the role of money in your identity? What areas of identity and religious awareness does it touch?
- Do you have a balance between your ability to give and your capacity to receive?
- "Who is rich? He who is happy with his lot" (Ethics of the Fathers 4:1). To what extent do you identify with this saying?
- What aspect of your lot in life makes you feel truly wealthy?

Chapter 10

Loneliness, Loving Relationships, and the Tree of Life

As we have seen, Professor Martin Seligman's research highlights that a key element of a good quality of life is being engaged in meaningful relationships. This insight is particularly relevant in our era, which is marked by loneliness, even in economically affluent societies and communities. Loneliness isn't just an emotional state; it's a significant human tragedy, often regarded as a modern "silent" epidemic. The UK has even appointed a minister to tackle loneliness. Research on social media usage, particularly on platforms like Facebook, indicates that loneliness can intensify despite the illusion of being surrounded by "friends."

The designation of loneliness as an epidemic is apt, considering its severe implications: it can double the risk of premature death, making it more lethal than obesity and comparable to the health risks of smoking. Loneliness triggers a stress response in the brain, weakening the immune system. It embodies the disparity between one's idealistic expectations and the reality of one's inability to fulfill them. Evidently, technology falls short in providing the most vital human experiences: the exchange of looks, deep listening, physical touch, and a genuine sense of belonging.

Loneliness isn't just the lot of single people; it also exists in relationships, often more hidden from view. The presence of a partner who doesn't respond as we expect can intensify feelings of loneliness, unintentionally reflecting back our own inner emotions. It's easy to blame our partner for our struggles, but that's often an escape from addressing the root issue: our internal sense of loneliness. At other times, loneliness in a relationship derives from the natural hope for sharing and connection with a partner who is "not there" emotionally. It stems from failed attempts to connect through both heart and mind to a loved one who is unable to provide the support we need.

The antidote to loneliness isn't found in fleeing into social interactions or engaging in often superficial conversations. These often take place in groups where people are essentially running away from themselves, much like digital social networks that draw our attention away from self-reflection.

Solitude and loneliness are distinct. Solitude can be a fulfilling experience, rich with intense inner life, deep listening, attentiveness, and even an openness to the world. Loneliness, however, is marked by a sense of emptiness, isolation, and distress. The issue of loneliness has been a focal point for many intellectuals. The Greek author Nikos Kazantzakis summed it up in his novel *Zorba the Greek* by saying that solitude is the "natural climate" of human beings, a sentiment echoed in various ways by many great writers and thinkers.

Indeed, this question has preoccupied humanity since its inception. The challenge of loneliness and how to cope with it is complex, and I don't presume to offer a solution. However, I will attempt to present an approach from the perspective of Tree of Life consciousness, which might provide a way to address one of the fundamental stumbling blocks of human existence.

One significant tool in dealing with loneliness is *hitbodedut*, a term from our ancient Hebrew sources, closely related to meditation. I began practicing this form of meditation quite late in life.

Maimonides' son Rabbi Avraham wrote extensively on solitude in his book *Hamaspik l'Ovdei Hashem*. He distinguishes between external solitude, which involves withdrawing from society to solitary places such as caves or prayer sites, and what he calls "solitude of the internal soul," which is more essential. In this form of solitude, a person delves into the inner self, isolating from external sensory distractions to find God within. Engaging in this introspection, we cease to focus on casting blame or external expectations. Instead, we explore our soul, uncovering various depths and layers. This exploration lessens the feeling of being a stranger to oneself; even in solitude, one is not lonely. It may reveal pain or emptiness, but often, in solitude, we discover inner vitality. Experiencing the life-giving breath that God has instilled within, we feel less alone, sensing the presence of the sublime in our life's journey.

The practice of *hitbodedut*, later regarded by Rabbi Nachman of Breslev as a crucial tool for life, can help a person approach relationships and social life from a place of fullness, rather than lack. Entering into a relationship, we don't become a mere energy source for our partner. Instead, we arrive as someone who has explored his or her soul and found added value and meaning in it. People who have encountered their own solitude may be ready and even eager to explore the realm of companionship and build shared spaces with their partners. Such a space, unique and exclusive to the couple, opens the door to "making a dwelling place for God in the lower realms," which is one of the purposes of creation, as we have seen earlier. As Rabbi Akiva was deeply engaged in the mysteries of the Torah, perhaps this is what meant in saying: "When husband and wife are worthy, the Divine Presence is between them" (*Sotah* 17a). When God is present in the loving space, this is a unique story and a manifestation of a high-quality connection.

Aloneness and Love in the Garden

In the Garden of Eden, as narrated in Genesis chapter 2, humanity began with a single individual. God created the garden for this lone man and placed him within it. The depiction of Eden, replete with abundance, security, and tranquility, initially served as a backdrop for the individual in solitude, not for a couple.

It appears that God intended for man to transform loneliness into solitude, relying solely on internal resources. Before the introduction of companionship, man had an awareness of rivers, trees, and the Divine Presence – elements that interact with and influence human solitude. These elements beckon us to engage with a consciousness rooted in abundance and security. This scenario embodies the hope that we all possess the ability to create, grow, and partner with the Creator in expanding and repairing the world. This vibrant, comforting perspective could alleviate loneliness. The person who figured out how to distill these elements and put them into a tablet would undoubtedly become one of the world's wealthiest individuals. A capsule that enables a person to feel seen, possessing abundance and security, fostering creation and a sense of significant self-worth, cannot be externally manufactured; it must emerge from within.

Interestingly, the story of Eden presents solitude as limited or potentially problematic, despite its benefits: "It is not good for the man to be alone" (Gen. 2:18). This observation likely comes after the individual has fully experienced the garden's abundant blessings. Yet even after the introduction of a partner, couples may still encounter significant periods of solitude. Acknowledging this is crucial for a sincere and healthy engagement with life.

In the garden, "It is not good for the man to be alone." Unlike the "good" that concludes each day of the first creation narrative, God recognized that living alone in the garden was "not good," as it lacked soul-opening dialogue, even amidst abundance and security. God aimed to introduce man to the social realm, integral to our consciousness of quality of life. The garden's abundance yearned for another to share and enhance it. Perhaps without a woman, who with her husband becomes one flesh, the true essence of intimacy – where one steps out toward another, forming a whole greater than its parts – cannot be realized. The Sages said: "A prisoner cannot free himself from prison" (*Berachot* 5b). Man needs another, intimate connection, because he is bound within his own complex identity.

As we've seen, in a world of blessing, dialogue and encounters are crucial. There's a significant difference between engaging with abundance against nature's forces and engaging with abundance with another human who, like you, was created in the image of God.

Before creating woman from his rib to address his solitude, God first formed animals from the earth and brought them to Adam, in hopes they might ease his loneliness. Perhaps there was an expectation that shepherding or animal care could help, a common notion in our world today. However, in Eden, this proved insufficient. The human potential for abundance is expansive and not fully realized through animal care alone. While such care may mitigate the feeling of solitude, it doesn't facilitate growth like an encounter with another person toward new meaning.[1]

---

1   According to the Sages, Adam lay with the animals that God had brought him (*Yevamot* 63a), but this did not satisfy his need to escape human loneliness.

Loneliness, Loving Relationships, and the Tree of Life

One of the foundational principles in the narrative of man and woman is that the woman was created from man's rib. This event is unique and serves the narrative of creation in Eden. Post-Eden, men and women meet coming from separate families. The initial state in Eden brought deep joy to Adam. His exclamation, "This is now bone of my bones, and flesh of my flesh; she will be called Woman, because she was taken out of Man" (Gen. 2:23), uniquely expresses Adam's self-discovery: the Hebrew word *etzem* (bone) also means "essence," implying that the woman reveals something about his own essence, perhaps even his strength. Interestingly, the Hebrew word for *etzem* also contains within it the word *etz* (tree). The woman, emerging from the man's solitude, represents an opportunity for man to taste and experience the essence of the Tree of Life, from which he did not eat. Within the challenges of partnership lie the elements of the Tree of Life and its blessings.

Christian and Jewish scholars and theologians debate over whether Adam and Eve had sexual relations while in the garden. The Christian stance is that they did not, as the first mention of such relations is post-expulsion: "And Adam knew Eve his wife; and she conceived, and bore" (Gen. 4:1). This view ties sexuality to guilt: in the idyllic life of Eden, there were no physical relations, and they are a consequence of sin and expulsion. Most Jewish interpretations disagree, viewing intimate relations as an essential part of couple's life and a part of life in Eden. This is despite the lack of explicit mention of such relations between Adam and Eve during their life in the garden.

I would like to suggest a different reading. In the Garden of Eden, Adam and Eve had sexual relations, but without childbirth. This unique state transcends our familiar concepts of time and commandments in the post-sin world. The verses in Eden talk about an intimate bond, "and will cleave to his wife" (Gen. 2:24), without the mandate of "be fruitful and multiply" present in the Genesis chapter 1 creation story. This unique circumstance opens up a scenario in which the initial encounter between man and woman, "This is now bone of my bones," symbolizes the profound connection between Adam and Eve, possibly representing their first union, yet without childbirth – and perhaps precisely due to its absence. This scenario is seen in couple relationships before and after child-rearing, in childless unions, in extended periods of infertility, or in later-life partnerships without mutual children. This unique situation invites a unique bond in which children are not the central elements defining the couple's intimacy.[2]

However, there was a cost. Despite Adam's amazement at the creation of woman, there is no description of dialogue between them. It seems Adam didn't fully "see" Eve, perhaps because they weren't truly distinct from each other. In the biblical narrative, she was created for him, and in Adam's perspective, she does not have a separate existence. In Eden, the element of "reflection," crucial in thriving partnerships, was absent. Nor were there eros and desire as we understand them today. These elements began only after the awareness brought by eating from the Tree of Knowledge. The hope for personal, touching conversation, to be seen, to desire, and to be desired in return are some of life's most meaningful experiences, which only emerged after leaving the garden.

Indeed, the intimate relationship outside Eden differs significantly from the experience inside: woman, distinct and coming from a different family and growth narrative, challenges the new partnership outside Eden. She calls for recognition of her independence before union, inviting personal dialogue that exposes and addresses the differences between partners. Proper vision, conversation, and listening can transform the intimate relationship into a mirror, reflecting each person's pains, dreams, unique existence, and place in the world.

Does the experience of "This is now bone of my bones" have a place in life outside the garden? Can a man and woman meet, despite the separate homes they came from, even without the framework of children? These are fundamental questions, and the answer to them is positive. However, it requires work to create a second innocence, one that comes after separate self-discovery. Within this self-discovery, there should be a mature understanding of the essence of separation from one's parents, allowing for mature intimacy. The intensity of our encounters could be even greater than those in the garden! This is a result of the new state of consciousness after eating from the Tree of Knowledge. Discovering the capabilities of intimate relationships in our

---

2   Nachmanides on Gen. 2:24 disagrees with Rashi, who interprets "one flesh" as expressing childbirth. Instead, Nachmanides says that this is an expression of creating a unique intimacy that is even greater than that of a family.

second innocence can lead to an especially high level of self-revelation. In this new space, a couple has the potential to reach a delight that is the result of shared work. Many couples who have completed the child-rearing stage find themselves at this crossroads. Can they touch this fundamental essence of "bone of my bones"?

Balancing Work and Family

Let's return to the story of Eden. A fascinating Midrash poses the question: Where was Adam when the serpent was conversing and tempting his wife?

> "And the woman said to the serpent" (Gen. 3:2). Where was Adam at that time? Abba bar Koreya said: He was engaged in intimate relations and then fell asleep. The Rabbis said: The Holy One, blessed be He, took him and showed him around the entire world, saying, "Here is a plantation, here is a sowing field." (*Midrash Genesis Rabbah* 19:3)

According to the first opinion, Adam fell asleep after having sexual relations with his wife. The language of the Midrash merits attention. "Engaged...and then fell asleep." It conveys a sense of a task performed and completed, and the ensuing desired sleep.

According to the second opinion, God took Adam on a tour of the garden's "industrial zone." He showed him all the potential work required of him, a structured work plan to fulfill the commandment "to till it and to keep it," while leaving the woman at home.

What is this debate about? According to the first opinion, the text offers an archetypal representation of a man's approach to sexuality. The male completes the act of union and then falls asleep. Indeed, there is an element of depletion that can create fatigue in the male sexual act. The concern here is that the "helpmeet opposite him" (Gen. 2:18) is reduced to being an object for satisfying the man's needs. The Midrash seemingly objects to this perception, calling for a higher consciousness in men, a different kind of alertness. Otherwise, a "serpent" – another aspect of reality with elements of darkness, surprise, and temptation – might enter. The woman, on the other hand, may experience the aftermath of the man's sexual union differently. The movement within her as a result of the encounter, as the one who has received her partner's seed, seeks alertness and connection. Sometimes silence, sometimes conversation, but mainly a desire for presence. These are very different gender mechanisms.

For a man, the sexual act may contain an element of completion. For a woman, however, there's an opening to new life. According to this view in the Midrash, this awareness is what the serpent aims to awaken. The *nachash* (serpent) *menachesh* (divines) and is present in the emotional gaps between man and woman.

According to the second perception, Adam was busy with work. He was touring the world with the Creator, learning where to build and where to plant. He observed amazing start-ups and deliberated where to invest. The Midrash protests his leaving the woman at home, indicating she isn't included in healing the world, repairing and refining creation outside her household. This problem, which also invites the serpent's appearance, points to an issue of inside and outside the home in the couple relationship.

Beyond the gender division itself, expressed in Talmudic language by defining the woman as "home,"[3] men often have trouble coming home. His conduct at home is different from his conduct outside. At home, a different world awaits him: the confined domestic spaces with diapers, laundry, squeaky door hinges that need oiling. More importantly, he must transition mentally to the inner world. He must respond to the woman's request for him to share about his day and listen to her report of hers. The inability to communicate and balance the outside and inside worlds is a significant human and relational challenge.

In recent years, I have been accompanying young entrepreneurs seeking to enter the realm of "being a blessing." One of the key issues for most people I meet is the desire to balance work life with family life. This balance is not just a matter of time allocation, although that is important. It's primarily a matter of the soul. We grapple with the question: Can one work, manage, create, and then come home and be truly present, living both worlds in integration and unity?

---

3   In Aramaic, the language of the Talmud, woman is called *d'beitahu* (his home).

This ability to correctly connect the external world with the concept of "woman-home" is a sign of blessing. In the Tree of Life, the purpose of love and the purpose of earning a living are one: a quest for abundant life in the broadest sense of the term. The capacity to be content with one's lot significantly links the external and internal worlds, work and home.[4]

In sensitive cases of imbalance, the serpent may enter, when a man is "asleep" or "busy, and not at home." The serpent invites motivations, downfalls, hidden pain, and consequently can lead to "concealment" of feelings, pains, hopes. It seeks to destabilize us in our most natural patterns. In the bigger picture of the garden and home, the serpent plays a crucial role in the consciousness of blessing. It represents the Sitra Achra (other side), which can surface in the absence of proper presence of the partners.[5]

In the language of the Tree of Life: the serpent invites us to a critical introspection, especially in those areas where we feel we are "fulfilling our role." The "serpent-like" nature, in a couple's context, is a call to reflect differently on the role of sexuality in life, and particularly on the quality of one's encounters with one's partner. A man who "falls asleep" is unaware of the life force of sexuality beyond pleasure. He doesn't truly see the woman. He isn't connected to the essence of pleasure and the Tree of Life consciousness in couple interaction.

A partner – man or woman – who doesn't know how to "return home in peace" after spending time in the external worlds isn't fulfilling a fundamental aspect of their role as "a helpmeet opposite." Indeed, the symbol of the serpent is critical to our existence, being present in places where we are imprecise. This imprecision is at the foundation of the creation of the Garden of Eden – an area the Creator left somewhat open in His creation, allowing the serpent to appear. Understanding the serpent and its place in the Garden of Eden story adds a depth of dimension to our motivations.

Our world outside the garden took a dramatic turn. New perceptions of female identity and status emerged, influencing lifestyles and consequently

---

4   The Talmud (*Ketubot* 63–64) shares stories about distinguished scholars who did not know how to come home on time or in peace. They failed to bring the creativity, passion, and sometimes the glory of their external world into the required intimacy of their homes.

5   In the modern world, where the traditional gender roles of men and women have undergone dramatic changes, we may translate the principles of this chapter into basic archetypes.

broader definitions. A world where both man and woman create, provide, and are present in the external-domestic sphere requires new tools for healthy relationships: abilities to share, quality time for encounters, and higher awareness to nurture the quality of their shared lives.

Can modern individuals, male or female, bring the realms of their worlds to each other? The outside isn't just the world of work, the gym, and other areas outside the home. The outside can also be external thoughts, anger, reflections, worries, childhood wounds, fantasies, and dreams. The ability to discuss these foundations is one of the components of blessing – and it's hardly simple.

One of the unique tools for couple communication is the "imago" method. Imago is the Latin word for "image." In Imago Relationship Therapy, imago refers specifically to an unconscious, idealized concept of familiar love that an individual develops during childhood, and which remains unchanged in adulthood. The basis of this approach is the assumption that we choose a partner based on unconscious motivations stemming from our imago – representations of significant relationships experienced in our childhood (usually with parents). That is, we choose a partner who possesses both positive and negative traits of influential figures in our lives. This pattern turns couple relationships into an opportunity for healing childhood wounds and for personal growth and development. Our relationship with our parents is always characterized by disappointments and hurts, and the couple relationship allows each partner to develop psychological areas neglected in childhood due to environmental demands and parental expectations. Furthermore, a loving relationship involves the possibility to engage with traits that we need to confront to achieve healing and renewed growth.

In the early stages of a relationship, we might feel and even fantasize that the partnership will allow us to love ourselves and feel unconditionally loved. However, as the relationship matures, we begin to realize that the very traits we fell in love with, due to our childhood deficiencies, are the ones that challenge us in everyday life. For instance, a woman from a boundary-less home with perceived weak parents may fall in love with a strong, authoritative man who, after the honeymoon phase, may seem rigid and domineering.

Consequently, we experience disappointment and frustration that our partner isn't fully meeting our needs, leading to power struggles. This phase occurs in almost every significant relationship. In some cases, it may disrupt or even destroy the couple's bond, but in others, it indeed forms the foundation for personal and couple growth.

The central technique of Imago Relationship Therapy is "intentional dialogue," based on the partners' commitment to create a dialogue rooted in deep listening. This authentic listening allows each partner to better understand why it's challenging to deal with certain traits of the other and how to respond to them anew. Partners learn how to transform their conversation into a meaningful dialogue in which both sides – the speaker and the listener – actively participate. This interaction enables empathy and constructive challenging of each other's views, fostering genuine listening and evolving a quality intimacy.

In Imago, three critical stages are identified: creating the couple's space, crossing the bridge, and deeply listening to the other. This deep, authentic listening and presence exemplifies the Tree of Life quality of being unified with and entirely devoted to the beloved.

Imago is just one tool, and there are many others. The crucial principle is that "I will make a helpmeet opposite him" is a defining moment in the Garden of Eden story and in human life after the expulsion from the garden. Couplehood is a life framework seeking Tree of Life consciousness and a space of blessing. It's not just a simple flow, but an understanding that the relationship encounter invites ongoing work to build connection throughout life.

Ba'al and Husband

The biblical Hebrew description of intimate relations draws a significant distinction between *be'ilah* (coitus, sexual intercourse) and *biah* ("coming toward"). The world of intercourse implies a desire to dominate and control, almost devoid of choice. The drive for life and survival, so deeply ingrained in human consciousness, may be reflected in the act of union. It is so natural, yet this element alone often lacks true intimacy and cannot by itself establish a quality, growing relationship. In contrast, the concept of "coming toward" involves gentleness, a quest for seeing, approaching. He comes to her.

The presence of the divine soul in a person asks a man to view the woman as a subject, not an object. This could be a correction for the sin of the "sons of Elohim" that we discussed in the opening chapters, which led to the Flood.

Be'ilah is from the essence of the Tree of Knowledge, while *biah*, "coming toward," is from the essence of the Tree of Life.

Honesty is required here. Both men and women have natural needs, recognized by Jewish culture. Perhaps this is why "the times [for marital relations] of scholars are from Sabbath eve to Sabbath eve" (*Ketubot* 62a), a statement that may seem to focus only on timing. However, I believe it primarily points to conscious intention: practicing marital relations on the Sabbath suggests a consciousness that distinguishes between cohabitation and "coming toward," thereby creating this distinction in our lives.

The Book of Hosea contains a prophecy describing days of peace between God and humanity and between man and woman, after a difficult period of infidelity and breakdown:

> And it will be at that day, says the Lord, you will call me *ishi* [my husband; literally, "my person"]; and you will call me no more *ba'ali* ["my master," from the root *ba'al*, meaning "ownership"]. (Hosea 2:18)

Hosea seems to reference a future state of "second innocence," after a couple relationship has experienced difficulties. The woman recognizes her separateness and from this independence seeks to touch a moment of the Eden experience, of the united man and woman. The Hebrew *ishi* means "my husband" and also "my person," and this evolved stage of the relationship seeks to remove the objectifying element implied by the word *ba'al* and to touch the personal relationship implied by *ishi*.

Jacob's Solitude

Despite living a tumultuous life and being married to many women, Jacob is one of the loneliest characters in the Torah. He loved Rachel at first sight and worked hard to earn her. Later, Leah became an unexpected yet significant figure in his life, along with two other maidservants, forming the foundation of our lineage. Yet it's hard not to sense his loneliness. In his poignant encounter with Pharaoh toward the end of his life, Jacob says: "Few and evil have been the days of the years of my life" (Gen. 47:9). These words, spoken by a man who experienced many hardships, seem to stem from a place of deep solitude.

From his youth, he wasn't a man of external communication, unlike his father Isaac, who "went out to meditate in the field" (Gen. 24:63) – the field being a common ground for Isaac and Esau and a root of Isaac's love for Esau. In contrast, Jacob was a quiet man, dwelling in tents, with a loving mother. Rebekah knew her younger son was the chosen one, as told to her by God during her difficult pregnancy. Yet she kept this knowledge secret, even from Isaac, her husband. This secret element of his interior life reinforced Jacob's sense of solitude. Solitary people often harbor an unresolved secret about themselves.

Rebekah dressed Jacob in Esau's hunting clothes, hoping he would receive Isaac's special blessing. Beyond the absurdity of wearing clothes that don't fit, this state symbolically indicates a person whose inner nakedness doesn't find appropriate external expression. This gap between inner bareness and ill-fitting attire further accentuates the feeling of aloneness.

Jacob never returned to his mother, who also didn't call him back as she had promised, for she died before she had an opportunity to do so. Later, he would encounter Esau, and in this meeting, he would understand the secret of wearing Esau's clothes. He would also come to terms with his connection to Leah. But the road to this significant encounter was long. Jacob fled from Esau, who sought to kill him. The first time Jacob expands his heart is in his initial meeting with Rachel at the well in Haran:

> And it came to pass, when Jacob saw Rachel the daughter of Laban
> his mother's brother, and the sheep of Laban his mother's brother,
> that Jacob went near, and rolled the stone from the well's mouth,
> and watered the flock of Laban his mother's brother. And Jacob
> kissed Rachel, and lifted up his voice, and wept. (Gen. 29:10–11)

Jacob's weeping is a profound breakdown of fear, pain, and – above all – loneliness. Perhaps Jacob's love for Rachel is an expression of the great pain of his loneliness, which he thought he could solve through a relationship with her. All the energy of his many years of work for her, his willingness to be deceived by Laban – he did all this for Rachel, thinking that she would redeem him from the distress of his family.

Was Jacob truly ready for a relationship at this stage of his life?

Two defining nocturnal stories are turning points in Jacob's life. The first is when he leaves his parents' house out of fear of Esau, who seeks to kill him. Jacob arrives at Beth-el toward nightfall. Alongside his fear of his brother, he carries the birthright that he purchased with a lentil stew and the blessing that he stole. This burden certainly does not help his mental state. On the contrary, a maturation process that involves such "gifts" is not easy and does not allow for a simple flow.

The fear originating from his complicated birth family and the uncertainty about the family he was supposed to establish is a familiar and difficult existential experience. This mental state can last many years, during which a person inquires, "Who am I?" as part of a powerful experience of exploring personal origins and destinations. Jacob is deeply present within his solitude. With the setting of the sun, he is filled with dread. His past lies heavy on him, and his future is shrouded in fog. Darkness falls.

In these moments, Jacob has a dream. In uncertain territory, God may communicate with human beings through a dream. In the dream, the ladder is set upon the earth, with the earth representing the existential place of the human being, the place that meets basic needs. Jacob's needs are the construction of a sense of identity, meaning, and security. He lacks all these. He is far from Eden and far from a sense of home. He has no choice but to work on building the foundations of his personality. When he can feel the earth beneath his feet, then his ascent can begin. At the top of the ladder, Jacob – and we along with him – encounters the question of meaning. God addresses him personally as "the God of Abraham your father and the God of Isaac" (Gen. 28:13). By questioning his origins, Jacob meets the God of his parents and discovers that there is significance to the home he comes from.

This revelation is not immediately clear to Jacob, nor to many of us. Jacob understands that his father's love for Esau does not replace Isaac's understanding that the principal blessing is intended for his son Jacob. For Jacob, the knowledge that his parents' home has a tangible significance for his destiny is a strong and comforting revelation. He begins to understand the foundations of his own home.

Jacob has a mission. From his confidence in the roots of his past, Jacob receives a blessing for the future that concludes with the promise made to his grandfather that all the families of the earth will be blessed through him and his seed. He is part of a broader story. There is hope for his future. This knowledge of origin and destiny gives meaning and purpose to the difficulties of the journey. Understanding our own narrative from origin to destiny connects us to a river of blessing.

Jacob awakens from the dream and reacts: "Surely the Lord is in this place, and I knew it not" (Gen. 28:16). An encounter with God in a specific place in a person's life is the moment of confrontation with the meaning of the crisis one is experiencing. The God Jacob met at Beth-El is the God of his fathers and now his God too. A connection to the past and future grants meaning to the present. "When a person knows that all the events of his life are for his benefit, this perception is like a taste of the World to Come" (Rabbi Nachman of Breslev).

The understanding that the story of one's life is not coincidental, that it has a past and thereby the individual is a link in a chain, pulls a person out of loneliness. We are not truly alone, because we have a perspective of roots and destiny. Without the feeling that the ground we walk upon has meaning, it is impossible to set up a ladder and ascend.

And despite this defining night, the dialogue with God ends with a condition:

> And Jacob vowed a vow, saying: "If God will be with me, and will keep me in this way that I go, and will give me bread to eat, and raiment to put on, so that I come back to my father's house in peace, then will the Lord be my God." (Gen. 28:20–21)

Something remains unresolved within Jacob, even after the dream full of insight and hope. Something is not at peace; he does not feel whole. This is true even though he has somewhat emerged from his loneliness. Perhaps in the night story at Beit-El, where he found within his personality a home for God, he is worthy to transition from loneliness to solitude. He is not redeemed yet but he has passed an important stage.

Be a Blessing

The *Zohar* understands the night experience in Beit-El as the story of Jacob's maturation. Jacob met himself in purity, with only the stone at his head and the heavens above. But he touches upon an important foundation that allows for the beginning of movement and maturity. This maturity will assist him in the next chapter, in his encounter with Rachel, and in the discovery of unknown strengths, which enable him to roll the stone from the well's mouth. The well represents the flow of living water from the depths. After many struggles, Jacob will be blessed with Rachel and later establish a large family.

Yet his personality unfolds slowly. The unresolved tension with his brother will soon be reflected through the tension and jealousy between his two wives, Rachel and Leah, who are sisters. Within this new home, his childhood wounds are revealed. Jacob understands that just as his wives are rival sisters, he too carries the pain of his brother. Perhaps, the primal story of Cain and Abel is present in these moments. The blessing he received from his father by deceit looms and troubles him.

Even Jacob's relationship with his wives is fundamentally different. Rachel had Jacob's love, while Leah bore him many sons. However, the tragedy in the story is that each woman desired what she did not have, what her sister had. Rachel wanted sons, while Leah sought his love.

The different connections between Jacob and Rachel, and his relationship with Leah, take us back to the two stories of the creation of man in the Book of Genesis, which relate to the essence of the relationship between man and woman. In the first story, the relationship described is for the purpose of procreation: "Be fruitful and multiply, and fill the earth," while in the second story, the intimate relationship between man and woman is a value in itself: "It is not good that the man should be alone… and will cleave to his wife, and they will be one flesh."

The human hope, rooted in the consciousness of the Tree of Life, is that it is possible to combine the foundation of family and fertility with the foundation of intimacy and love in one woman, without division.

We return to our story: Jacob establishes a family. Yet something within him is still incomplete. As he leaves Beit-El for the journey of his life, during which he will establish an extensive family, he seeks to "return in peace to my father's house," as Rebecca promised before his flight. At his father's house, he recognizes his parents, but also his brother, as part of the familial system. Jacob is not granted a reunion with his parents. Perhaps precisely because of this tragic fact, the later meeting with Esau, his brother, is so significant and thus inevitable. It is necessary for Jacob to become a complete person. The need for resolution of tension between brothers is present even after establishing a large family. In the first part of the book, we spoke of the existential fracture in humanity since the first fraternal conflict, resulting in the murder of Abel. Jacob feels a deep need to heal his relationship with his brother Esau. This healing is crucial to be a model for his sons and the nation that will descend from them.

The narrative continues to another defining story, which also takes place at night – the crossing of the Jabbok.

The backdrop of this story is entirely different from that night at Beit-El. Jacob arrives at Jabbok as a married man and father of a large family. On one hand, this gives him confidence. He has achieved something in life. He has built a family and strengthened himself. On the other hand, the measure of his success might intensify the rivalry with Esau, raising the question of which brother is indeed the blessed one. Even if Esau has reconciled with the deception and lost the desired blessing, Jacob still has to make amends with his brother. This amendment will strive for a meeting that involves "reflection" for Jacob, leading to greater closeness. This reflection is fundamental to the fellowship between siblings, a fellowship of social ties. It is present in the foundation of the biblical story and is at the root of the promise made to Jacob's grandfather Abraham that he will "be a blessing." The ability to see in the other a reflection of ourselves creates a connection as opposed to estrangement.

There is a great difference between a meeting of emptiness and a meeting of fullness. In Beit-El, Jacob met himself with a great void. He was filled with fear, alone, without a home of origin and without a future home. The meeting with Esau at the Jabbok crossing is fundamentally different. Two brothers arrive with the products of their lives, with large families and wealth. Below is the passage that describes the night at the Jabbok crossing:

> And Jacob was left alone; and there wrestled a man with him until the breaking of the day. And when he saw that he did not prevail

against him, he touched the hollow of his thigh; and the hollow of Jacob's thigh was strained, as he wrestled with him. And he said: "Let me go, for the day breaks." And he said: "I will not let you go, until you bless me." And he said to him: "What is your name?" And he said: "Jacob." And he said: "Your name will be called no more Jacob, but Israel; for you have striven with God and with men and have prevailed." And Jacob asked him, and said: "Tell me, I pray you, your name." And he said: "Why do you ask my name?" And he blessed him there. And Jacob called the name of the place P'ni-El: "for I have seen God face to face, and my life is preserved." And the sun rose upon him as he passed over P'ni-El, and he limped upon his thigh. (Gen. 32:25–32)

A mysterious story unfolds. In contrast to his initial encounter at Beit-El, where Jacob felt loneliness, he is described in the second encounter as being left "alone," despite being surrounded by family. This solitude is swiftly replaced by a struggle with a man that persists throughout the night. The unique aspect of this conflict is its indecisiveness and lack of bloodshed.

Unlike the swift and somewhat ambiguous murder between the first brothers, Cain and Abel, this is a prolonged struggle, symbolizing the recognition of "the other." In this context, the other refers to an angry brother seeking revenge. Before the night at the Jabbok crossing, Jacob says, "I will appease him with the present that goes before me" (Gen. 32:21). The mysterious figure wrestling with Jacob is later revealed, as dawn approaches, to be an angel, perhaps representing Esau – a divine messenger.

The struggle recalls the jostling of these brothers while they were still twins in the womb of their mother, Rebekah. The grasping of the heel at birth converses with the dislocation of Jacob's hip during the struggle, but in reverse – this time, it seems as if the angel is grappling with Jacob's heel. Something has turned around.

This reversal symbolizes a rebirth for Jacob. This time, he leads as the stronger one, aware of the limits of his power. Unlike the story of Cain and Abel, this struggle leads to life, not death. Jacob will wrestle throughout the entire night, not with the aim of victory. At the Jabbok crossing, Jacob confronts the Esau character within his personality. He internalizes the strength of his brother. This is a critical condition for their real encounter in the following verses. Only through complete identification with the adversary can one truly reach a living solution, rather than a deadly conclusion.

In the language of the *Zohar*, there is a certain element of *hitkalelut* or "integration" in this story. However, unlike in the story of Abraham and Isaac, where both were mutually integrated,[6] Esau himself is absent from the Jabbok encounter. Esau's absence only underscores Jacob's uniqueness in internalizing parts of his brother's personality, knowing that his brother might not be undergoing a similar process. This ability to integrate is foundational to the blessing, as it expands a person's consciousness of appeasement toward the other, as in Jacob's words: "I will appease him with the present that goes before me; and afterward, I will see his face; perhaps he will accept me" (Gen. 32:20).

Jacob seeks Esau's face. Only when Jacob encounters the face as a kind of mirror to himself, his brother's strength within him, and makes amends, can he truly see Esau's real face. Then he can truly look his brother in the eye. Jacob lived under the shadow of his parents' split love for their sons and his own internal division. Now he manages to create a new and unified self-identity by meeting the Esau within him. He is ready for familial healing.

The story of the Jabbok crossing can thus be seen as a correction to the story of Cain and Abel. Through this internalization at the Jabbok crossing, Jacob can love Leah in maturity, as someone who has walked a long and hard path. Notably, it is Leah who becomes his love in the second part of his life and is buried beside him.

The story of Jabbok represents a significant development from the encounter with God in the dream at Beit-El. Jacob develops confidence and a compass for his path, as well as the internal ability to meet his brother and thereby recognize parts of his own personality. This is a higher level of communication, an expression of being a blessing.

A Struggle of Blessing

In the heart of the struggle, the angel requests Jacob to release his hold. Jacob consents, but not before he explicitly demands from the angel, "I will not let

---

6   See the section on the Binding of Isaac in chapter 16, where we describe the integration created between Abraham and his son.

you go, until you bless me" (Gen. 32:27). This encounter presents a unique form of struggle that seeks not victory but blessing. The goal of this prolonged engagement is not to overpower the other, but to seek his blessing.

The angel does not bless Jacob immediately. Instead, he first asks for Jacob's name. This moment is in stark contrast to Jacob's earlier encounter with his father Isaac, during which he lied about his identity and masqueraded as Esau to obtain a blessing. This time, Jacob simply and truthfully responds with his own name: "Jacob." The simplicity and honesty of stating his own name must have been a profound relief for Jacob. It highlights the beauty and peace in accepting yourself as you are and being at ease with your own identity.

Then, perhaps surprisingly, Jacob's blessing is a change of name. However, after integrating the "Esau-ness" within his personality, this change of name is fitting. "Israel" is the new essence of Jacob. He is no longer the simple man dwelling in tents. Jacob's ability to genuinely encounter the other marks the completion of his maturation and his emergence from solitude.

This new name, "Israel," also embodies our essence as a people – engaging actively with the challenges of a broken world, while understanding that we are all composed of fractured pieces. Vulnerability is an inseparable part of life. The crossing of the Jabbok will be etched in our memory as a place where embracing vulnerability is possible and perhaps necessary. This vulnerability may lead to a struggle ending in blessing.

In changing his name, Jacob fulfills God's blessing to Abraham: "And I will make…your name great; and you shall be a blessing" (Gen. 12:2). This time, it's not a blessing he received through the cunning plan of his mother, but through his own merit. It is due to the significant work he has done on himself and his readiness to be alone. The man who steps out of the tent – into the field, into a life filled with challenges – is blessed with a new name.

The night comes to an end. "And the sun rose upon him" (Gen 32:32). The face of Jacob-Israel has changed. He is now ready for the practical encounter with his brother, to close the wounded familial circle. Reborn on this night, Jacob has rightfully earned his birthright and blessing – through merit and honesty. Therefore, he is rewarded with the honor of continuing God's covenant with Abraham. Jacob is limping. A limping man needs to slow his pace. There is a cost to the struggle, but also a sense of immense satisfaction and meaning.

It's unclear how the experience of the Jabbok crossing influenced his relationships. This encounter occurred long after he had established a large family. It seems that the fundamental relationship with siblings, the question of "Am I my brother's keeper?" persists throughout a person's life. In life, one does not always enter a relationship "complete." Emotional life is not linear.

As the Sages say, "The deeds of the fathers are a sign for the children." Jacob experiences loneliness, acknowledges solitude, and achieves a face-to-face encounter. The path to being a blessing in the world goes through territories similar to Jacob's life journey.

Jacob is granted a unique gift – he is able to bless all his children, although they have undergone severe conflicts among themselves and also against their father. The conclusion of the Book of Genesis is the moment when Jacob's children achieve reconciliation among themselves. They are indeed a family, soon to give birth to a nation. Therefore, his blessing of the children before his death is a powerful moment, sealing the Book of Genesis and its focus on the issues of sibling relationships.

Many individuals experience anxiety during the transition from their identity as a child of their parents to an uncharted new identity. During this phase, we are invited to a night of dreams and ladders, with angels of God. It's a moment to remember that despite change and complexity during growth, we have received blessing from our parents. This blessing continues to accompany us into the unknown territories of our lives.

Moreover, everyone encounters an individual Jabbok crossing. These are pivotal life moments that occur after we have matured, established ourselves, and achieved success. It is a time for introspection and clarifying our essence. We ponder how we have evolved from the foundational Jacob within us to the Israel aspect, capable of wrestling, discerning, and being blessed. The act of the weak seeking a blessing from the strong is remarkable and deeply meaningful. It emerges from a place of significant freedom and substantial emotional flexibility. Our life's struggles are not meant to defeat us or our opponents but to nurture us into a new form of blessing.

Questions for Reflection

• Reflect on whether you recognize your "Jabbok."

- Think about a crisis in your life that may have concluded with a blessing. Try to recount the story and consider what lessons can be learned from it.
- What more you can do in the future to have a renewed encounter with your sibling? How can you transform tension into blessed reflection?

Chapter 11

Blessed Speech

In 2014, I met with one of Facebook's executives at the company's Silicon Valley headquarters in California. I wanted to interest him in Kolot and explore the potential for supporting our organization's activities. After a long and exhausting flight, I arrived at Menlo Park near Palo Alto. Following a security check, my host insisted on giving me a tour of the headquarters. I observed calm people in transparent rooms beside inviting kitchens with an abundance of healthy food. The complex also included a gym, a counselor/psychologist, and other fascinating "effects" to help make the workplace feel like home. When we returned to the office, I noticed we only had fifteen minutes left, and the next person on his schedule had already arrived. Quickly I changed the subject and asked, "Is there a price the world pays due to Facebook?" He inquired whether I came from Israel to talk about Facebook or Kolot. I asked him to please consider my question.

He then called over a young woman who was conducting post-doctoral research at Stanford and asked her to share it with me. After confirming that I was not a Google agent, she revealed that she had studied over twenty-six hundred youths on the West Coast of the United States who used Facebook. She found that many of them lacked the ability to have face-to-face conversations with close contacts, including family and friends. They struggled to share personal observations about their inner well-being. She concluded, "For them, words are merely instrumental."

I was disturbed by this statement. I looked at the clock, and unfortunately, our time was up. At the office door, as we said our goodbyes, I told him that we might discuss Kolot another time. I briefly shared that "being a blessing" raises questions regarding the costs of social media compared with the hopes for its potential. I emphasized the Jewish belief in the power of words, in speech as a tool for connection and healing, and the quality of face-to-face encounters. He looked at me curiously as we parted. Later, it turned out that this odd meeting brought us closer, and he invited me to teach the subject of "Face to Face" interactions at Facebook and even donated to Kolot for several years.

One of the repercussions of media, particularly social media, is its impact on the caliber of human discourse. The capacity to forge conversations that are meaningful, engaging, and connective is increasingly compromised. In a realm in which speech is predominantly utilitarian, the essence of human communication experiences a significant decline.

Historically, speech has been perceived as a quintessential human attribute, traditionally associated with the vibrancy of the soul. Philosophers and thinkers across the ages – notably Socrates and Freud, each within their respective times and frameworks – have identified speech as the primary conduit for therapeutic intervention. Socrates regarded dialogue as a tool for the pursuit of philosophical truth, while Freud considered conversation a critical component of psychological healing. Freudian therapeutic discourse, distinct from Socratic dialogue, is more associative than logical, unearthing facets of the individual's inner realm that are often repressed or distorted. Freud posited that exposure to one's psychological realities could empower people to reconfigure their emotional existence. While speech may not alter the laws of nature, it holds an essential role in sculpting an individual's spiritual landscape.

Despite this distinct human characteristic, many of us grapple with feelings of being misunderstood. We exert considerable effort in the pursuit of understanding ourselves and others. The anguish associated with the quality of our communication is intensifying. Our endeavors to clarify our intended meanings are often accompanied by a profound frustration arising from words that fall short of conveying our genuine, heartfelt sentiments.

As Rabbi Nachman of Breslev says: "Through speech, the soul moves from potential to action" (*Likutei Moharan* 31:9). The human soul yearns for connection and presence in the world. Rabbi Nachman posits that speech is the tangible manifestation of this deep-seated desire within our souls. Its essence is to communicate longing, a profound request. Indeed, people crave a medium through which their souls can find expression. At times, however, the soul may become ensconced in the depths of concealment and silence, rendering us incapable of articulating our innermost experiences. The quality of our speech, therefore, is a reflection of our state of being and vitality, acting as a mirror to our very existence.

Yet achieving such precision in speech is a complex endeavor. The *Zohar* delves deeply into the existential state of voice devoid of speech, highlighting scenarios in life where an individual is unable to fully express the soul's intent. People whose soul's longing does not find expression can emit only a voice, a sigh, a general inclination, without the ability to produce clear, articulate speech that accurately conveys their condition and emotions.

This is a familiar experience for many of us. It's the feeling that the words we speak don't fully express our inner desires, that something within us is not quite ready to engage with the world, or perhaps even with ourselves. Sometimes, these gaps in our speech reflect our own struggles in leading or guiding ourselves. "One can gauge one's spiritual position by the clarity of one's speech" (Rabbi Avraham Yitzhak Hacohen Kook, *Orot Hakodesh* 3:293).

We find ourselves in a time when a vast chasm exists between the swift advancement of technology and the evolution of the human spirit. The allure of technology is potent, widening the gap between our connection to our souls, our innermost selves, and the pursuit of recognition and casual "likes" on social media. Despite its inherent potential to foster intimacy, human speech confronts one of its most significant challenges in a world dominated by social media. Consequently, theories on deep listening are gaining prominence in our era, responding to the lack of quality listening that further compounds the challenges of verbal communication.

The proverb "Death and life are in the power of the tongue" (Prov. 18:21) captures the extreme potentials of speech: to bring forth either life or death, and everything in between. This perspective suggests that speech can profoundly impact us, either invigorating or diminishing our spirit.

The onset of COVID-19 significantly amplified the realm of ZOOM and virtual communication, proving to be quite effective in various domains, including workplaces, the education system, and beyond. The challenges brought forth by COVID-19 lead us to a fundamental inquiry: What is the true purpose of communication? Is it merely to efficiently transmit professional messages or educational content? Or, as suggested by the earlier

Facebook study, are we at risk of losing an element in speech that facilitates encounters that encourage intimacy?

In the upcoming discussion, my goal is to return speech to its core essence. I will delineate the distinction between speech rooted in the consciousness of the Tree of Life and speech characterized by the qualities of the Tree of Knowledge. Additionally, I will offer insights into the markers of what constitutes "blessed" speech.

The Origin of Human Speech

> Then the Lord God formed man of the dust of the ground, and breathed into his nostrils the breath of life; and man became a living soul. (Gen. 2:7)

This verse describes the human as a composite of earthly dust and a divine element – the breath of life – with the union of these elements transforming man into a living soul.

On the term *living soul, Targum Onkelos*[1] comments: "He breathed into his nostrils the breath of life, and man became a speaking spirit." The phrase "a living soul" is interpreted here as a "speaking spirit," a unique descriptor that defines speech. This interpretation reinforces the idea that the power of speech is a distinctive characteristic of humans, a gift directly endowed by the Creator. Among all creatures in the animal kingdom, it is humans who possess this particular trait, making speech a profoundly special aspect of our personality.

Speech that embodies the qualities of the Tree of Life is centered around fostering life and cultivating constructive dialogues with others. It encompasses elements of surprise and personal touch, expressing deep emotions and striving for a soulful connection. This form of speech transitions from isolation to active engagement with others.

On the other hand, speech that emanates from the Tree of Knowledge is more concerned with analysis, decision making, praise, and critique. It seeks

---

1   *Targum Onkelos* is the primary Jewish Aramaic *targum* (translation) of the Torah, accepted as an authoritative translated text of the Five Books of Moses and thought to have been written in the early second century CE.

to understand and interpret the world through the dualistic lens of good and evil. This form of speech navigates the realms of right and wrong, emphasizing the ability to discern differences among people. It serves a functional purpose, allowing us to communicate needs and expectations to others effectively.

Both types of speech play essential roles in the world. The speech of knowledge is crucial for articulating viewpoints, fostering debates, and facilitating practical engagement in worldly affairs. It enables the world of action to function with efficiency. However, this kind of speech has another dimension to it. Some individuals resort to defensive mechanisms such as cynicism, sarcasm, or excessive sophistication in their speech.

In contrast, there's another kind of speech that originates from the soul, emanating from a deeper, more primal place. This speech aims to connect with life's mysteries and essences that transcend mere knowledge. Rabbi Kook articulates this beautifully: "Every uttered word opens a channel in the soul, channeling that content from which speech is carved" (*Orot Hakodesh* 3:281).

In the late nineteenth century, Rabbi Israel Meir Kagan of Radin, known as the Chafetz Chaim, authored *Shemirat Halashon* (Guarding the Tongue) in Poland. This work, which has become a cornerstone in Orthodox Jewish education, focuses on human words. It delineates the boundaries of speech, outlining what is permissible and what is forbidden. This guide to proper speech effectively opened the gates to understanding the Tree of Knowledge of Good and Evil in the realm of speech. The Chafetz Chaim recognized the immense challenge of maintaining clean speech, avoiding gossip and slander. He therefore emphasized guarding one's speech and observing the prohibitions against slander and gossip, not only as moral imperatives but as halachic practices. He urged Jews to study and meticulously observe these laws and ethical teachings, with the same rigor applied to observing kosher and Shabbat laws.

He delved into aspects such as the extent of the prohibition against slander, differentiating it from gossip, and the ban on defamation. The Chafetz Chaim's goal was to cleanse the Jewish world of the early twentieth century from speech that was harmful and weakening. From this perspective, his endeavor was significant and impactful, resonating with Jewish communities globally.

However, the focus of the book was primarily on the negative, destructive aspects of speech, rather than on promoting intimate and connecting speech.

In contrast, a key part of the current era is the aspiration to heal speech from its years of "exile." This idea is also pertinent in the context of the modern return to Zion, which revitalized the Hebrew language (a significant achievement of Zionism). Many thinkers, however, advocate beyond this for restoring speech to its original, life-affirming purpose. They emphasize the need for speech that genuinely creates life, infuses the soul with color, and illuminates the face. Rabbi Shimon Gershon Rosenberg (also known by his initials as Rabbi Shagar) wrote, "Through language, a person can overcome loneliness, connect to another soul, and break the encasing shell of estrangement."[2]

Sefer Yetzirah (The Book of Formation) stands as one of the earliest texts in Jewish mystical literature. It depicts the creation of the world through letters and words, aiming not only to elucidate divine creation via speech but also to serve as a blueprint for human emulation and activity. The book posits the idea that humans, through their language and speech, possess the power to create worlds. This notion marks a profound difference from merely being cautious with permissible speech, as emphasized in guarding the tongue. It reintroduces an ancient yet renewed understanding of the power of words to forge new realities, to pierce through the mundane and arid, to imbue the world and others with flowing, life-giving waters.

Take, for instance, the unique words spoken during the sanctification of a marriage in a wedding ceremony: "Behold, you are betrothed to me with this ring." These words do not merely reflect reality; they actively create it. There are instances when words can generate sanctity, covenant, and life. The wedding expresses a unique hope for connection to the Tree of Life, and these words that create the connection come from this world.

In the sections below, I will outline areas of speech that emerge from the consciousness of the Tree of Life.

Blessing in Speech

One striking example of the power of speech is the act of blessing. In the biblical context, blessings transcend mere well-wishes or hopes for someone to attain what the blessing describes, as is commonly perceived today. In the

---

2   Rabbi Shimon Gershon Rosenberg, *Panecha Avakesh* (Efrat: The Institute for the Advancement of Rabbi Shagar's Writings, 2005), 67.

Bible, a blessing embodies a state of abundance; through the words of the blessing, there is an intent to create a new reality. The one bestowing the blessing endeavors to convey prosperity to another. In this profound human experience, the person issuing the blessing feels an internal surge of life and abundance, and the words of the blessing aim to materialize a similar reality for the recipient.[3] The act of laying hands on the head of the one being blessed serves as a tangible conduit, transferring the abundance articulated in the words of the blessing.

For instance, Isaac's blessing to his sons is given through a feeling of physical satiety. Isaac instructs his son Esau: "And make me savory food, such as I love, and bring it to me, that I may eat; that my soul may bless you before I die" (Gen. 27:4). He asks his son to go out into the field. What is it about the field that is essential for the words of the blessing? The answer lies in the blessing given to Jacob in Esau's disguise: "And he came near, and kissed him; and he smelled the smell of his raiment, and blessed him, and said: 'See, the smell of my son is like the smell of a field which the Lord has blessed'" (Gen. 27:27).

Significantly, the following verse speaks of material abundance:

> And God give you of the dew of heaven, and of the fat places of
> the earth, and plenty of corn and wine. (Gen. 27:28)

In the field, God's blessing dwells without barriers or intermediaries, reminiscent of the abundance in the Garden of Eden.[4] The aroma of a blessed field triggers within Isaac a gateway to blessing, a sensation that intensifies as he consumes the savory food. It is only when Isaac is imbued with a sense of God's blessing that he feels empowered to bless his son. This blessing is intimately connected to a state of consciousness and the experience of abundance.

In a venerable Jewish tradition, parents bestow blessings upon their children before the Kiddush on Shabbat eve. A blessing is not just a hopeful utterance. At its origin, it emanates from a place of fullness and a deep-seated

---

3   See chapter 4 above, on the essence of blessing in Boaz's dialogue with the laborers in his field.

4   "He smelled the smell of his raiment...and said, 'See, the smell of my son'" – when Jacob came in, he brought the scent of the Garden of Eden with him, and he was wearing Adam's clothes (*Zohar*, Parashat Bo 138).

desire to give. The parents recognize the abundance within themselves, experiencing a flow akin to a river of material or spiritual vitality, which they seek to impart to their children. The blessing, articulated through words and conveyed with a gentle touch, becomes a medium for transferring this abundance to their loved ones. The act of blessing children on Shabbat eve mirrors the Creator's blessing following the six days of creation. Parents reflect on the week that has passed, attune themselves to the abundance they feel within, and bless their children with this sense of fullness.

Speech Devoted to Experience

Another example that reflects on the power of speech through the paradigm of the trees of the garden is this well-known Talmudic source:

> The Sages taught: How should one dance before the bride?
>
> Beit Shammai say: "The bride as she is."
> And Beit Hillel say: "A beautiful and graceful bride."
> Beit Shammai said to Beit Hillel: "If she was lame or blind, would you say to her: 'A beautiful and graceful bride'? As the Torah said, 'Stay far away from a false matter' [Ex. 23:7]!"
> Beit Hillel said to Beit Shammai: "According to your words, if someone bought a bad purchase from the market, should he praise it [to the seller] or degrade it? You must say he should praise it!"
> Based on this, the Sages said: A person's mind should always be concerned with humanity. (*Ketubot* 16b)

The scene depicted here involves guests dancing before the bride and groom at a traditional marriage ceremony, likely occurring as the couple exits the *yichud* room, where they have just spent their first private moments together. This moment is a crucial opportunity to bolster the emotional bond between the couple, following the formalization of their marriage contract. In this Jewish ceremony, the celebration goes beyond mere singing and dancing. It includes spoken words of praise directed at the bride and groom, presumably to bolster and encourage them in their newfound marital covenant and the sacred union they have just embarked upon. In these moments, words carry profound significance, serving not only as expressions of joy but also as affirmations of the couple's commitment and the sanctity of their relationship.

Beit Hillel advocates for the guests at a marriage celebration to use a standardized phrase: "A beautiful and graceful bride," while Beit Shammai proposes speaking the truth as perceived: "The bride as she is." The implication is that observers should express what they genuinely see in that moment.

This story – and the dispute it encapsulates – can be interpreted in various ways. Many perceive it as a classic tension between the advocates of peace and truth, a theme common in many disputes between Beit Shammai and Beit Hillel. Beit Hillel aims to preserve the couple's harmony, whereas Beit Shammai prioritizes the principle of truth, regardless of the potential immediate repercussions. However, Hillel's metaphor, "If someone bought a bad purchase from the market, should he praise it or degrade it?" guides us toward a different understanding. In this analogy, Hillel suggests that we are no longer in the pre-wedding phase of deliberation and engagement, which can sometimes be fraught with tension. Instead, we have moved into the post-chuppah reality. Accepting the reality of the other at this juncture is a decisive act, calling for a level of acquiescence from the observer. Theoretical hesitations give way to a profound desire to affirm and reinforce the decision just solemnized by the ceremony.

I'd like to offer a slightly different interpretation of this story. Rather than a conflict or debate between truth and peace, I see it as representing two ways of understanding truth. Hillel's perspective is that on her wedding day, every bride is indeed beautiful. This view challenges the notion of an absolute, objective standard of beauty, which Shammai seems to uphold to the very end.

Hillel perceives the situation through the lens of the Tree of Life. A wedding is not just an event; it is a foundational experience deeply rooted in the Garden of Eden. This connection is echoed in the seven blessings of the wedding ceremony, many of which refer back to the act of creation. One blessing poignantly states: "Delight the beloved companions as You delighted Your creation in the Garden of Eden of old." In this context, Shammai's conception of knowledge, or that of any other wedding guest, is irrelevant. During these moments, everyone is symbolically invited back to the Garden of Eden, if only briefly. In this sacred space and time, indeed, every bride is perceived as beautiful and graceful.

Shammai struggles with the idea of entering the Garden of Eden, even momentarily. He is not prepared to abandon the consciousness associated with the Tree of Knowledge of Good and Evil. Shammai contends that embracing the Edenic state in the tangible world of a wedding is a dangerous precedent, cautioning against relinquishing the lenses of knowledge, discernment, and judgment. At the core of Shammai's perspective is the belief that our world, in its unredeemed state, does not allow us to forsake the distinction between good and evil. According to him, these discernments are the essential tools for navigating life. He rejects the notion of indulging in illusory romanticism or fanciful imaginations. "The bride as she is" represents an adherence to observable reality, to what the eyes can see and verify.

In contrast, the Tree of Life perspective suggests that our fractured world contains distinct oases in which life can be experienced in its fullness. The human challenge lies in identifying these oases and then cautiously yet confidently extending their reach into additional realms of our existence.

"A beautiful and graceful bride" – certainly. The wedding canopy represents a moment of profound blessing, an opportunity to lay down a hopeful foundation for the couple's future and, by extension, for the world at large.

Rebuke That Can Be Heard

The commandment of rebuke is a notable area in which we can discern the contrasting qualities of the two trees. Rebuke is inherently uncomfortable for most people, and with good reason. It often carries an air of judgment and can feel like an unwelcome intrusion into someone's personal space.

In each class I conduct on the topic of rebuke, I begin by asking participants: *What does the concept of rebuke evoke for you?* Typically, the response is one of discomfort or unease. Despite this, rebuke holds a significant place in Torah. Moreover, the Sages stated: "Any love that does not include rebuke is not love" (*Midrash Genesis Rabbah* 54:3). This intricate interplay between love and rebuke will be the central theme of our exploration. We'll delve into how rebuke, when rooted in love and understanding, transcends mere criticism and becomes a pivotal component of caring and meaningful relationships.

Blessed Speech

The commandment of rebuke appears in the Torah in Parashat Kedoshim, which commences with the directive "You shall be holy; for I, the Lord your God, am holy" (Lev. 19:2). A closer examination of the subsequent verses reveals that holiness, according to these teachings, is primarily expressed in the mundane aspects of life: leaving the corners of the field for the poor and the stranger, not delaying wages, and refraining from placing a stumbling block before the blind.

This portion reaches a pivotal moment with the following verses:

> You shall not go up and down as a tale-bearer among your people; neither shall you stand idly by the blood of your neighbor: I am the Lord. You shall not hate your brother in your heart; you will surely rebuke your neighbor, and not bear sin because of him. You shall not take vengeance, nor bear any grudge against the children of your people, but you shall love your neighbor as yourself: I am the Lord. (Lev. 19:16–18)

These verses present a cohesive narrative, threading together various commandments: the prohibitions against tale bearing, standing idly by your neighbor's blood, harboring hatred in your heart, taking vengeance, and bearing a grudge. Interspersed among these are the positive commandments of rebuke and the injunction to love your neighbor as yourself. In this interpretation, the journey to achieving "love your neighbor as yourself" navigates through the preceding mandates. It is this interpretive lens that intricately links the acts of rebuke and love, suggesting that true love for one's neighbor encompasses the willingness to offer constructive rebuke. This connection underscores the complex but essential relationship between guiding others toward better paths and genuinely caring for their well-being.

However, in several places in the Talmud, the Sages expressed skepticism about the ability to fulfill the commandment of rebuke:

> Rabbi Tarfon said: I wonder if there is anyone in this generation who can accept rebuke. If someone tells him to remove a splinter from his eye, he would retort to remove the beam from his own eye.

Be a Blessing

Rabbi Elazar ben Azariah said: I wonder if there is anyone in this generation who knows how to rebuke.

Rabbi Akiva said: I wonder if there is anyone in this generation fit to rebuke. (*Arachin* 16b)

In the period following the destruction of the Second Temple, the Sages expressed skepticism regarding the practicality of fulfilling this biblical commandment of rebuke. Their concerns stemmed from various factors: the potential inability of the recipient to accept and internalize the rebuke, the possibility of an inappropriate or ineffective method of delivering the rebuke, and doubts about the authority or legitimacy of the person offering the criticism. This hesitancy highlights the complexities inherent in the act of rebuking, underscoring the delicate balance required to ensure it is both meaningful and constructive.

Often, we find that our attempts at criticism fail to make the intended impression.[5] We have seen how the Sages found it challenging to implement this biblical ideal.

The absence of rebuke, however, comes at a cost. It results in relationships marked by incomplete communication, devoid of the capacity for authentic dialogue. In such relationships, expressions of pain, hurt, and need are conspicuously absent. People refrain from offering rebuke, thereby overlooking the profound request it embodies. Parents may overly praise their children while failing to set boundaries; couples might engage only in superficial interactions or resort to silence. Even during conflicts, communication remains flawed.

Despite these challenges, rebuke has the potential to be a powerful tool for fostering complete, personal, and deeply connecting dialogue. But how can this be effectively achieved? How can rebuke lead to love?

The Ba'al Shem Tov and his disciples breathed new life into the concept of rebuke, approaching it from the Tree of Life perspective. For them, rebuke is

---

5   The Sages summarized the matter as follows: "Just as it is a commandment for a person to say something that will be heeded, so too it is a commandment for a person not to say something that will not be heeded. Rabbi Abba says: It is an obligation, as it is stated: 'Do not reprove a scoffer, lest he hate you; reprove a wise man, and he will love you'" (*Yevamot* 65b).

deeply connected with presence – in both language and the inner soul – and is underpinned by empathy. In their view, rebuke should not stem from the judgmental stance of the Tree of Knowledge. Instead, it should arise from a place of understanding and connection, aiming to heal and improve the relationship.

Rabbi Isaac bar Sheshet (Ribash) said to a righteous man of his generation, who frequently admonished many: "How can you know how to rebuke when throughout your entire life you are unaware of sin, and you do not interact with people to understand their sins?" (*Amtachat Binyamin*, Kohelet).

Rebuke that is impactful and connecting can only come from someone who has truly been present in the tangible environment of the transgression. It requires empathy with the situation, the temptation, and the accompanying pain. Only a person who has experienced such circumstances firsthand and understands the context intimately is qualified to offer admonishment. Criticism delivered from a position of distance, alienation, or, worse, from a pedestal of lofty righteousness is unlikely to forge a genuine connection.

To navigate the realm of rebuke effectively, one needs to approach it from a place of presence and identification, embodying a shared consciousness rooted in the Tree of Life. This approach forms the essential first step toward offering meaningful and empathetic guidance.

Yet there's another vital step to rebuke:

> The Ba'al Shem Tov, whose soul resides in the heavenly treasuries, taught that a complete tzaddik, devoid of evil within himself, sees no evil in any person. This is like looking into a mirror: if one's face is dirty, one sees it reflected in the mirror, and if it's clean, one sees no flaw. As one is, so one perceives oneself. (Rabbi Menachem Nachum of Chernobyl, *Me'or Einayim*, Chukat)[6]

This insight leads to significant internal reflection. When one is disturbed or triggered by a trait in another, it's essential to introspect and identify

---

6   Rabbi Ya'akov Yosef of Polnoye describes the process of a preacher's rebuke to his congregation as a process of connection between them, where ultimately the reprover criticizes himself, and through his attempts to rectify his own flaws, he inspires the congregation to rectify theirs. This is an outward speech that essentially turns inward.

where similar aspects of that issue may reside within oneself. As the Sages wisely noted, "Whoever disqualifies does so with his own flaw" (*Kiddushin* 70a). These elements may not be identical to those observed in the person being admonished but often relate to similar psychological or emotional underpinnings.

Consider the example of a young religious woman I once spoke with, who was in search of a husband. She was vehement in her assertion that she would never marry someone with eating disorders – a perfectly valid preference. However, her intense aversion led me to ask if she recognized any aspect of this disorder in herself. After initial hesitation and embarrassment, she acknowledged that she did. Acknowledging the presence of a challenging trait we see in others within ourselves doesn't necessarily alter our views, but it enables us to connect with a foundation of empathy, compassion, and possibly even humor. Most crucially, this recognition shifts our perspective and dialogue from a judgmental, Tree of Knowledge–based approach to a more inclusive, Tree of Life–oriented stance.

The mirror concept significantly enriches the Tree of Life consciousness. Rebuke, as an act of speech, serves as a reflective mirror toward others. It's intriguing that our eyes are designed to perceive everything but our own flaws, leading us into a deeply human process that has the potential to forge strong connections. This process commences with recognizing a "flaw" in someone else as a mirror of our own self. This reflection often brings us face to face with unresolved aspects within us that we might be hesitant to address.

Rather than projecting these issues onto others, we introduce them into the conversation as a form of candid and engaged dialogue. It's possible that the other person is grappling with similar issues, creating a shared understanding. This mutual recognition paves the way for a new type of interaction that nurtures closeness and partnership and has the potential to transform rebuke into an avenue for rediscovering love.

The journey of this form of communication is both demanding and fulfilling. It's challenging to confront our own shortcomings, yet it's immensely rewarding when two individuals discover they share personal experiences, leading to profound companionship. This is the essence of love in its varied expressions. It invites individuals to step out of their comfort zones, shaped by their past and various life experiences, and embrace the revitalizing aspects of the Tree of Life. In this state, individuals take ownership of their wounds rather than projecting their pains onto others.

Thus, a discourse of rebuke, when it emerges from the Tree of Life perspective and acts as a human mirror, can be a powerful tool for fostering new, meaningful human communication.

Tree of Life Approach to Confession

Rabbi Nachman presents a distinctive approach to life through speech, viewing our existence as a story, or more precisely, a play. In this narrative framework, he portrays the Supreme Director – God – as the architect of a plot intricately woven for our individual benefit. He states: "When a person knows that all his experiences are for his own benefit, this perspective is akin to the World to Come" (*Likutei Moharan* 4:1).

From this vantage point, events in our lives are not classified through a dualistic lens of good or evil. Instead, each occurrence holds positive significance, contributing to the richness of life's tapestry. This perspective values every experience, aligning with the Talmudic notion that in the future, people will offer blessings for adverse events just as readily as they do for favorable ones.[7]

Achieving a unified consciousness, as Rabbi Nachman explains, involves lifting our materialistic perceptions of reality to a higher plane in which everything is genuinely governed by God, Who inherently seeks life. This process is intrinsically linked to Tree of Life consciousness. It demands recognizing the divine essence within every crisis, acknowledging that each challenge holds an invitation to find deeper meaning and growth. This task, though formidable, is crucial for the transition from the consciousness rooted in this world to the enlightened perspective of the World to Come. It requires a profound shift in perception, so that even the most trying circumstances are seen as part of a larger, divinely orchestrated narrative, guiding us toward growth and understanding.

Rabbi Nachman introduces a practical approach: "It's impossible to restore the kingdom to God, except through confession of words to a Torah scholar" (*Likutei Moharan* 1:4). This suggests that to grasp the meaning in

---

7   *Pesachim* 50a, and see chapter 16 on trials and the Tree of Life.

what happens to you, you should confess to a Torah scholar. This confession, however, is not merely recounting sins. It represents an open-hearted sharing of your personal narrative, embracing its honesty and complexity. Rabbi Shagar clarifies this, stating, "Speech has the role of externalizing the subject. Speaking about things takes us out of our subjective space, allowing us to see them as external to us."[8] The ability to examine ourselves from an external perspective allows us to break free from narrow consciousness to a broader one nourished by the Tree of Life.

The ideal Torah scholar, as conceptualized by Rabbi Nachman, embodies deep listening skills. Their wisdom manifests not in original insights but through authentic identification with the learner. Rabbi Nachman describes sins and failings as if they are ingrained into our very bones. Through confession, complemented by the Torah scholar's unique listening ability, individuals can liberate themselves from these deep-seated marks in their psyches, enabling them to break free from limiting self-perceptions.

Professor Otto Scharmer of the Sloan School of Management at MIT developed "U Theory," which outlines five levels of listening for an organizational leader.[9] He asserts that deep listening fosters profound insights, helping to cast aside habitual thoughts and responses, and paves the way for listening from the perspective of an emerging future, thus facilitating the creation of a new reality. The act of verbal sharing, especially with a receptive listener to whom one can reveal the core of one's existence, including failures and aspirations, is transformative for the sharer. This process can lead to newfound self-awareness and a significant liberation from entrenched behavioral habit patterns.

Speech rooted in the Tree of Life inspires us to forge a world that is vibrant and hopeful. Just as a seed's potential brings forth life and connection, speech influenced by the Tree of Life can cultivate a world teeming with vigor and optimism. This form of speech has the power to establish genuine connections with others, broadening the bonds of intimacy among people. It introduces

---

8   Rabbi Shagar, *Shi'urim al Likutei Moharan*, 5775, part 4, 31.

9   In 2006, Scharmer and his colleagues founded The Presencing Institute "to create an action research platform at the intersection of science, consciousness, and profound social and organizational change." See www.presencing.com.

into our world, often dominated by dichotomies of good and evil, an elemental life force – the "speaking spirit" from the Garden of Eden – capable of effecting tangible transformations in our lives.

Exercise

- Try to be aware of the quality of your speech for a few hours. When does it come from the Tree of Knowledge mindset, and in which situations does it stem from the Tree of Life mindset?
- Try practicing rebuke from the mirror perspective. Start with someone you know well, and gradually move to people who represent a higher risk level.

Chapter 12

Eating from Both Trees

Food, a fundamental necessity, is not just a basic biological requirement like the oxygen we breathe. It transcends mere sustenance, enveloping aspects of comfort and compensation for various non-nutritional internal needs. We find ourselves inundated with an endless stream of information and research on dietary habits, from diet recommendations to alarming studies about widespread weight issues among children in the USA, alongside concerns about anorexic teenagers and the general populace grappling with existential food-related issues.

The pursuit of an ideal physical appearance and the yearning for positive body image are intimately linked to diet. In recent years, the significance of food has been elevated, evidenced by the ubiquity of cooking shows and culinary competitions. These not only showcase a sense of abundance but also a yearning for creativity in our gastronomic experiences. Similarly, in the realm of spirit and consciousness, there's a growing awareness around the quality of food we consume. This sentiment is echoed by Jewish spiritual luminaries, including Maimonides, Rabbi Isaiah Halevi Horowitz (the Shelah), A. D. Gordon, Rabbi Kook, and contemporary figures in Israel such as Rabbi Yuval Asherov, who advocate for a conscientious approach to our dietary choices.

The narrative of the Garden of Eden, with its central focus on the Tree of Knowledge and the forbidden fruit, highlights the significance of food as an elemental aspect of existence and blessing. A fascinating passage from the Jerusalem Talmud states: "In the future, a person will be held accountable for everything his eyes saw and he did not eat" (*Kiddushin* 4:12). The

Korban Ha'edah's commentary[1] on this passage offers an intriguing perspective: "And did not eat – he sinned against himself by unnecessarily denying himself." This interpretation suggests that the essence of this judgment is not merely about the pleasures one denied oneself but rather about a deeper disconnection between the body and the soul. The soul seeks fulfillment and expression; it yearns to experience and taste all that our eyes behold. Hence, excessive restraint in eating can be seen as constricting the soul, denying it the fullness of its desired expression.[2]

The narrative of Eden places a significant emphasis on food, notably through the directive to avoid eating from the Tree of Knowledge. This early instruction in our collective history underscores the importance of mindful eating. It encourages an awareness of choosing foods that genuinely nourish us, distinguishing between consumption patterns influenced by the Tree of Knowledge – emphasizing need, dependency, and prohibitions – and those aligned with the Tree of Life, emphasizing the joy of food.

Eating in the spirit of the Tree of Life is characterized by the enjoyment and pleasure derived from the act of eating. Here, the focus extends beyond just the type and quantity of food, which is often the central concern in diets, to include the consciousness we bring to the experience of eating. From this viewpoint, occasionally indulging in a delicious ice cream or a cinnamon croissant is justifiable, even if their nutritional value is low. The key lies in the pleasure and satisfaction derived from these foods.

This chapter aims to delve deeper into the relationship between food and pleasure. We will explore how defining food as a source of pleasure can reshape our approach to eating.

We have seen that eating occupies a central place in life in the Garden of Eden:

---

1 A commentary on the Jerusalem Talmud by Rabbi Naftali Frankel, chief rabbi of Berlin in the eighteenth century.

2 A similar principle appears in *Ta'anit* 11a, where Shmuel states: "Anyone who sits in fast is called a sinner.... One should always practice self-moderation as if the Divine Presence resides within one's innards, as it is said, 'Your Holy One is within you, and I will not enter the city' [Hos. 11:9]." This teaching emphasizes the importance of taking care of one's body, seen as a vessel containing holiness, rather than denying or harming it through unnecessary fasting.

And the Lord God planted a garden eastward in Eden; and there He put the man whom He had formed. And out of the ground made the Lord God to grow every tree that is pleasant to the sight, and good for food; the Tree of Life also in the midst of the garden, and the Tree of Knowledge of good and evil. (Gen. 2:8–9)

After describing the creation of the great rivers, God commands:

And the Lord God took the man, and put him into the Garden of Eden to dress it and to keep it. And the Lord God commanded the man, saying, "Of every tree of the garden you may freely eat: But of the Tree of Knowledge of Good and Evil, you shall not eat; for the day you eat from it, you shall surely die." (Gen. 2:15–17)

Man, initially created outside the Garden of Eden, is placed within it after the Creator prepares a foundation rich in trees and water, catering to all his nutritional needs. The divine command to eat from all the trees, indicated by the Hebrew phrase *achol tochel* ("you will surely eat," with repetition of the verb for emphasis), underscores eating as a central aspect of life in the garden, characterizing the Edenic existence as one deeply connected with nourishment. However, amidst this abundance, a singular restriction exists: the prohibition of one tree. This command, ultimately defied by man, who consumes the forbidden fruit, introduces the concept of restraint and choice within the otherwise nurturing environment of the garden.

What makes eating so foundational in the infrastructure of the Garden of Eden? Eating has an intrinsically dual nature of nourishment and dependency. It transcends mere sustenance; food engages the senses through its taste, appearance, and scent. Moreover, it awakens desire and appetite, intrinsic human traits present from birth to death. The Israelites' intense craving for meat in the desert, overpowering their reason and faith, exemplifies the compelling force of such desires. Eating represents the internalization of the external world, integrating it into our being. This process of absorbing from outside to inside invites contemplation and mindfulness. In contrast, as explored in the previous chapter, speech operates from the inside out, projecting internal thoughts and feelings into the external world.

The distinctive aspect of food-related desire is its ability to be satisfied independently, unlike other impulses such as interpersonal communication, sexual relations, the quest for honor, or envy, which inherently involve others. This unique attribute, combined with its vital role in our survival, underscores why food is so central in the Garden of Eden narrative. However, the act of eating also encompasses an element of "the other" or community, a topic we will explore further below.

The *Zohar* emphasizes the significance of eating "from every tree of the garden," suggesting an expectation that man would partake from the Tree of Life. According to the *Zohar*, Adam's transgression was not solely in consuming the fruit of the Tree of Knowledge but also in his failure to eat from the Tree of Life. Partaking from this tree would have connected him to the divine essence of his soul ("and He breathed into his nostrils the breath of life"), influencing his core personality. The act of eating from the Tree of Life was intended to shape his approach to nourishment and his relationship with food in the world, contrasting with sustenance from other sources.

What does eating from the Tree of Life mean in terms of a consciousness of blessing? This type of eating suggests a heightened sensory and conscious experience of food. This elevated consciousness of food could extend to other aspects of our lives, including touch, sight, meaningful conversation, and more. Embracing the concept of *oneg* in our eating can play a central role in our dietary choices and impact other bodily experiences such as listening, speaking, seeing, and smelling. While the actual Tree of Life may have been left behind in the garden, the consciousness associated with it remains accessible to us if we choose to adopt it in our lives.

Our world is replete with food, and not just from trees. After the Flood, we were permitted to eat meat.[3] We enjoy a vast diversity of field crops, as well as endless manmade products.

After eating from the Tree of Knowledge of Good and Evil, man was exiled from the garden, leaving the Tree of Life behind. This exile changed our eating habits, and our consciousness now centers around food from the Tree of

---

3   The connection between vegetarianism and the Tree of Life deserves a separate discussion, in the spirit of Rabbi Kook's essay "The Vision of Vegetarianism and Peace" [in Hebrew], in *Afikim ba'Negev* (Jerusalem: Hapeles, 1913), 35–46.

Knowledge. Furthermore, while before the sin Adam ate from all the trees of the garden, after the sin it is said, "And you will eat the herb of the field" (Gen. 3:18). At this point, humanity's primary sustenance comes from crops.

The shift from eating from trees to consuming the grass of the field, similar to the way animals eat, carries significant symbolism. Symbolically, trees relate to the spiritual, higher aspect of a person. The Sages wrote:

> Rabbi Joshua ben Levi said: When the Holy One, blessed be He, told Adam, "Thorns and thistles will it bring forth to you," his eyes shed tears. He said before Him: "Master of the Universe, will I and my donkey eat from the same trough?" (*Pesachim* 118a)

As a punishment, man received a "measure for measure" consequence. After succumbing to the serpent's temptation, which originated from the dust, he partook of the Tree of Knowledge, symbolizing the earthly aspect of his creation. As a result, his new existence is bound to earthly concerns. Eating the grass of the field aligns with the stature of animals, grounding them without the ability to aspire to spiritual elevation. In contrast, trees grow vertically and are suitable for human stature, as expressed in the verse "For man is a tree of the field" (Deut. 20:19).

Moreover, in the Edenic setting, there were moments when man had to lift his head upward to pluck fruits from the tree, fostering a connection to the heavens through his gaze. This was the ideal image: mindful consumption while standing upright. However, after partaking of the Tree of Knowledge, man's stature is likened to that of animals that graze on grass from the field. This transformation signifies a disruption of balance and man's inclination toward the earthly aspect of his existence, neglecting the spiritual within him. This is the familiar depiction of food for us: sustenance that represents earthly substance, necessity, and survival, lacking a connection to the concept of *oneg*, one of the attributes of blessing.

The serpent has the lowest status of all. After eating from the Tree of Knowledge, God decreed: "Upon your belly you will go, and dust you will eat all the days of your life" (Gen. 3:14). Crawling on the dust and eating from it represents the lowest level – there is no deeper descent than this.

Furthermore, trees and grasses differ in their growth patterns. Vegetables and grasses are seasonal, delicate, and have relatively short lifespans. In contrast, trees are less reliant on irrigation because of their deep roots, and they typically bear fruit across multiple seasons.

Interestingly, we observe that Egypt, blessed with field grasses thanks to the irrigation provided by the Nile, is not known for its abundance of trees and their fruits. The prevalence of field grasses, which do not require looking upward for harvesting and lack the awareness that this act inspires, could potentially lead to a sense of stagnation.[4] In contrast, the tree symbolizes aspiration toward height and a meaningful life.

The hope of the Garden of Eden was that man, like the tree of the field, would establish deep roots within his identity by partaking of the Tree of Life and then partaking of the other trees in the garden. The upright stature of man would connect him with the Creator's proximity, granting him security and balance in his relationship with the abundance in his life.

Eating in the Tree of Life consciousness arises organically from sensing the garden. The river flows, nourishing the trees, and their fruits are absorbed within us. This is not eating born of necessity and scarcity but rather from a place of simple attention to the life force within the body.

Eaters and Eating

Eating with *oneg* is expressed in several dimensions in our practical lives. In the dimension of time, it finds manifestation in the unique eating customs observed on Shabbat and holidays.[5] In the dimension of place, it is expressed in eating in Jerusalem, during the pilgrimage three times a year, and in eating at the Temple before God.[6] This eating resembles the eating in the original garden and invites even those living outside the Land of Israel to experience its special quality. The bringing of the first fruits on the festival of Shavuot

---

4   This temptation led Lot to choose Sodom, which was irrigated like Egypt. In both places, there was a direct connection between economics and moral delinquency of the residents.

5   See chapter 6 on the *oneg* experience of Shabbat.

6   On the connection between the Temple and the Garden of Eden, see chapter 19 on Jerusalem.

is another significant expression of experiencing eating through garden consciousness.

Another meaningful dimension is the social aspect of eating. Eating with others requires a special consciousness. The Mishnah in Ethics of the Fathers says:

> Rabbi Shimon says: Three who ate at one table and did not speak words of Torah, it is as if they ate from the sacrifices of the dead, as it is said: "For all their tables are full of vomit, without a place." (Ethics of the Fathers 3:3)

Three people dining together around a single table beckon a different level of engagement in consciousness. This situation resembles a heavenly table, symbolizing God's presence in the garden. When eating is coupled with spiritual discourse, the meal is elevated to a higher plane of awareness. However, all of this presupposes that these actions are carried out with mindfulness and intention, not mechanically or as a mere fulfillment of commandments. Eating without Torah discussion is likened to offerings of the deceased. This stern expression, reminiscent of the element of death in the Tree of Knowledge, conveys a sense of weightiness. Instead of revitalizing us, the food burdens us.

At times, dining with others can have the opposite effect, where the communal setting can actually intensify the indulgence in food, sometimes leading to physical heaviness afterward. This phenomenon was observed in certain celebrations of the ancient Roman world, and it remains familiar to us in our contemporary context during unrestrained feasts on special occasions.

The invitation to bless after the meal, the *zimmun*, is an invitation for the participants to pay attention to the potential of the communal experience. Eating with ten people, a minyan, signifies an added dimension, seeking a tangible divine presence in the meal. In the language of the *zimmun*, when ten individuals are present, we add the words "our God": "Blessed is our God from Whose food we have eaten and by Whose goodness we live," as opposed to the wording used in the presence of three men: "Blessed is He from Whose food we have eaten and by Whose goodness we live." A minyan calls for a consciousness of communal eating. Just as praying with a minyan elevates the status of prayer, the community creates a different context for eating, in the presence of God.

As we saw previously,[7] food on Shabbat is associated with the term *seudah* (feast), in contrast to the *aruchah* (meal) of weekdays. What's the difference? The Shelah (in his commentary on *Shabbat*, Ner Mitzvah 37) writes:

> The main way to delight in Shabbat is not by filling one's belly like a horse or mule, senselessly consuming whatever tastes good. Overeating leads to drowsiness and dulls the mind. Such people are not delighting in Shabbat but rather indulging themselves (their stomachs) on Shabbat.... The point is to eat and drink joyfully and with good cheer, enjoying well-prepared, delicious, easily digestible food, focusing on quality over quantity, without overeating, and drinking two or three glasses of wine to gladden the heart, all according to one's personal capacity.

The Shelah discusses food not solely as a source of personal pleasure but as a means to honor the Sabbath. He views food as an integral component of a broader purpose, a part of the larger canvas of rest and enjoyment on Shabbat, rather than a mere pursuit of self-gratification. Just as work in the Garden of Eden was about fulfilling human purpose and not solely about earning a livelihood, this experience delves into the deeper significance of eating, going beyond the idea of merely "filling one's belly like a horse or mule."

As previously mentioned, eating within the consciousness of the Tree of Life is intricately linked to a wider awareness encompassing dimensions of time, place, and society. These dimensions beckon us to perceive eating as an experience of delight, a way to embrace the earthly aspects of life within a broader framework of consciousness. This transformative process mirrors changes in other areas explored in the book, such as money, the power of speech, sexuality, the fear of death, and repentance. Each of these facets extends an invitation to a new realm of consciousness, enabling the Tree of Life within us to guide the Tree of Knowledge.

---

7   See chapter 6 on Shabbat *oneg.*

As we have explored in previous chapters, in the Torah, a "blessing" signifies the presence of abundance that an individual experiences in life. A blessed person aspires to share this abundance with others. Similar to many concepts that underwent significant changes after the destruction of the Second Temple, the notion of "blessing" also evolved in the new spiritual landscape. The Sages of the Mishnah formulated a series of blessings for food, both before and after consumption, categorizing food into various types. This categorization is intriguing, demanding precision and intention based on the type of food we partake in.

Growing up in a religious environment, my late father's question, "Did you say a blessing on the ice cream?" instilled in me the perception of blessings as a tool for religious discipline, emphasizing the priority of acknowledging God before indulging in earthly pleasures. It served as a powerful lesson in restraint. Even the Talmud, while seeking a scriptural source for the obligation to bless before eating, concludes: "It is forbidden for a person to benefit from this world without a blessing" (*Berachot* 35a). This perspective views food and the enjoyment of it as distinct from us, with the blessing essentially granting us permission to savor the pleasures of this world. The concept of abundance and vitality is replaced by a sense of distance from abundance. This viewpoint is reinforced later in the same discussion: "The Sages taught: It is forbidden for a person to benefit from this world without a blessing, and whoever does so is performing a form of sacrilege" (ibid.). In this view, food is regarded as sacred property belonging to the Creator. The blessing permits us to enter the Creator's world and enjoy the food.[8]

The concept of a blessing as a permit to eat without constraint or awareness of one's body, rooted solely in pleasure, exemplifies a form of consumption aligned with the Tree of Knowledge of Good and Evil. Some individuals may diligently recite blessings, yet their eating habits may still reflect this particular mindset. Washing one's hands, reciting the blessing over the food, and then overeating thousands of calories of unhealthy foods does not represent a blessed mindset.

---

8 Rabbi Yosef Dov Soloveitchik expresses a similar concept in *Shiurim Le-Zecher Abba Mari* (Jerusalem: Rav Kook Institute, 2003) part 2, Birkat Hatorah, 113–16.

Blessings on Food

I propose a practical approach to conscious eating, rooted in the Tree of Life, that relates to the traditional blessings associated with food.

Blessings before eating. These blessings vary depending on the type of food we are about to consume. They serve to open our awareness to what is entering our bodies. We consider where this food comes from and how it integrates with our body. This applies to everyday food items as well as special ones, such as the blessing over wine. Is the wine meant for a ceremonial transition, as in Kiddush or Havdalah? Is it intended to alleviate the burdens of life, creating a sense of lightness and possibly promoting an open heart? Or is it seen as an escape from reality? These distinct blessings before eating are designed to heighten our attention to the food and, in turn, foster awareness and choice regarding what we consume.

Blessing after eating. The post-meal blessing, based on the Torah verse "When you have eaten and are satisfied, you will bless" (Deut. 8:10), centers on gratitude. This sense of gratitude is intricately linked to the Tree of Life, urging us to direct our gaze toward the source of life. This, in turn, creates a circular movement of gratitude that begins with the Creator of the food, extends through human efforts in harvesting, cooking, and eating, and culminates in the expression of gratitude at the meal's conclusion.

Blessing after bodily functions. This blessing, recited after using the bathroom, serves as an expression of awe and gratitude for the proper functioning of our digestive system. It delves into the intricate details of this system and, in doing so, completes the cycle by acknowledging our bodies, including the process of waste elimination.

Being mindful of the sequence of these three blessings – before eating, after eating, and after using the restroom – forms a sort of blessed dietary practice that can connect us to delightful eating and, of course, promote a healthy body.

In the second innocence of our lives, marked by newfound mature awareness, there lies hope for bridging the gap between body and soul, inviting the consciousness of the Tree of Life. Within this framework, we discover a fresh invitation to unite blessings and food, beckoning us to connect with the

Garden of Eden and to fuse the religious discipline of the blessing with the experience of pleasure.

Questions for Reflection

- Consider when you last ate with Tree of Life consciousness as opposed to Tree of Knowledge consciousness. What characterizes each type of eating?
- What do you experience when you eat in the company of others?

PART FOUR

Curses Transformed into Blessings

"When a person knows that all his experiences are for his benefit, this perception is akin to the World to Come." (*Likutei Moharan* 4:1)

Chapter 13

Repentance and the Tree of Life

One of the side effects of the politicization of religion in Israel is the loss of the original meaning of central terms in ancient Hebrew, leading to superficial usage in everyday language. A prime example is the transformation of the concept of teshuvah, which means repentance. Literally, the word means "return" and also "response, answer." Originally, this fundamental Jewish term denoting the capacity for movement, return to an original state, and hope for change, has gradually become a label for a societal transition. Being a *ba'al teshuvah* ("one who has returned" or a newly religious Jew) today often signifies a shift from a secular to a religious lifestyle. In Israel, this is sometimes described metaphorically as a move from secular Tel Aviv to religious Jerusalem.

The term *ba'al teshuvah* as commonly used implies reaching a destination, an arrival. Consequently, a *ba'al teshuvah* knows how to give a response. In this process, modern Hebrew and contemporary Judaism have lost one of the most inviting and beautiful concepts available to a person in our culture. The concept of repentance in Judaism is fundamentally different from its Christian counterpart. It generally contributes to an optimistic view of the future and a strong belief in human dynamism. In this chapter, we will discuss this precious concept in detail, analyzing it in the context of the discourse of trees in the Garden of Eden. We aim to demonstrate that teshuvah is not merely (or even primarily) a behavioral change, but first and foremost a shift in consciousness, a return to Tree of Life consciousness that leads to behavior stemming from self-acceptance and, consequently, a return to one's roots.

Be a Blessing

Lech Lecha – The Journey Inward

After the Flood, God acknowledged that "the nature of man's heart is evil from his youth" (Gen. 8:21). This recognition has led many in the world to the perception that a person cannot truly change. We came from the earth (Gen. 2:7) and we will return to it, and in the meantime, there isn't much that is new under the sun. Family backgrounds and fundamental experiences shape who we are, and there seems to be little room for freedom. Indeed, human existence manifests a deep determinism. There's something honest and straightforward about this perception. It prevents self-delusion and unrealistic hopes for change. Determinism accepts reality with a relative calm and understanding, and it describes our reality more than we sometimes care to admit.

In contrast to this human perception, many Jewish sources indicate the possibility of an alternative. The ability to change and transform is at the core of the concept of teshuvah, which is a foundational belief of Jewish culture. Moreover, teshuvah is rooted in the Jewish narrative. *Lech lecha*, "Go forth" – those first words spoken to Abraham, our forefather, are, according to various commentators, spoken to each one of us.[1]

Lech lecha invites us on a journey that requires courage to leave our comfort zones and familiar surroundings. We face uncertainty, heading toward an uncharted land. This movement, as mentioned in the verses addressing Abraham, forms an integral part of the process of becoming a blessing. This foundational aspect of the Jewish journey predates the formation of the nation and the covenant at Sinai. Being a Hebrew (*ivri* – from the root *ever* or "beyond," implying movement) or a Jew involves a willingness to embrace movement across various life dimensions.

---

1   Hillel Zeitlin wrote: "The voice of God calls out to every person, in every place and at every time: 'Please, human being, please leave behind the desires of the flesh to which you are bound, leave behind all the habits through which you are tied to the world limited by senses, leave behind the pride of your heart, leave your family relations, leave your preconceived notions and the vain beliefs that you hold. Go and seek a distant land, a higher land, a land of the heavens. Where will you seek it? Where will you find it? Go and search!'" (*Safran shel yehidim* [Jerusalem: Rav Kook Institute, 1979]. See also Sefat Emet commentary on Parashat Lech Lecha, 5632/1872).

Repentance and the Tree of Life

Is repentance just about correcting sins? While this is partly true, moral transgression represents a distortion in need of rectification. In our post–Tree of Knowledge world, we require order and justice, the ability to discern between good and evil, and the responsibility to rectify evil actions while striving continually toward good deeds.

This moral form of repentance, moving from evil to good, is a realistic goal in our world, though not always easy to achieve. The Sages warn that "one transgression leads to another," and people often find themselves deeply entrenched in challenging habits. Nevertheless, we see many individuals who have successfully turned away from their wrongful paths. This kind of repentance is characteristic of the Tree of Knowledge, representing a conscious choice between good and evil. Breaking free from the grip of desire, setting limits, and ending harmful behaviors are significant achievements.

However, does this understanding truly encapsulate the full essence of repentance? Is it necessary to sin in order to repent, and is repentance solely reliant on the feeling of correcting evil?

An ancient Mishnah[2] lists the entities that preceded the creation of the world, among which repentance is included. Such a concept elevates repentance beyond a reaction to sin, which emerged after creation. It suggests repentance as a foundational and essential aspect of the world, profoundly shaping the essence of life.

As explained, the Hebrew term *teshuvah* (repentance) contains an inherent notion of "return." Yet this return extends beyond the moral decisions of choosing good over evil, typically associated with the Tree of Knowledge. Instead, it encompasses a deeper journey back to one's core self, echoing the original state in the Garden of Eden, related to the Tree of Life. Every individual shares a fundamental connection with Adam, the first human, suggesting a universal journey of returning to one's true essence.

In the literature of the Sages, Adam is portrayed as a being who could see from one end of the world to the other. He is described as having astonishing dimensions in height and breadth, hinting to a larger perspective beyond the physical. These descriptions symbolize Adam as a microcosm of all humanity.

---

2   *Pesachim* 54b.

Every person born contains an element of this first human, who possessed an exceptionally expansive and illuminating vision.[3]

The *Zohar* adds another dimension to these descriptions.[4] In this mystical text, we learn that every person carries within an imprint of Adam. This hidden figure encompasses each individual's potential, as it existed before eating from the Tree of Knowledge, before the mixture of good and evil and other motives that hinder our growth. In the journey of repentance, a person is called to connect with the inner Adam, to the vast potential of life forces within. As we have seen, the tree and the river are part of Adam's environment. The ability to change calls for us to expand our consciousness and connect it to this primal landscape and movement. Repentance that springs from our connection to the Tree of Life invites us to taste and return to the air of Eden hidden within us.

One of the qualities of this form of repentance is its constant evolution, reflecting the fact that we are alive. Similar to the river flowing from Eden, which is continually emerging and receding, the tree also evolves continuously, albeit at a different pace and often imperceptibly. The individual need only awaken and listen to this movement.

According to this perspective, any focus on performing moral acts or commandments or engaging in spiritual practices that does not connect us to the root of our being lacks an essential element of return and therefore misses the essence of repentance. On the contrary, excessive preoccupation with guilt can distance us from recognizing our potential for growth.

---

3   Rav Judah said in the name of Rav: "Adam, the first man, spanned from one end of the world to the other, as it is said, 'From the day that God created man upon the earth, from one end of heaven to the other' [Deut. 4:32]. When he sinned, the Holy One, blessed be He, placed His hand upon him and diminished him, as it is said, 'And Your hand was heavy upon me' [Ps. 32:4]" (*Chagigah* 12a).

4   "Come and see, a person does not depart from this world until he sees Adam, the first man. Adam asks him why he is leaving the world and how his soul is departing. The person then says to him, 'Alas, because of you I left the world,' meaning because of Adam's sin with the Tree of Knowledge, death was decreed upon mankind. Adam then replies: 'My son, I transgressed one commandment and was punished for it. You see how many transgressions and how many commandments of your Master you have transgressed and not fulfilled'" (*Zohar*, Bereshit 59).

What does it mean to return to oneself, to the root of one's essence, to the Tree of Life within?

The Tree of Life represents an undivided entity, with a connection between its roots, branches, and fruit. Repentance in the shade of the Tree of Life is based on self-acceptance – accepting one's life story. It involves recognizing one's childhood and understanding that moments of happiness, alongside childhood wounds, are an inseparable part of who we are. The more we recognize and acknowledge their role in shaping our lives, the more we can embrace them without allowing them to control us. This acceptance can sweeten the foundational pains of our existence.

This type of repentance reveals the hidden secrets of our personality. Sometimes, it touches the elements of chaos and void within our identity. It has the ability to navigate through the good and evil within us, touching both the revealed and the hidden aspects simultaneously. This repentance, which preceded the world, constitutes a way of life.

In the story of the Garden of Eden, which is also the story of the beginning of our consciousness, there was a simple and direct connection between Adam and the Creator. By eating from the Tree of Knowledge, Adam chose separateness. This was also the serpent's aspiration, to create a divide between human and God. The primary desire of the first human in eating from the forbidden tree was the desire for individuality. After all, the ability to make free choices is only possible at a certain distance from God.

Accepting Sin

In the realm of the psyche, the issue of repentance is formulated as follows: Is repentance a correction of sin, leading to change, following a mistaken choice? Or is the essence of repentance found in the desire to move beyond the duality of good and evil, with its primary quality being self-acceptance and recognition, a sort of surrender to God, as in the original state in the Garden of Eden? On this issue, we find a fascinating distinction between Maimonides and Rabbi Tzadok Hacohen of Lublin.[5]

Maimonides states:

---

5   This distinction was made by Rabbi Shagar, *Shuvi nafshi* (Alon Shvut: The Institute for the Advancement of Rabbi Shagar's Writings, 2001), chapter 7.

What is repentance? It is when the sinner abandons his sin, removes it from his thoughts, and resolves in his heart that he will not do it again, as it is said, "Let the wicked forsake his way," etc. Similarly, he should feel remorse for what he has done, as it is said, "For after I had turned away, I repented." And he should testify before the One Who knows all hidden things that he will never return to this sin again, as it is said, "And we will no more call our handiwork our gods," etc. (*Mishneh Torah*, Laws of Repentance 2:2).

Here we find a clear effort to abandon the sin – in action, thought, and heart. The individual acknowledges internally that he has departed from a certain way of living, with the resolve never to repeat that sin. Furthermore:

One of the ways of repentance is for the penitent to constantly cry out before the Lord with weeping and supplications, and to give charity according to his ability. He should distance himself greatly from the thing in which he sinned, even change his name as if to say, "I am another person and not the same one who committed those acts." He should change all his deeds for the good and to the straight path, and exile himself from his place of residence, because exile atones for sin as it causes him to be humble and lowly in spirit. (Maimonides, *Mishneh Torah*, Laws of Repentance 2:4)

Maimonides focuses on a fundamental change that begins within the individual. First he cries out before the Lord, then he moves to another stage, saying "I am another and not the same person." Finally, he changes his name, which reflects an inner transformation.

Why is a change of name important? Changing one's name represents an attempt to make a fundamental transformation in our original nature. Parents have a kind of intuition when naming their children, whereas changing one's name comes from desire to alter something in one's original essence, to transition from one name to another. In this sense, such repentance acknowledges that a person's childhood name may lead to certain life sins; changing the name corrects childhood foibles, paving the way for mature transformation. Here, we recognize a gap, and sometimes alienation, between the different parts of a person's life, manifested through a change of name. The process concludes with exile, as Maimonides sees changing location as an essential foundation for repentance.

In this state, free choice reaches its pinnacle of expression. It starts with a significant effort to change actions, then proceeds to a transformation in consciousness – the realization that I am a different person – a change of name, and ultimately exile. The individual manages to undergo a transformation in all components of identity, to be reborn anew.

Rabbi Tzadok Hacohen of Lublin[6] offers a different perspective:

> The essence of repentance is until the Lord enlightens one's eyes so that intentional sins become like merits, meaning: to recognize and understand that everything he sinned was also by the will of the blessed Lord…. When a person attains this profound enlightenment, then all his intentional sins, not deviating from the deep knowledge of the Lord, are unified with him, his knowledge, and his will. Since the Lord willed it, everything is merits, and he merits complete atonement on Yom Kippur…. All transgressions and concealments are by the will of the blessed Lord. (*Tzidkat Hatzaddik* 40)

This is a radical perception that requires deep reflection. Rabbi Tzadok believes that an individual's narrative – the way one recounts one's life story – may be revealed as an intentional design of the Creator's will. Every part of your life, including the difficult and less pleasant ones, is part of God's plan for you. This is not an ideology that encourages committing transgressions and delving into forbidden things, as the Sabbatean movement brought into the world. A person is obliged to differentiate between good and evil and to choose good.

The Tree of Knowledge of Good and Evil is a substantial part of our lives, embodying the duty to distinguish between good and evil, the permissible

---

6   One of the most creative and productive thinkers of the Chasidic movement (1823–1900).

and the forbidden. However, if we fall, we have the opportunity to see retrospectively in the work of repentance how everything was directed with providence and reason by the Creator of the world. This is a complex perception. It acknowledges the Tree of Knowledge, boundaries, and responsibility for sin, and asks the person to move to the Tree of Life in that stage of repentance.

In this perception, individuals must accept themselves, including the parts that pushed them to betray their inner essence and sometimes even commit external sins. This involves a deep psychological understanding that behind the external guise that appeared as sin, there is an essence of life that the individual seeks to recognize, embrace, and refine. This is not a struggle against oneself but a movement toward liberation: we cast our lot with God, declaring, "I was created in Your image!" This movement is not passive. It begins with self-recognition and acceptance and continues with the knowledge that our pain, wounds, and damaged parts need not dictate our existence in the world. We find here an organic minimizing of guilt, channeling it to the initial part of the teshuvah process and not allowing it to define us. The focus of the experience is not on disconnection from the past but rather on a connection to the life roots rather than the events of the past.

This quality of teshuvah represents a second, mature kind of innocence, in which we connect all parts of ourselves. This is a state of unknowing, expressing a plea, as in the prayer recited during the Ten Days of Repentance between Rosh Hashanah and Yom Kippur: "Our Father, our King, be gracious to us and answer us, for we have no deeds; deal with us in charity and kindness and save us." With full understanding of our own life story, we cast our lot with the Creator, saying: "See me, accept me with all my parts." We do not live in an illusion of power or of completely free choice. On the contrary, we recognize the roots of our identity with gentle submission, accepting ourselves and releasing to the Creator. These are all indeed elements of the same person.

On the concept of name change in repentance, note that in the initial verses of Lech Lecha, an interesting element appears: "Go forth from your country…and I will…make your name great" (Gen. 12:1–2). The Hebrew here is *va'agadlah shemecha* – literally, "I will make your name grow." What does it mean to have a name that grows? A blessed person can feel how one's original name grows not by changing it but by giving new meaning to it. Our original name is renewed through the process of teshuvah, gaining additional color and life.

The citation from Maimonides above refers to changing the name as part of the process of teshuvah, indicating a fundamental change in the person. He is no longer the same individual, and his name no longer accompanies him. However, in Rabbi Tzadok's perspective, changing the name might not be necessary. On the contrary, the person seeks a new perspective on the name given by his or her parents.

I recall attending a rebirthing workshop some years ago. Connecting with various aspects of the workshop was challenging for me. One evening at dinner, I found myself facing a young woman who looked at me with a probing expression. As I sat there, feeling uneasy and silently hoping for the vegan meal to conclude, she said: "Mordechai, why do you introduce yourself as Moti? You're much more of a Mordechai." I didn't reply, and that brief exchange was the only conversation we ever had. However, it marked a significant moment for me.

Her words felt like an invitation to step fully into the name Mordechai, the name my parents chose for me. Embracing this process wasn't easy. It meant moving away from the familiar nickname that people were used to, including my grandchildren, who affectionately called me Grandpa Moti. Amidst this transition, I also learned to appreciate the "Moti" aspect of my identity. Yet clearly, "Mordechai" is my true name, demanding a deeper level of self-work.

This experience taught me that sometimes, as we evolve and change, revisiting our given name can be a powerful exercise. We can return to our full name, finding in it new meaning and charm.

Repentance and Choice

The story of Joseph's sale by his brothers is a distinct example of the relationship between the two trees in the process of repentance. This story is regarded as one of the gravest sins in the biblical narrative. Not only does it initiate a long scriptural trajectory filled with twists and turns, but it also ultimately leads to the descent of the children of Israel into Egypt and their prolonged enslavement. In later sources, the sale of Joseph is referred to as the "original sin" that precipitated the fate of the Ten Martyrs, those Sages who suffered brutal deaths at the hands of the Roman authorities during and after the destruction of the Second Temple.

In this difficult story, there is a process of *tikkun* or repair that illustrates the approach we mentioned. Initially, the brothers express regret for selling Joseph and feel guilty:

> And they said one to another: "We are verily guilty concerning our brother, in that we saw the distress of his soul, when he besought us, and we would not hear; therefore is this distress come upon us." (Gen. 42:21)

At this stage, emphasizing guilt is important, to acknowledge full responsibility for the sin.

In the next stage, the brothers repent for their actions, showing willingness to sacrifice themselves in the story of Benjamin, Joseph's brother. They refuse to leave Benjamin to his fate in Egypt, as they did Joseph. Judah leads this rectification with his strong presence. This correction is crucial from the perspective of the Tree of Knowledge. The sinner repents from his wrongdoing through clear and measurable actions that demonstrate the change he has undergone.

However, the process does not end there. During this process, Joseph can no longer restrain himself and reveals his identity to his brothers:

> And Joseph said to his brethren, "Come near to me, I pray you." And they came near. And he said, "I am Joseph your brother, whom you sold into Egypt. And now, be not grieved, nor angry with yourselves, that you sold me to here: for God did send me before you to preserve life. For these two years the famine has been in the land: and yet there are five years, in which there will be neither plowing nor harvest. And God sent me before you to preserve you a remnant on the earth, and to save your lives by a great deliverance. So now it was not you that sent me here, but God: and he has made me a father to Pharaoh, and lord of all his house, and a ruler throughout all the land of Egypt." (Gen. 45:4–8)

Let's notice the fascinating stages. In the first stage, Joseph describes the harsh reality: "whom you sold into Egypt." This is the realistic stage of our world, corresponding to the Tree of Knowledge of Good and Evil. The brothers are responsible for the severe act they committed. They sold him, their brother, and they must accept responsibility for this harsh deed. However, after they start the process of rectification, a new stage arrives: "Be not grieved...for God did send me before you to preserve life." This stage acknowledges the problematic act but identifies a direction in which all is for the best. The sale of Joseph led to the economic well-being of Jacob's family.

Then comes the final stage: "So now it was not you that sent me here, but God." In other words, the act is under God's ownership, by His providence and intention. God has a broader plan, beyond the story of the brothers' sale. This stage moves from the world of sin and free choice to the world of the Tree of Life, where the entire process is connected to the God Who examines our deepest motivations, in a unified perception.

The process culminates in a central statement from Rabbi Nachman of Breslov's teachings:

> When a person knows that all his experiences are for his benefit, this perception is akin to the World to Come. (*Likutei Moharan* 1:4)

This passage invites a person to understand that everything happening to him is under God's individual providence, and each event in our lives has a meaning that we need to connect to our narrative. According to Rabbi Nachman, a person should walk in the world with the perception that all aspects of his life are a kind of invitation to accept oneself, not just for the sake of completion, but in order to experience self-acceptance as a new life force. This offers another understanding of the nature of the Tree of Life. All parts of a person are part of his conscious life story. A person can understand how the pictures connect into a spiritual backbone. The past and present create a continuum toward the future.

The story of Joseph and his brothers leads us to another insight into the ability to forgive. Forgiveness is a crucial emotional and psychological mechanism for cleansing the soul, relieving burdens, and improving mental health. The ability to forgive can help us move closer to ourselves and others.

However, often the mechanism of forgiveness does not operate, is underdeveloped, or even becomes stuck. Sometimes, this is linked to deep emotional wounds that we carry, which are not always directly related to the matter of forgiveness at hand. Often these are remnants of memories from broken places in our lives that are reactivated, dimming and weakening the capacity to forgive.

When Joseph was thrown into the pit and later sold to the Ishmaelites, it is likely that a deep wound opened within him. One can only imagine: the fear of death, immense anger toward his brothers. Perhaps during his years of separation from his family, he painfully realizes that he might be part of a family narrative in which the beloved son is rejected. He might interpret his fate as similar to that of Ishmael and Esau and assume that he is not the central bearer of the blessings of his father's lineage. It's hard to imagine a greater sense of abandonment and invisibility, especially considering his father's love for him, his beauty, his resemblance to his mother Rachel, the special nurturing he received, and the coat of many colors. Joseph had every reason not to forgive.

However, Joseph understands very early in his life that God is guiding reality. He possesses a unique consciousness that allows him a different perspective on what is happening in his life, enabling him to step out of himself and see things from an additional viewpoint. This is his way throughout the story. He knows that his experiences are for his good. Perhaps Joseph also learns during his years of exile to forgive himself for his arrogance and his sense of separateness from his brothers. Self-forgiveness is critical for forgiving others.

When Joseph sees that his brothers are caring for Benjamin, he realizes they have made amends for selling him. This is a fundamental and necessary prerequisite to be worthy of forgiveness. Here lies the necessity of the Tree of Knowledge in our lives – to recognize that the one who caused harm knows how to make amends. Then forgiveness reveals its full glory. Joseph tells his trembling brothers that there is another perspective, another force guiding reality, and his sale was destined for a greater purpose – for good and blessing. The story concludes with great compassion and forgiveness, which enables Jacob to bless his sons before his death. This brings healing and repair to the story of Cain and Abel, the tragic story that began life after expulsion from the garden.

I would like to illustrate the connection between the trees of the garden and the concept of repentance through a Talmudic story about Bruriah and her husband Rabbi Meir:

> In Rabbi Meir's neighborhood, there were thugs who caused him much distress. He prayed for them to die. His wife Bruriah said to him: "What are you thinking? Is it because it is written, 'Let sins cease'? Note that it says 'sins,' not 'sinners.' Also, consider the rest of the verse: 'and the wicked will be no more' (Ps. 104:35), meaning that once sins cease, there will no longer be wicked people. You should pray for the end of their wickedness, not for the end of the wicked themselves. Rather, pray for them to receive mercy, that they may repent." Rabbi Meir prayed for them, and they repented. (*Berachot* 10a)

Rabbi Meir was distressed by thugs who were abusing him, and he prayed for their death. Rabbi Meir was entirely in the realm of the Tree of Knowledge of Good and Evil. For him, the evil associated with death was caused by the actions of the evil ones toward him, the good one, and this was a reason to pray for their demise. Bruriah, however, was in a different world. She understood that the thugs were not connected to their inner selves, and this was the root of their negative behavior. She believed in the potential for human rectification and in their roots in the Tree of Life. What would help them connect to their true inner selves and stop the violence? The connection of her husband Rabbi Meir to himself! She saw a deep connection between the thugs and her husband. It was no coincidence that they were tormenting specifically him. His life was not random, and if thugs were bothering him, there must be a personal reason for him. The rectification of the negative act is not judgment and punishment, but a reason for internal contemplation.

Bruriah asks Rabbi Meir to change his approach and pray for the thugs who have been tormenting him. Instead of praying for their demise, she urges him to pray for their repentance. Bruriah's request highlights a profound lesson: Rabbi Meir's transformation from a judgmental stance to a more compassionate one is crucial. His initial prayers reflect a view of God as a strict judge, but Bruriah guides him toward a gentler perception of God that encourages repentance and connection. This shift from a punitive to a compassionate view of God mirrors the transition from the Tree of Knowledge to the Tree of Life. It's a journey from seeing the world as a dichotomy of good and evil to seeing it as a place of understanding and empathy.[7] Bruriah's ability to influence her husband's perspective showcases not only their deep connection but also her wisdom.

This change in Rabbi Meir's prayers represents a return to a more nurturing and life-affirming relationship with God, highlighting the divine preference for growth and life over punishment and death. God is a king Who desires life.

Admitting Mistakes as Tree of Life Consciousness

Judah earned the distinction of being the progenitor of the tribe that established the monarchy. The Jewish people are named after him, rather than Joseph. What about his character made him so significant?

Judah is the one who suggested to his brothers that they sell Joseph to the Ishmaelites, saving him from the fate of the pit, asserting that "he is our brother, our flesh" (Gen. 37:27). However, upon seeing Joseph's bloodstained coat, Jacob did not see in Judah the potential of an heir. "And all his sons and all his daughters rose up to comfort him; but he refused to be comforted; and he said: 'Nay, but I will go down to the grave to my son mourning.' And his father wept for him" (Gen. 37:35). There was no consolation. No replacement for Joseph. Unsurprisingly, the next chapter begins with "And it came to pass at that time, that Judah went down from his brethren, and turned into a certain Adullamite, whose name was Hirah" (Gen. 38:1). Judah realizes there's nothing for him at Jacob's home. He seeks to rebuild his life far from his family of origin. This is Judah's *lech lecha* story.

Far physically and emotionally from his brothers and the traditions of his family, Judah undergoes a complex and problematic saga with Tamar. An entire strange and disconnected chapter interrupts the drama of Joseph's narrative, like a long commercial break in a suspenseful series.

---

7 This reflects an understanding of prayer as expressing the hope for change from Tree of Knowledge consciousness to Tree of Life consciousness.

This story about Judah is difficult. He marries a Canaanite woman and they have three sons. Over the years, he finds Tamar as a wife for his firstborn son, Er, who is then killed by God. Due to the law of levirate marriage, his second son, Onan, then marries Tamar but avoids impregnating her and is also killed by God.[8] Judah perceives Tamar as a "deadly woman" and tells her to wait in her father's house until his youngest son, Shelah, grows up. However, to himself he thinks, "Lest he also die like his brethren" (Gen. 38:11).

Judah sees Tamar as the problem, similar to Adam who shifts the responsibility for eating from the Tree of Knowledge onto Eve. This is despite the clear fact that God killed Er and Onan for their own actions, unrelated to Tamar. These sons corrupted their seed, not being attentive to the life force within them. They are far removed from the Tree of Life, deeply immersed in the Tree of Knowledge, especially its evil aspect. Onan spills his seed, and Er (which, spelled backward in Hebrew, is *ra*, meaning "evil") wanted one woman for procreation and another for sexuality – "so her body would not deteriorate" (*Yevamot* 34b, Rashi there). They are close to death in their lifestyle and indeed are killed.

The problem in this family lies in the consciousness and behavior of the men. Their sin resembles that of the "sons of Elohim" in Genesis, who saw women as objects. Judah has a significant responsibility as the head of the family and the initiator of the entire process.

In stark contrast to the men around her, Tamar is desperate for life and yearns to create life within herself. She actively takes control of her destiny, refusing to succumb to a victim mentality and accepting responsibility for her own redemption, representing a Tree of Life movement. She rejects the notion that she is the cause of the problem, as portrayed by her father-in-law. Disguising herself as a prostitute, she has an encounter with Judah, who is still mourning his wife's death and is unaware of Tamar's identity. This liaison results in Tamar's pregnancy.

At the pivotal moment, when she is about to be executed for supposedly being "with child by harlotry," Tamar reveals Judah's signet, cord, and staff,

---

8   It would be worthwhile to hold a separate discussion on the problematic personalities of Er and Onan and their attitude toward sexuality under the rubric of the Tree of Knowledge instead of the Tree of Life.

and challenges him: "Discern, I pray you, whose are these" (Gen. 38:25). In this moment, Judah faces a crucial choice. He could deny everything, in line with the norms of ancient times, and let the execution proceed. However, Judah chooses differently. He acknowledges, "She is more righteous than I; forasmuch as I gave her not to Shelah my son" (Gen. 38:26). With this statement, Judah recognizes and admits that the fault lies not with her, but with himself.

This is a defining moment, in which Judah recognizes his mistake and takes responsibility. The story is instantly transformed thanks to Judah's ability to admit his mistake, which opens the flow of hope and enables him to return home to his father, with renewed strength.

Judah's admission of his mistake is a dramatic moment in the biblical story. From this pregnancy, Perez and Zerah are born, ancestors of the tribe of Judah for generations to come. Many years later, when Ruth the Moabite marries Boaz, the people of Bethlehem bless them, saying, "And let thy house be like the house of Perez, whom Tamar bore to Judah" (Ruth 4:12). The story of Judah, who left his family for Adullam and his union with Tamar, is recalled in a positive context as a blessing for Boaz and Ruth, the forebears of King David.

How does a tragic, alien story transform into one of redemption and blessing? It's due to Tamar's boldness on the one hand, and Judah's acceptance of responsibility for his mistake on the other. Admitting a mistake is the moment of transition from the Tree of Knowledge core of our identity to the Tree of Life within us. There is something powerful about this ability to admit fault, a reflection of the great freedom of a person who recognizes that he can change a natural reaction and create a different reality. Tamar, recognizing the potential for life within her, and Judah, recognizing the magnitude of his potential for rectification, are two different branches of the Tree of Life.

We see the same dynamic in the meeting of Boaz and Ruth – Boaz as the blessed homeowner, and Ruth on her long *lech lecha* journey. But while in the story of the Book of Ruth, high-quality love develops slowly, leading to the redemption of the woman and the establishment of a home, the story of Tamar and Judah begins without love, with a courageous pregnancy initiated by Tamar and a poignant clarification by Judah of his mistake.

Repentance and the Tree of Life

The ability to admit a mistake is a significant foundation of leadership and human development. Admitting a mistake is not just a learned tactic; it indicates a psychological foundation of dynamic movement. Who I was in the morning does not have to dictate who I will be in the evening. A constant readiness to examine the principles I trust, the foundational assumption from which I approach life's challenges, is a central element of being Jewish. The linguistic connection between admission (*hoda'ah*) of a mistake and the name Judah (Yehudah) is found in various translations of the Bible, particularly in *Targum Yonatan*. Regarding the verse in Jacob's blessing, "Judah, you will your brethren praise" (Gen. 49:8), the Targum states:

> Judah, you admitted your actions with Tamar. Therefore, your brothers will praise you, and they will be called Jews [Yehudim] after your name.

This implies that being Jewish is connected to the ability to admit a mistake – a profound point.[9] Judah's ability to admit his mistake surpasses the centrality of Joseph the Righteous in the biblical narrative.

The ability to admit mistakes also characterizes King David. He was able to say, "I have sinned against the Lord," and to bear responsibility for his sin with Bathsheba, leading to the death of their child, as well as the challenges in his subsequent life. King David of Israel is eternally relevant, because he opens the Jewish world to the language of repentance,[10] to that movement of internal change that becomes a defining element of being Jewish. The ability to repair is identified with the forces of life, driven by the movement of the Tree of Life. David is a *ba'al teshuvah*, a penitent, and his repentance grants him eternity and offers us, his descendants, new meaning to our lives and the knowledge that the gates of repentance are always open.

---

9   A similar concept is found in a Midrash discussing Jacob's blessings to his sons before his death: "Shimon and Levi were also anxious, and Judah was afraid that his father might recall the incident with Tamar. Jacob began by addressing him: 'Judah, your brothers shall praise you.' God said to him: 'You admitted your mistake in the incident with Tamar, therefore your brothers will acknowledge you as their king'" (*Midrash Genesis Rabbah* 99:8). Thus, Judah's ability to admit his mistake led to his kingship over his brothers.

10   "Who established an offering of repentance" (*Avodah Zarah* 5a).

Questions for Reflection

- Do you feel the concept of repentance in your life as a movement toward your true self? Is the feeling of guilt (and its connection to the Tree of Knowledge) central in your life?
- How do you assess your ability to admit a mistake as a fundamental part of your identity?

Chapter 14

The Tree of Life and Fear of Death

But of the Tree of Knowledge of Good and Evil, you will not eat of it; for on the day that you eat thereof, you will surely die. (Gen. 2:17)

Death came into the world as a result of eating from the Tree of Knowledge. Death is one of the mysteries of life, perhaps the greatest of all.[1] Its certainty, alongside the inability to truly imagine it, evokes wonder, fear, and a sense of mystery. In the play *Chefetz*, Hanoch Levin wrote that "no one wants to die, but someone has to do the job."

"Fear of death" is a phrase used to describe a permanent freeze. Some see excessive worry as a form of fear of death. There are people who are paralyzed by the dread of death, manifested in despair and depression. These are usually people who feel that their lives are souring, as they are not frequently in situations that bring them satisfaction. People who fear the suffering associated with death tend to develop hypochondria or specific phobias such as fear of flying or fear of heights.

However, fear of death does not only cause paralysis – it is also a powerful engine for action, growth, and creation. In the words of psychiatrist Irvin Yalom: "Although the physicality of death destroys man, the idea of death saves him."[2] Yalom means that life without the awareness of death is boring and degenerate, without growth. Perhaps this is why after Adam ate from the

---

1   This chapter is offered in memory of Anat Gov.
2   Irvin Yalom, *Existential Psychotherapy* (New York: Basic Books, 1980), 30..

Tree of Knowledge, he and Eve were forbidden to eat from the Tree of Life, which promises eternal life. After they ate from the Tree of Knowledge, death became an inseparable part of life and a life of blessing.

Death can lead to two opposing directions: stagnation and waste, or development and creation. In light of Yalom's words, we may find great advantage in eating from the Tree of Knowledge, as the awareness of death can be a significant driver for a person's healing and improvement. He further writes:

> The fear of death ordinarily goes underground from about six to puberty, the same years Freud designated as the period of latent sexuality. Then, during adolescence, death anxiety erupts in force: teenagers often become preoccupied with death; a few consider suicide. Many adolescents today may respond to death anxiety by becoming masters and dispensers of death in their second life in violent video games. Others defy death with gallows humor and death-taunting songs, or by watching horror films with friends.[3]

The fear of death is a defining trait of our era, even though life expectancy is longer now than at any other time in human history.

I recall a time when I was involved with organizations that provided spiritual support to the severely ill and dying. In discussions with professionals, it became apparent that confronting death should not be limited to moments of sickness or old age. It should be integrated into our way of life from an early age, perhaps even from birth. Dealing with death appropriately as a life philosophy can impact other areas of life, including our eating habits, sexuality, and the way we communicate and listen. It can shift these aspects from mere survival to a life filled with meaning. This is where the Tree of Life intersects with the fear of death. Our modern world, from East to West, supports a vast industry of surgeries and cosmetic companies, all attempting to distance us from the sensation of aging, and, ostensibly, from death. However, it seems unlikely that we can truly address aging through anti-aging measures. This concept is not only hard to grasp but practically unfeasible. In the terms of this book, it leads us directly into the shadow of the Tree of Knowledge of

---

3 Irwin Yalom, *Staring at the Sun* (San Francisco: Jossey-Bass, 2008), 3–4.

Good and Evil. Rather than offering a solution that revitalizes the soul, it often simply clogs the soul's pores, preventing our inner light from shining through.

The fear of death can unconsciously influence conservative attitudes, an adherence to the status quo, and a pessimistic view regarding the potential for change and improvement. It accompanies us even when we are not aware of it, leading to situations for which we have no explanation other than the unconscious and unprocessed fear of death.

Perceiving death through the consciousness of the Tree of Life offers a different approach to dealing with death.

Charity Delivers us from Fear of Death

Anat Gov was a renowned Israeli brilliant playwright and social activist, and a special woman in many ways. She was also a friend and a long-time student of mine in Kolot. On January 22, 2013, I received the following email from Anat. The subject line was "A good end." I thought Anat was sharing details about a recent play she wrote with that title about her battle with cancer. The play, in her typical style, dealt incisively with how she coped with the disease. The play was well received in Israel and abroad, and I assumed that was what her email was about.

To my surprise, this is what I read in the body of the email:

> My dear Moti,
>
> I feel that my end is near. It's a matter of a few weeks. I'm still functioning. The pain is severe, but my mind is working. I would love it if you could come visit with me, Gidi,[4] and the children. I want to plan the funeral arrangements, and I would like to ask you to conduct the ceremony. When can you come?
> Anat

Just like that. Simple and direct. In her way. Within a few days, we met along with Gidi and the family and finalized the various details. Simple and straightforward, with open eyes, subtle humor, and while she was in home

---

4   Gidi Gov, Anat's husband, is a well-known Israel singer and actor.

hospice, exactly as she requested. Our conversation took place against the backdrop of morphine boxes that Gidi had just bought, intended to alleviate her pain.

There were surreal moments when I thought I was witnessing the writing of her next play unfold before my eyes, moments that alternated with a strong realization that I was invited to an immensely meaningful yet complex experience. Anat flowed with her death and accepted it, yet she also planned it carefully, and her attempt to control the end of her life was extraordinary.

From that meeting until our last conversation on Friday afternoon, mere hours before her passing, Anat remained connected to life, with a focus on caring for her loved ones, almost without succumbing to the energy of the approaching death. She even comforted mourners around her, before her own demise.

In reference to Jacob our forefather, the Bible says, "And the days of Israel drew near to die, and he called to his son Joseph" (Gen. 47:29). Just as Jacob, with great clarity, blessed his sons when he felt his end was near, so Anat wished to part with a blessing from the world, especially from her loved ones and her family, while maintaining her dignity.

Anat's unique relationship with death had been an existential issue for her for many years, even when she was at the peak of her fitness and health. About fifteen years earlier, we studied together the following Talmudic story, and she expressed her original and bold perspective.

> Rabbi Akiva had a daughter. But astrologers said to him, "On the day she enters the bridal chamber, a snake will bite her and she will die." On the night of her marriage, she removed a brooch and stuck it into the wall. When she pulled it out the following morning, a poisonous snake came trailing after it; the pin had penetrated into the eye of the serpent.
>
> "Was there anything special that you did yesterday?" her father asked her.
>
> "A poor man came to our door in the evening," she replied. "Everybody was busy at the banquet, and there was none to attend to him. So I took the portion of food that was given to me and gave it to him."

The Tree of Life and Fear of Death

Thereupon Rabbi Akiva went out and declared: "Righteousness delivers from death – and not just from an untimely death, but even from death itself." (*Shabbat* 156b)

Rabbi Akiva took the astrologers' prediction about his daughter's death on her wedding day seriously.[5] When I first read the story, I thought to myself that every time his daughter returned from an unsuccessful date, he must have been secretly relieved.

Yet one day, she indeed got married. Rabbi Akiva stood outside his daughter's bridal chamber, waiting for news of her death. There is something dramatic in this waiting around the bridal chamber – an act of love that signifies life (Tree of Life) is intertwined with the impending danger of death (Tree of Knowledge).

Her safe emergence from the room with a dead snake wrapped around her pin led him to ask her, by what merit? What deed did you perform that nullified the *mazal* that was decreed upon you? She simply explained that she saw a poor man at the doorway, during the wedding feast the previous night, and gave him her special portion to eat. Rabbi Akiva then went out and taught his students: "'Righteousness delivers from death' [Prov. 10:2] – and not just from an untimely death, but even from death itself."

What is it about Rabbi Akiva's daughter that enables her to act in such a way in the world in the face of death? When I taught the story, in 1998, to my students in the first cohort of Kolot, which included Anat, Rabbi Akiva's interpretation at the end of the story aroused skepticism among the learners. After all, we all know righteous people who die in their time, and even before their time. The connection between good deeds and being saved from death was unclear. This is not the reality we see in the world. The students protested. As the group's teacher, I found myself unable to respond.

Then we turned our attention to Anat. Anat had an exceptional intelligence, a wellspring of life perspectives that we eagerly awaited whenever we faced difficulty interpreting a challenging or perplexing text. With deep

---

5   This issue also addresses the concept of *ein mazal l'Yisrael* (literally, "astrology does not affect the Jewish people"). On one hand, this indicates a serious consideration of astrological influences, and on the other hand, a belief that human action can overcome luck or the astrological element in one's life.

insight, she said: Rabbi Akiva's daughter had a unique human capacity for perception, originating from a primal and natural place within her. Her vision was direct and immediate; anyone she faced was with her in the same moment of existence. She saw the poor man as plainly as she saw her own hand. The fact that she was a bride on her wedding night, the least likely person to notice a poor man at the door, had no bearing on her ability to see others. Her simple act of giving was a natural extension of this perception. A person in such a state of giving experiences a liberated and direct connection with others. One who lives with such a quality of giving transcends the fear of death by the very essence of his or her life. Plus, they are not afraid of snakes, she concluded with a smile.

As we have seen in previous chapters, in unique situations of closeness, there is a type of connection between the giver and the receiver that essentially nullifies the fundamental definitions of their identities. The fact that Rabbi Akiva's daughter was a bride, the center of attention, did not separate her for a moment from her existential connection to the poor man. Despite all eyes being on her during the wedding feast, she was the first and perhaps the only one to see him. Her giving did not stem merely from a moral obligation to help the weak but from a primal understanding that all parts of creation are interconnected and in need of one another. Like in the Garden of Eden.

Such a quality of vision frees a person from the fear of death because it is connected to the foundations of the garden, before the eating from the Tree of Knowledge, which split oneness into duality and brought the fear of death into our world.

Rabbi Akiva held a normative ethical mindset, believing that if one does *x*, then *y* will happen, symbolizing the Tree of Knowledge. This belief fueled his worries over the years, prompting him to seek an explanation for his daughter's safe return from the bridal chamber. His daughter, however, represents the consciousness of the Tree of Life through her perception and actions. Her unique ability is a further manifestation of being a blessing. The act of her pin entering the snake's eye is almost instinctive, certainly not a conscious decision on her part. In triumphing over the snake awaiting her, she symbolically rectifies the fall of Eve, who succumbed to the temptation of the primordial serpent to eat from the Tree of Knowledge. The snake and its symbolism are the personifications of the world's hindrances, duality, and estrangement.

Connecting to the Tree of Life allows one to rise above the snake and its symbolism. There is indeed a quality of giving that signifies a direct link with the essence of life, encompassing a wider perspective. In this state, there's no need for knowledge, ethics, or fear of death. Rabbi Akiva's daughter is simply in tune with life.

Ritual Impurity, Purity, and the Tree of Life

The concept of the Tree of Life, which is fundamental to this book, speaks of a connection to life of the highest quality. Being connected to the Tree of Life means being in a state of continual becoming and development. In such a life, there is a polar difference between death – symbolized by the Tree of Knowledge – and life under the shade of the Tree of Life.

In Jewish culture, death is associated with the concept of *tumah* (ritual impurity). The dead human body is considered *avi avot hatumah* (literally "the father of the fathers of impurity"), the highest level of impurity. Unlike other religions, Jews do not bury their dead around places of worship (such as monasteries or mosques), and contact with the dead is seen as a physical distancing from holiness and life. Saving a life takes precedence over observing the Sabbath. Once a person has passed away, the body, devoid of the soul, seeks to return to the earth, and on the Sabbath, the corpse is considered *muktzeh*, forbidden to even be touched.[6]

Ritual impurity and purity are not connected to the ethical world of good and evil. Impurity is not "bad," and purity is not "good" in the moral sense of the word. They are related to a consciousness of life (*taharah* or "purity") or a consciousness of death (*tumah* or "impurity"). Indeed, states of *tumah* in life represent the absence of potential or life energy. In contrast, *taharah* is fundamentally associated with vitality and the giving of life.

The author of *Mei Hashiloach* adds a fascinating dimension to this definition. Purity, he asserts, is a person's ability to connect with "flow" and self-improvement – finding the strength for cognitive and behavioral changes in life. Opposite to this state, *tumah* is related to a sort of stagnation, an inability to initiate change. Death is a severe form of *tumah*, *avi avot hatumah*, as it is the

---

6   A miraculous story in the Talmud illustrates this transition regarding King David's death (Shabbat 30a–30b).

ultimate expression of the deceased's inability to make further corrections in this world. According to his view, the essence of death is the end of potential for improvement and vitality.[7]

This explanation adds a new and precise dimension to the concept of death, the meaning of mourning, and the return to life of the living after the mourning period. The deceased can no longer repent or experience a renewal of life. This is essentially what we mourn. The emergence from mourning, the return to life, is tied to the fact that the living have the potential for internal renewal and *tikkun*. Hence, the period of mourning is limited. The mourner is asked to accept the judgment that death brings, then gradually detach from the energy of death and continue with the evolution of his or her own life.

Thus, connecting to the Tree of Life and blessing consciousness enables us to expand the languages and tools with which we approach the reality of our lives, which fundamentally seek evolution and change.

From this perspective, it would be worthwhile to ask ourselves: When are we in an energy of *tumah* (death) during our day, and when are we in a consciousness of *taharah* (life)? These questions invite a reflection on our way of life, beyond the moral questions of good and evil. Being aware of states of purity within us invites emotional capabilities of gratitude, generosity, forgiveness, optimism, and even the ability to judge everyone favorably. In other words, it's an energy of being in the frequency of love, characterized by these qualities.

Conversely, a person who engages in or listens to gossip or is drawn to excessive criticism, cynicism as a way of life, and the like enters a kind of impurity, not because of the ethical implications of failed or false speech, but because the energy created by unrectified speech weakens the soul's immune system and partially deadens us. Cynicism creates a negative reality in the world, distancing its bearer from the stream of life.

Reintegrating the concepts of *taharah* and *tumah* in the sense of energies of life or death into our modern lives can add a unique layer to the meaning of our lives. In our existence, negative and positive energies are frequently

---

7   See *Mei Hashiloach*, part 1, Parashat Emor, 123, s.v. "*Emor el hakohanim*"; part 2, Parashat Ki Tetzei, 246, s.v. "*Zachor et asher asah lecha Amalek.*"

intermingled, and acknowledging this can lead to a way of life with a different kind of vitality.

Snake, Dust, and Fear of Death

The snake in the story of Rabbi Akiva's daughter waits for her in the bridal chamber. It aims to intrude with the dust and death it represents (Tree of Knowledge) at the intimate moment of the newlywed couple (Tree of Life). This snake is connected to the primordial snake. After God punished Adam and Eve separately for eating from the Tree of Knowledge, He expelled them from the garden. The reason for the expulsion is encapsulated in the following verses that conclude the story:

> And the Lord God said, Behold, the man is become as one of us, to know good and evil; and now, lest he put forth his hand, and take also of the Tree of Life, and eat, and live forever. (Gen. 3:22).

Remaining in the garden and eating from the Tree of Life would have enabled eternal life. So, what changed? Why, before eating from the Tree of Knowledge, was there hope for eating from the Tree of Life – "Of every tree of the garden thou mayest freely eat" (Gen. 2:16) – but now there is a fear of this eating, to the point of expulsion?

To understand this issue, we need to comprehend what the snake's actual request was. The snake said to Eve:

> And the serpent said to the woman, "You will not surely die. For God knows that on the day you eat thereof, then your eyes will be opened, and you shall be as gods, knowing good and evil." (Gen. 3:4–5)

It appears that the snake sought to create an image of a god in competition with its creator. The statements "You will not surely die" and "and you shall be as gods, knowing good and evil" entice Adam and Eve into a sort of competition with the Creator, concerning the knowledge of good and evil, while promising eternal life. Moreover, the snake attempts to tarnish the image of the God in the garden, Who desires life for His creations, turning Him into a deity of the Tree of Knowledge, primarily interested in good and evil – a god of ethics. The snake, emerging from the dust, is the ultimate embodiment of death, of cunning movement, devoid of vitality.

We often see that being diagnosed with a serious illness becomes a turning point for many, leading them to seek additional purpose and meaning in their lives. Yet our understanding that a person "is from dust and to dust will return" should impact us from the earliest stages of our existence. This knowledge of human mortality should, from the outset of our lives, bring into focus the fear of death on one hand and the desire to live meaningful and fulfilling lives on the other. It would be ill-advised to eat from a literal Tree of Life and live forever. It's precisely this realization that underscores the significance of the consciousness of the Tree of Life in our world where death is a reality. This consciousness allows us to create a quality of life that encompasses an awareness of death, providing tools to manage the fear of death and to lead a meaningful life until our end.[8]

Rabbi Kook addresses the fear of death, suggesting that it can be confronted:

> The fear of death is a general human ailment that follows sin. Sin created death, and repentance is the sole remedy to eradicate it from the world. (*Orot Hakodesh* 2:41)

He continues:

> The very guidance for removing the fear of death should come through the habituation of loving life for its true value. (Ibid.)

In more familiar words: Everything a person does, consciously or unconsciously, is an attempt to escape death, and the relative liberation from this

---

8   In this respect, the author of Ecclesiastes was right in saying: "It is better to go to the house of mourning than to go to the house of feasting, for that is the end of all men, and the living will lay it to his heart" (7:2). There is a preciseness about the house of mourning, as the finitude of man touches the essence of humility within us. Sometimes, at funerals or in the house of mourning, I encounter people with whom I have unresolved tensions, and suddenly all the tension dissolves in the face of human mortality. Other people have shared similar experiences with me.

fear is enabled by connecting to the qualities of the Tree of Life, an act of repair that brings vitality to our lives. Animals are devoid of the fear of death because they lack consciousness and knowledge; they simply live their lives. However, humans, unlike animals, carry an immense weight from the knowledge of death. Therefore, we have no choice but to try to touch upon the love of life for its true value. This invites us to expand the realms of the Tree of Life in our world.

Righteous Ones in Their Death Are Called Alive

At the funeral of Anat Gov, may she rest in peace, I eulogized her, feeling that she departed this world in a state of vitality. A Talmudic story opens the discussion about the definition of "life" and "death," concluding with the statement "Righteous ones in their death are called alive, whereas the wicked, even in their lifetime, are called dead."[9] This phrase demands clarification. Who are the righteous people being referred to, and what is the state in which they are called alive in their death?

On a simple level, a righteous person is one who does good. In the world of the Tree of Knowledge of Good and Evil, they belong to the good branch. Even in their death, they are alive in consciousness, knowing that they will be judged favorably in the heavenly court due to their actions, and they experience in their world the power of doing good deeds. In their death, they merit a world that is entirely good. There is a reward for their actions. Wicked people, on the other hand, due to their actions, experience a lower quality of life, connected to death.

In contrast to this understanding of righteousness, the following Midrash offers a different definition of righteous and wicked:

> Rather, the wicked in their lifetime are considered as dead, because they see the sun shining and do not bless the Creator of light, it sets and they do not bless the One Who brings evenings, they eat and drink and do not bless upon it. But the righteous bless everything they eat, drink, see, and hear. Not only in their lifetime but

---

9   *Berachot* 19b.

even in their death, they bless and give thanks before the Holy
One, blessed be He. (*Midrash Tanchuma, Vezot Haberachah* 6)

The righteous, according to this Midrash, are those who bless the sunrise and
sunset and the experiences they encounter. They are people who experience
life itself, its flow and sensuality, with a consciousness of gratitude to their
Creator. This gratitude is not just an experience of fulfilling a commandment.
It's a consciousness that looks at the world with constant wonder. These fundamental movements and consciousness bring a person to a state in which
"even in their death, they bless and give thanks before the Holy One, blessed
be He." Recognizing gratitude as a leading movement into eternity can free us
from the fear of death, allowing us even in moments of death to bless and give
thanks, as the world, like God, is in a state of constant becoming. Connecting
to this becoming on a spiritual and conscious level liberates us from the fear
of death.

Consciousness of gratitude and blessing, as a way of life, creates a continuous and lively frequency and connection between the grateful person,
the Creator, and the broader world. This movement reduces the ego and the
need for control, which are the results of eating from the Tree of Knowledge.
Furthermore, the righteous "bless everything they eat, drink, see, and hear."
All senses are enveloped in gratitude and become an inseparable part of the
flow of the river of life.

According to this, the "wicked" person is not inherently evil, but simply
unaware. What is the nature of a person who does not bless sunset and sunrise or bodily pleasures? Such a person does not feel an inseparable part of a
continuously evolving existence. Eating, drinking, smelling, witnessing the
sunset – all these happen in our encounter with the world. It is appropriate
to bless such encounters, as they are signs of life, of a living dialogue. The
absence of such an encounter creates static energy. The Midrash identifies this
lack as an expression of a quality of death that is present even in the ordinary
stages of such a wicked person's life.

This definition of righteous and wicked moves beyond the ethical world
of the Tree of Knowledge and enters a consciousness closer to the Tree of
Life. This consciousness views a person's blessing of nature as an alertness to
continuous becoming.

The Tree of Life and Fear of Death

Rabbi Ashlag offers a further, somewhat revolutionary level of interpretation:

> This can explain what is meant by "the wicked in their lifetime are called dead," because everything they receive is through vessels of reception, which causes separation.... Therefore, they said "the wicked in their lifetime are called dead." From this, we understand by implication that "the righteous in their lifetime are called alive," because they receive the filling of the vessel, meaning the light and pleasure, in vessels of bestowal. Through this, they are connected to everlasting life, even though they become receivers.[10]

To explain Rabbi Ashlag's interpretation: a wicked person is not morally evil. Rather, the wicked keep what they receive to themselves – receiving for the sake of receiving (what Rabbi Ashlag refers to as "vessels of reception"). In contrast, a righteous person is someone who "receives in order to give." In the language of the Garden of Eden, a righteous person lives according to the consciousness of the river of life. What the righteous receive passes through them with *oneg* that they pass on. They do not hoard money, talent, or any other form of abundance. Boaz and Rabbi Akiva's daughter, whom we discussed, exemplify this quality.

Rabbi Ashlag's perspective is quite radical, because it abandons the conventional definitions of righteous and wicked and does not merely settle for awareness of one's surroundings as presented in the Midrash above. He introduces a new distinction related to the language of blessing, a consciousness of "receiving in order to give." Therefore, according to Jewish law, even a poor person who receives charity is obligated to give charity.[11] The act of giving continues and even amplifies the movement of life.

According to Rabbi Ashlag's view, the ability to give and receive as a central foundation in life brings one to a state in which, despite being aware

---

10 "*Madua hachayim nechlakim l'shtei bechinot* [Why is life divided into two aspects]," in Rabbi Baruch Shalom Halevi Ashlag (son of Rabbi Yehuda Leib Ashlag), *Kitvei Ravash*, article 1.

11 In the Talmud (*Gittin* 7b), Mar Zutra states: "Even a poor person who is sustained by charity should perform acts of charity." Additionally, in the *Mishneh Torah*, Hilchot Matnot Ani'im 7:5, Maimonides writes: "Even a poor person who is sustained by charity is obligated to give charity to another."

of mortality, one lives fully through constant giving. As we saw with Rabbi Akiva's daughter, this experience has a special vitality, helping one cope with life in the shadow of death.

The balance between receiving and giving is the dance of the Tree of Life. Understanding this model of receiving in order to give frees us at least partially from the fear of death.

At the end of a Jewish funeral service, we recite the verse "He will swallow up death forever" (Is. 25:8). Jews have an interest in conquering death, in the sense of not allowing the Tree of Knowledge to lead our lives. Judaism believes in life, and God is called "the King Who desires life." The Tree of Life consciousness in our world can assist in this victory.

Questions for Reflection

- Do you feel moments of purity and impurity in your life?
- What underlies the emergence of these feelings?
- Does the fear of death occupy a central place in your life? What helps you cope with this fear?
- Do you feel a balance between your ability to give and your ability to receive?

Chapter 15

Lack as a Foundation of Blessing

In the same way a person's deficiency is found, within that same aspect and by its own nature lies his merit. (*Tzidkat Hatzaddik*, part 1)

One of the early participants in Kolot was Professor Amitai Ziv. Amitai is a former Israel Air Force fighter pilot who pursued a career in medicine after his military service and is now a senior professor at Sheba Medical Center in Tel Hashomer. His significant contribution to the world is the founding of the Medical Simulation Center (MSR) within Sheba Medical Center. This center trains medical personnel in clinical and communication simulations within a simulated medical environment. It is an experiential setting that enhances learning, enabling structured and safe experiences through documentation, investigation, and immediate feedback to trainees, all without posing unnecessary risks to patients.[1]

A central principle in the world of MSR is the ability to learn from mistakes, since medical errors are one of the leading causes of death worldwide, ranking third after cancer and heart problems. Amitai applied his experience from the air force, particularly its culture of investigations, to the medical field. This approach, focusing on investigation – identifying errors, acknowledging them, and learning from them – can reduce deaths due to medical errors.

---

1   Over 190,000 people in the medical and paramedical professions have undergone training at the center, in numerous projects.

I was deeply touched by the concept of acknowledging and learning from mistakes. I think that if I had acknowledged my mistakes earlier, my life would have been better. If the human ability to admit mistakes were a way of life, the world would be a better place, not to mention how leaders, who often struggle to initiate such movement, could benefit.[2] Moreover, as we've seen, one of the foundations of being Jewish, and the root of the name Judah, comes from the ability to admit a mistake.[3] For this reason, I felt a profound connection to Amitai's work.

One day, I met with Amitai, who had become a dear friend, for a brainstorming session on the possibility of creating a joint initiative between MSR and Kolot. This collaboration led to the creation of the Fracture and Repair program, a year-long program that brought together therapists from the fields of medicine, nursing, mental health, and social welfare. The concept behind the program was that the combination of engaging with ancient texts in a seminar-like, study hall atmosphere, along with personal and group reflective processes using simulation tools, would inspire deeper introspection, enhancing the participants' work quality. Additionally, the program offered participants a spiritual resource to share the emotional burden their work demanded.

The program extensively dealt with the theme of brokenness in our lives. It touched upon issues such as brokenness as an immanent part of creation,[4] acknowledging mistakes, the fundamentals of human encounter in Buber's philosophy, and the importance of direct human interaction in professional relationships. The program included learning days at MSR during which participants engaged with the concepts of brokenness and repair in their lives.

---

2   As the *Mei Hashiloach* explains the significance of the leaders of the tribes of Israel: "Each one understood his own deficiency, and then their completeness was evident…for the primary completeness of a person is when he recognizes his deficiency." *Mei Hashiloach*, part 1, Numbers, chapter 6, s.v. "And the Lord spoke to Moses and to Aaron, saying."

3   See also chapter 13 above, on repentance and the Tree of Life, focusing on the centrality of acknowledging mistakes as a fundamental cause for the kingship of David and the tribe of Judah.

4   Jewish commentators wrote about brokenness in the description of creation in Genesis chapter 1, and the Ari's kabbalistic commentary describes broken vessels as part of ordinary existence.

Lack as a Foundation of Blessing

For many participants, the program provided support and often profound internal healing as well as practical tools for their work.

Eventually, I realized that I had erred somewhat in not embedding the Fracture and Repair program into Kolot's main program, leaving it as a separate initiative instead. I realized that the principles of this program are essential for any engagement with Judaism — indeed, for all spiritual growth – and should be woven into the very fabric of the organization. My aim was to introduce a more personal dialogue among learners and to elevate the learning process to deeper existential levels, but I was unable to fully achieve this. However, I knew that these principles of the program would continue to influence my personal life and learning approach, and I hoped that someday I would revisit the themes of brokenness and repair, possibly extending them into my professional realm. That understanding informs this chapter.

Over the years, I realized that the concept of brokenness extends far beyond what we discussed in the program. I discovered that in certain Chasidic teachings, there is a well-structured doctrine dealing with a concept similar to admitting mistakes, namely *chisaron* (lack or deficiency). This perspective considers the recognition of one's own deficiencies as a necessary base for significant personal growth and a crucial part of being a blessing. A complete blessing is impossible without acknowledging personal shortcomings. Recognizing these deficiencies can lead to a more comfortable acknowledgment of mistakes, as they both originate from the same psychological framework. If to err is an integral part of our lives, then the recognition of deficiency lies at the core of this understanding.

Everyone Has a Deficiency

In this section, I explore the teachings of renowned Chasidic scholar Rabbi Mordechai Yosef of Izbica and his seminal work *Mei Hashiloach*.[5] The core of *Mei Hashiloach* is to shift the reader's consciousness from the conventional to a perspective of standing before God in an intimate, personal I-Thou

---

5   Some of the ideas in this chapter were inspired by Dr. Aviezer Cohen's doctoral dissertation, "*Toda'ah atzmit ba'sefer Mei Hashiloah k'kli l'kiyum hazikah she'bein ha'El v'ha'adam*" [Self-consciousness in *Mei Hashiloach* as a tool for maintaining the connection between God and Man], University of Be'er Sheva, 2006. I am grateful to him for introducing me to this concept and for his innovative approach.

relationship, profoundly meaningful in nature. This shift is achieved by reflecting on and identifying the drivers of our actions and the role of the ego in daily life, described as barriers between an individual and divine will in the world.

Recently, we have witnessed a surge of interest in Rabbi Mordechai Yosef and his philosophy, driven by a yearning to move beyond the conventional and embrace a more radical, introspective Jewish discourse. A key tenet of Rabbi Mordechai Yosef's teachings is the necessity for individuals to recognize their deficiency. This deficiency can be seen as a wound or existential pain inherent in every person: "For each person has a deficiency in his nature which he must rectify."[6] This concept is rooted in the kabbalistic teachings of the Ari, which describe the world's creation as originating from a "break" or flaw. According to this view, creation itself contains inherent flaws or deficiencies that create a sense of restlessness in the world and human existence. This break is not about societal or cosmic repair but is deeply personal, pertaining to individual deficiencies that we carry from the moment of creation.[7] It underscores a vital personal process, fundamental to any broader social or cosmic endeavors.

The Torah was given to humans, not to angels, precisely because humans inherently possess deficiencies.

> The Torah was granted to Israel due to their deficiencies.... Without it, they would be significantly lacking, hence the Torah wasn't given to angels.[8]

This concept of deficiency is evident in the story of the Garden of Eden. Adam, despite his considerable potential for influence, was created with an inherent flaw, as evidenced by the prohibition against eating from the Tree

---

6   *Mei Hashiloach*, part 1, Parashat Korach, s.v. "*v'eved*," 157.

7   In another expression: "Humility is the recognition of deficiency.... Fear is the completion of the deficiency" (*Likutei Mei Hashiloach*, 261 [in the name of *Dover Tzedek* 25b, s.v. "*v'hineh*"]).

8   *Mei Hashiloach*, part 2, *Berachot* 40a, s.v. "*v'amar*," 181; part 1, *Shabbat* 88b, s.v. "*v'amar*," 242.

of Knowledge. This prohibition implies a deficiency in Adam, although the exact nature of this flaw is not explicitly stated.

The deficiency in Eve, however, is more discernible and is linked to her creation to address Adam's loneliness. After fulfilling her role in alleviating her husband's solitude, she sought presence and connection herself. Left alone, she desired context and companionship.[9] This created a vacuum or deficiency within her, which the serpent exploited to tempt her. The serpent's suggestion, "you will be like gods," highlights the woman's "shadow," a state of dependence and powerlessness she was experiencing.

Deficiency manifests as a person's point of weakness, the very place where one is most likely to falter.

> The Torah was given to address the inherent deficiency in a person from birth. Using the commandment to Adam, "But of the Tree of Knowledge of Good and Evil, you will not eat of it" (Gen. 2:17), the serpent seized this void as an opportunity. The way of an enemy is to target the deficiency in the one he opposes, to ensnare him in his weakness. The prohibition against eating from the Tree of Knowledge addressed a deficiency in this aspect of eating for Adam. Indeed, Adam himself feared this, and God had to define it for him, as will be explained, and therefore the serpent pounced and caused him to fail in this respect.[10]

Key points emerge from this:

1. The Torah was given to heal the innate deficiency present from birth. This concept is a profound statement about the Torah's essence. Judaism aims to heal the individual and the world, addressing the fundamental human flaw.

2. The serpent identifies the point of deficiency. It senses the most effective way a person can be drawn into his or her deficiency. In our lives, the serpent symbolizes any area in which our wounds remain unaddressed, a place of unawareness of our own shortcomings. Ignoring or failing to work on our

---

9   See chapter 10 on relationships, and see the Midrash on Adam's absence.

10   *Mei Hashiloach*, part 1, Parashat Bereshit, s.v. *"va'omer,"* 15.

deficiencies invites the serpent-like elements in our lives to exacerbate the pain at the site of our wound.[11]

Tree of Life consciousness suggests that individuals need to engage with the entirety of their personalities, including their areas of deficiency. Each person carries within an archetype of primordial man, representing the full potential of one's personality. This encompasses areas of abundance and pleasure, as well as a wounded part; in Tree of Life consciousness, these aspects are not separate but interconnected. Recognizing our deficiencies as part of our being and using them to understand our motivations in the world can enhance our growth and the sense of joy within us.[12] Neglecting our deficits leads to the predominance of the knowledge of good and evil, leaving the wound unaddressed and untreated. Avoiding this self-work is a conscious choice that limits our potential for growth.

> The deficiency embedded in a person from birth is his or her greatest challenge; God does not create a deficiency in a person beyond what the individual has the capacity to heal.[13]

This deficiency is not a minor detail but a significant aspect of a person's being. The Creator assigns each of us a deficiency of a size that we are capable of discovering, acknowledging, and embracing in order to work toward healing.

Recognizing a deficiency enables its correction, creating a cycle of cause and effect: acknowledging the deficiency is the first step toward rectification. Yet this recognition is just one phase in the broader healing process of life. Below, I will propose several approaches to this work. The following Midrash illuminates another dimension of deficiency:

---

11 For more on the serpent and fear of death, see chapter 14 on the Tree of Life and fear of death.

12 *Sefer Hayetzirah* (chapter 2) notes the connection between the Hebrew word *nega* ("affliction") and *oneg*, which is related to healing the *nega* within us.

13 *Mei Hashiloach*, part 1, *Bechorot* 8b, s.v. "*mashrei*," 274. See also part 2, Yehoshua 2, s.v. "*va'nichtam*," 138, "*ki l'varer shorsho v'chisaron hanitba bo.*"

Rabbi Abba bar Yudan said: Everything that the Holy One, blessed be He, disqualified in an animal [for sacrifice], He deemed fit in a human. He disqualified in an animal "blind, or broken, or maimed, or having a wen" (Lev. 22:22), but He deemed fit in a human "a broken and a contrite heart" (Ps. 51:19).

Rabbi Alexandri said: For an ordinary person, using broken vessels is a disgrace. But for the Holy One, blessed be He, His vessels of use are broken – as it is said: "The Lord is near to them that are of a broken heart" (Ps. 34:18), "He heals the broken in heart" (Ps. 147:3), "And revives the spirit of the humble" (Is. 57:15).
(*Midrash Leviticus Rabbah* 7:2)

Given that fracture is a fundamental element of divine creation, God is especially present with those who have broken hearts.[14] Moreover, as described by *Mei Hashiloach*, a lack of awareness of one's own deficiencies is akin to neglect and a loss of understanding. It indicates an inability to recognize oneself and, consequently, one's purpose in the world. This unawareness is more common among those who conform to the normative crowd, following a simple path. In this context, those guided by Tree of Knowledge consciousness might completely lose touch with their deficiencies. Paradoxically, their confidence in their lives can prevent them from experiencing significant, transformative moments.

Additionally, people who encounter pain, absence, and occasional failures in life are likely to connect more quickly with their deficiencies. Those who proceed with unquestioned certainty may hide their true motivations and remain deeply entrenched in their egos, regardless of their outward adherence to commandments or moral living. The awareness of one's deficiencies needs to be transparent. Individuals must be able to introspect, to view themselves objectively. Transforming the self into a subject of reflection is a trait characteristic of people who are able to view themselves with humor.

---

14 "The Holy One, blessed be He, dwells only in a place that is broken, in a broken vessel, as it is written, 'And to revive the spirit of the humble' (Is. 57:15). For one who recognizes their deficiency, the Holy One, blessed be He, illuminates them to complete their deficiency, as it is written, 'The Lord is near to them that are of a broken heart, and saves such as are of a contrite spirit' (Ps. 34:19)" (*Mei Hashiloach* 2:153).

Ways to Recognize Deficiency

Awareness alone is not enough. *Mei Hashiloach* suggests several methods for engaging with our deficiencies. Following are some of them.

Learning through Events in the World

The approach of learning from this world posits that every event in a person's life has personal significance, including seemingly random incidents and unintentional actions.[15] An example is given from the story of Joseph and Benjamin. Judah says,

> "What will we say to my lord? What will we speak? Or how will we clear ourselves? God hath found out the iniquity of thy servants; behold, we are my lord's bondmen, both we, and he also with whom the cup is found." (Gen. 44:16)

Regarding "God hath found out," as *Mei Hashiloach* explains: Judah understood that despite their innocence in the moral sense (i.e., they did not actually steal the cup, which would have been a violation of the rules of the Tree of Knowledge), the mere fact that they were suspected points to a divine intervention. This suggests that there are no coincidences and that we need to introspect and address some deficiency within ourselves, even if the external suspicion is unfounded.[16]

This interpretation reveals that personal deficiencies often come to light in situations in which we feel blameless. When we are free from the judgment of the Tree of Knowledge, the work on addressing these deficiencies, rooted in the Tree of Life, begins. According to Martin Buber, everything that happens to us is like a direct call to us. The human experience of which we are a part is a call to us, as something that affects us.[17]

---

15   *Mei Hashiloach*, part 2, Parashat Korach, s.v. "*ketiv*," 103. See also chapter 13 on repentance and the Tree of Life, which expands on this perception.

16   *Mei Hashiloach*, part 2, Parashat Miketz, s.v. "*ha'elohim*," 33.

17   Martin Buber, *B'sod siach – al ha'adam v'amidato nochach hachavayah* (Jerusalem: Mossad Bialik, 1973), 118.

Lack as a Foundation of Blessing

Learning from Mistakes
The concept of learning from mistakes was a key theme in the Fracture and Repair project. We encouraged deep reflection on one's errors, aiming to understand their origins and how they can reveal personal deficiencies. Such an approach is also employed in the Medical Simulation Center, similar to practices in the Israel Air Force, where mistakes are reconstructed and analyzed. Delving into the brokenness one has caused in the world demands engagement with the "lacking" elements of the psyche, prompting the question: What is the wound that led to this mistake?

Consider an individual in an unfulfilling life situation, whether in relationships, friendships, or work. The suffering person might sense something isn't right. The crucial question is: What purpose did remaining in that situation serve? What inner deficiency allowed this prolonged error?

> The individual should search for that fundamental core, understanding that their biography is a kind of therapy for them. Until the person reaches this realization, it can be said that they are living with a deficiency. Naturally, this recognition enables a person to correct the deficiency and turn it into a destiny, meaning a prism through which they live their lives. Essentially, this is the revelation of the person's "self."[18]

Reducing External Activities
It's challenging to touch upon core inner deficiencies without dedicating quality time for inner reflection, a state achieved by deliberately limiting one's external actions. In my life experience, I've learned that a sabbatical year, when properly observed, can be a valuable tool for facilitating this connection. Of course, there are many other ways to achieve the necessary reduction.

> A person who minimizes external activities, stepping out of routine and even sacrificing personal honor for the sake of heavenly honor, is considered a Chasid.[19]

---

18   Aviezer Cohen, *Toda'ah atzmit*, 450.

19   *Mei Hashiloach*, part 2, *Berachot* 4a, s.v. "*l'David*," 172.

The Chasid understands that alongside professional and creative successes, self-limitation is necessary to identify and integrate one's personal deficiencies into one's life.

Some individuals are capable of being in a constant state of "expansion," meaning they maintain a broad presence of encompassing generosity. These are people who walk hand in hand with their wounds and are always conscious of their inner deficiency. As King David says, "My sin is ever before me" (Ps. 51:5), indicating an awareness that the sins of his life dance with him in a constant spiral movement. Although he has is no longer controlled by his sins, he has integrated his deficiencies into his life such that he feels connected to them yet free from them. Such people are rare. This ability to navigate the world with a broad and influential presence is fascinating. However, most of us require periods of reduction. Those who understand the secret of reduction, accepting the presence of personal sin and deficiency, can later return to reality with expansion, re-embracing a wide scope of giving and influence. Perhaps this is part of the concept of the Sabbath and the sabbatical year in our lives – to slightly reduce our creativity and giving, in order to touch freshly upon our deficiencies.

Focusing on One Mitzvah

One way to engage with our deficiencies in the world can be by focusing on performing a specific commandment that directly relates to our personal wounds.[20]

For example, the Talmud relates a story about a man who was particularly careful about the mitzvah of tzitzit (the commandment to wear fringes on a four-cornered garment). He saw a special personal significance in fulfilling this commandment. This man, who was also very lustful, arranged a meeting

---

20 "'For the commandment is a lamp; and the law is light' (Prov. 6:23) – The Torah is likened to light because its illumination is very great, and the commandment to a lamp, whose light is very small. However, there is an advantage to a lamp over light, as a lamp can be brought into holes and crevices, unlike light. Indeed, the Torah purifies the entire person, but in an area where one is aware of a deficiency, one needs a specific commandment to grasp. As we find in the Talmud (*Shabbat* 118b), 'What was your father most careful with? He said, with the mitzvah of tzitzit.' He needed this mitzvah according to his understanding, and through this, his deficiency was completed" (*Mei Hashiloach*, part 1, Prov. 6, s.v. "*ki*," 221).

with an expensive prostitute. As he was undressing for the intimate encounter, he saw his tzitzit, bringing him back to his values, and this saved him from lying with her. Regarding tzitzit, it is written:

> And it will be to you for a fringe, that you may look upon it, and remember all the commandments of the Lord, and do them; and that you go not about after your own heart and your own eyes, after which you used to go astray. (Num. 15:39)

On a basic level, the protagonist's adherence to the mitzvah of tzitzit touched upon a significant lustful element in his personality, and seeing the tzitzit saved him from falling into sin. However, the story itself contains another unique moment of mental breakdown. The text relates that "the man collapsed to the ground from the high bed he was on with the woman, and she fell to the ground after him." This act brought him into deep contact with his wound, and his ability to touch his wound also led her to touch hers. She realized that even a beautiful woman with exceptional power has deep inner pain – in this case driving her to live her life as a top-class prostitute.

This separate touch on the deficiencies of both the man and the woman in the story, during a joint act, led them to develop a deep closeness, and they married. The end of the story relates: "All the beds she had prepared for him illicitly, she now prepared for him lawfully." In this story, touching the deficiency is not just a personal act but forms the basis for a very special intimate relationship.

The ability to touch upon the root of one's deficiency through adherence to a specific commandment that resonates with it allows for a shift of focus from the commandments as a whole to one particularly relevant one. This focused attention on an area of significance to us can reveal much about our required inner work. Often, we can learn a great deal from understanding the limits of our comfort zone.

The Shadow and Deficiency

According to Carl Gustav Jung, the shadow is one of the four central archetypes (alongside the self, the persona, and the anima/animus) in human psychology. This archetype represents the aspects of one's personality that do not conform to societal expectations or collective morality, and hence, one tries to hide or disguise them. This is the darker half of a person, housing primitive instincts present in everyone. Jung suggests that confronting the shadow typically occurs in the second half of life, when we learn to acknowledge ourselves fully, without denying our negative and egoistic aspects. The shadow also embodies creativity and uniqueness in an individual.

I once heard of an interpretation in the *Mei Hashiloach*[21] of the verse "The Lord is your shade upon your right hand" (Ps. 121:5) – this means that God is particularly present in the shadow that darkens our wounds.

The following Midrash reinforces the connection between God and our shadow:

> God said to Moses: Go tell Israel that My name is "I will be what I will be."
>
> What does "I will be what I will be" mean?
>
> Just as you are present with me, so am I present with you.
>
> And so, David said: "The Lord is your shade upon your right hand."
>
> What does "The Lord is your shade" mean? Like your shadow –
>
> If you play, it plays with you;
>
> if you cry, it cries opposite you;
>
> if you show it a stern or thoughtful face, it reflects the same.
>
> Similarly, God is "your shade": as you are with Him, He is with you. (Midrash cited in *Nefesh Hachaim* 1:7)[22]

Just as the shadow communicates with our visible parts, at a higher level of consciousness, connecting with the Tree of Life and touching upon our deficiency, the shadow reveals our wounds and the ability to work with them.

---

21   I heard this from Rabbi Ya'akov Wershevsky, but I was not able to verify the source in *Mei Hashiloach*.

22   Cited earlier in Ibn Gabbai, *Avodat Hakodesh* 2:16.

Lack as a Foundation of Blessing

Deficiency as Blessing in Our Lives

Living life without engaging with personal deficiency is possible, and most people seem to do so. However, the expanded consciousness inherent in the purpose of *ve'heyeh berachah* requires us to touch the broadest aspect of our personal image, tasting the quality of life in the Garden of Eden. In this world, there is also deficiency, an inseparable part of the foundation of the world with humanity at its center.

In recent years, a movement called "F..kup Nights" has emerged, originating entirely by accident in a bar in Mexico in 2012, after a few too many tequila chasers. Four young people, tired of hearing only American-style success stories, decided to share their biggest failures, sparking keen interest among other bar patrons. A week later, they found themselves sharing their failure stories onstage at that bar, invited by the owner. The phenomenon quickly spread to dozens of countries, including Israel. Four individuals take the stage to talk about their biggest failure for about ten minutes, with time for questions after each sharing. The idea is to encourage entrepreneurship and creativity, while learning from failure. I once participated in such an evening in Tel Aviv, and I found something comforting about seeing people share their failures or embarrassments. A sense of human connection and humor permeates the atmosphere. I can understand how a world focused on excellence and competitiveness finds a quiet and fertile space for reflection in these evenings.

However, there is still a certain distance between sharing a story of failure and recognizing deficiency. Recognizing a deficiency touches the most intimate core of one's personality, a place of great vulnerability. It's not something to be shared on a stage. The ability to reveal one's wounded places to a loved one is an integral part of the quality of the encounter.

A connection of love that also touches upon deficiency is an expression of "healthy nakedness" or exposure, as in the Garden of Eden. In the world of communication within couples, the ability to expose a wound in an environment of listening and trust can deepen the relationship and contribute to the quality of intimacy. A meeting that includes all aspects of a person invites a unique experience of sweetening the wound through a partner. In special moments of connection, it can transform the wound into an experience of *oneg*,[23] as it sweetens our deficiencies into a tool for life.

As we move beyond the personal sphere, caution is needed in working with deficiency. The ability to bring forth one's deficiencies requires a sense of security, and the external world does not always provide this. A lack of security can make us all more vulnerable, especially those who are touching their deficiencies.

In recent years, I have developed a small circle of friends; we are able to share a bit of our deficiencies, particularly in times of disagreement. The danger in sharing our deficiencies, even with someone we love, is that the person who is aware of our deficiencies may use them against us during conflicts. Therefore, sharing deficiencies requires a clear commitment to keeping the shared information within the "holy ark" of the friendship or relationship, and any discussion about it should only occur in a loving and safe space.[24]

A family can develop a special humor around the deficiencies of its family members, creating a dialogue and connection in which the deficiency is present. Such a state allows family members to bring themselves closer to each other. Perhaps it is up to the parents to demonstrate this in their relationship, to enable the rest of the family members to connect to this unique melody.

When my sister Chava turned seventy, my sister Ruth and I took her on a trip to Sinai for three days, something we had never done before. It was just a few weeks before the outbreak of the COVID-19 pandemic. Until that trip, the three of us had a reasonable relationship, but we'd known difficult years of tension, anger, and even estrangements. Mainly, we got along by bypassing issues of anger and pain.

Something happened in Sinai. One evening, while discussing the Trees of Knowledge and Life in our lives, we decided to share some of our deficiencies – not just to talk about unresolved tensions, but to touch deeply, to share childhood pain and open up on a personal level. Something happened during that encounter, which allowed for better communication and much

---

23 *Sefer Yetzirah*, chapter 2, says that there is nothing lower than a wound and nothing more lofty than pleasure: "There is nothing better above than pleasure, and nothing worse below than a wound."

24 See the discussion of the Imago workshop in chapter 10, on relationships and solitude, as an example of a unique, safe form of dialogue about painful topics.

compassion. I left Sinai, and we left our personal Egypt, feeling that we had met at some deep point that was revealed to us. A new quality of connection gave us a sense of confident presence. The competitive aspect that is unconsciously present among siblings was replaced with joy and a desire to genuinely share in each other's well-being. Since then, our conversations have had a different quality.

The differences between Cain and Abel in their personal and professional worlds led to fratricide. Recognizing the deficiency can bring great healing among siblings. Cain and Abel chose silence, which led to violence. We chose direct and honest communication.

In the professional world, this can manifest in an employee's ability to reveal weaknesses – sharing all parts of his or her life, and not just the areas of excellence. Sometimes, this very deficiency can lead to creative thinking, allowing a different perspective on professional challenges. It certainly gives the work environment a more relaxed feeling, minimizing the gap between home and work.

Can we imagine a school where teachers develop such a dialogue among themselves? It would differ from a couple's conversation seeking intimacy, requiring boundaries suitable for a staff room, not a parental home. However, fostering such a language could give teachers a sense of personal ease. More importantly, it could develop a special sensitivity in identifying shortcomings in students. Thus, students too could bring their whole selves to school, greatly contributing to their growth.

Can we envision a community or society where there's a discourse about deficiency? At first glance, it seems impossible, perhaps even inappropriate. Yet particularly in the context of the Jewish people, there's a case for creating a formative wound, namely the experience of slavery in Egypt – a pivotal pain of centuries of harsh persecution for a nation just starting its journey. This slavery was part of a divine plan revealed to Abraham during the Covenant between the Parts. Each year during Passover, we reopen this wound. Only those who recognize their personal and collective deficiencies can sweeten the pains and fight against the various sophisticated forms of human bondage today, turning bitterness into sweetness.

The ability to expose our wounds is a sign of being free, part of living in an era in which we can expand the narrow consciousness of exile (its peak being the Egyptian slavery and the Holocaust) to a new consciousness in our time, opening new spaces for humanity.

Recognizing our deficiency is an integral part of being a blessing and perhaps even one of its key elements.

Questions for Reflection

- Do you acknowledge a long-standing deficiency within yourself?
- Are you familiar with it?
- How do you manage it in different areas of your life?

Chapter 16

Chapter 16

The Flaming Sword – Transformations

In May 2019, I was invited by a division of the Israel Ministry of Defense to conduct a workshop for bereaved parents, in preparation for Memorial Day. I was asked to carefully touch on the topic of blessing for people who had lost their dearest ones. I was full of apprehensions about the possibility of addressing such a sensitive and nearly impossible topic for people who had experienced the hardest of trials. I consulted with my colleague and friend Tzvika Gilat. He suggested I focus on the opening verses of Lech Lecha and walk with them through their journeys since their bereavement, and only in the last hour of the four-hour workshop, to carefully touch upon the end of God's promise to Abraham, *ve'heyeh berachah.*

I was seized with anxiety. In my preparation, I focused on midrashim on the topic of journeys, prepared various questions and exercises, and did not touch at all on the matter of blessing. When I entered the Ministry of Defense on the morning of the workshop, the social worker informed me that, naturally, they had no control over the type of people who would attend. I wasn't even granted the limit of twelve people I had requested; seventeen people came.

I entered the room and met with people who were experiencing pain and sadness. There were parents who had lost their daughter, who had served in the police, in a terror attack just a few months earlier, making this their first personal Memorial Day. There was a sister who lost her brother in the First Lebanon War at Sultan Yacoub, parents who lost children, and a daughter who lost her father. In the opening round, I heard harsh words about Arabs, the IDF's weakness, and the government's insensitivity. The social worker gave me a knowing and compassionate look as if to say, "I told you it wouldn't be easy."

After the opening round, I asked one of the older fathers to read the first verses of Lech Lecha. I hoped he would get through the many verses with the root *bet-resh-chaf* (*b-r-ch*, "blessing"); however, when he reached the words *ve'heyeh berachah*, he exclaimed, "Blessing – this goal is hard to accomplish!"

We began with stories of journeys following the participants' bereavement. They shared how they viewed the change in their lives since that terrible day when they lost their loved one. But contrary to the original plan, we quickly reached the topic of being a blessing. Thus, I found myself leading three hours of heated discussion, with tears as well as moments of laughter, revolving around the concept of blessing. Some participants vehemently opposed seeing any blessing in their personal *lech lecha*. They absolutely refused to use this term, even if they had recovered and rebuilt their lives after their tragedy. However, others shared the blessing they had seen in their lives as a result of the disaster.

To my surprise, I noticed a sharp gender divide in their responses. The men showed resistance to the concept, sometimes responding in blunt and angry language, while the women spoke of significant positive changes following their bereavement. According to some of the women, the bereavement gradually became a catalyst for personal growth. One woman said her sense of vitality had increased since experiencing death, stating that the changes she made because of the tragedy enhanced her will to live with vitality and meaning.

After the workshop, I remained with some of the participants to talk for a while. They wanted to explore further the language of blessing I proposed. I have maintained contact with two of them. From these individuals, I learned that within the Israeli family of bereaved individuals, some view their departed loved ones as a gift that was bestowed on them, albeit for a short time. They see it as a privilege to have had their loved ones in their lives for several decades; the very fact that these individuals existed in this world is not taken for granted. The concepts of life and death have gained new meaning for them. This recognition exists alongside an existential pain that they will always bear.

In this poignant workshop, I encountered narratives that embodied the Tree of Life concept, shared by people who might have been expected to live overshadowed by the Tree of Knowledge – the symbol of death's entry into the world. These conversations were nuanced and challenging to fully capture in writing. This workshop stands out as one of my most impactful experiences, offering profound insights into the interplay between the Tree of Life and the Tree of Knowledge. Specifically, it illuminated how the Tree of Life consciousness enables us to live and even grow, despite the pervasive presence of death in our lives.

In this chapter, I aim to explore further the Tree of Life theme and how the challenges posed by the flaming, turning sword that guards the way of the Tree of Life continuously tests us throughout our lives. I have met individuals who find a deep dialogue between the pain of death and questions of meaning and hope for blessing in their lives and in the State of Israel. Especially poignant are the experiences of the individuals and families I've recently been mentoring, who have tragically lost their beloved family members in the aftermath of the events of October 7, 2023.

Blessing Adversity

The Tree of Life consciousness and the earthly life vision of *ve'heyeh berachah* call for a connection to a unique frequency. This frequency seeks to provide tools that connect people to their life potentials and their full personalities, touching the vitality that brings a meaningful life experience. However, the concept of blessing might give the impression of a guaranteed life of constant celebration. This is not an accurate understanding of being a blessing. Our lives are filled with trials, difficulties, and unexpected painful surprises. As we saw in the previous chapter, which addressed the concept of deficiency, touching our areas of pain is essential to fully realizing our potential. It is an inseparable part of Tree of Life consciousness.

The Midrash narrates regarding Jacob that after enduring difficult experiences, including fleeing from his brother, separating from his parents, and surviving challenging encounters with his father-in-law, he sought to finally "dwell in tranquility," to spend the rest of his life in peace and calm. He had been through enough:

"And Jacob dwelt in the land of his father's sojournings." Jacob sought to live in tranquility, but the turmoil of Joseph sprang upon him. God said: Is it not enough for the righteous what is prepared for them in the world to come, that they seek to dwell in tranquility in this world too? (Midrash, cited in Rashi, Gen. 37:1).

As we recall, Jacob then thinks he has lost his beloved son Joseph and refuses to be consoled for the many long years when he didn't see him. Can Jacob's tumultuous life be seen as a "blessed life"?

The Sages have a saying: "The deeds of the fathers are a sign for the children." Our forefather Jacob is an archetypal figure within us, symbolizing recognition of trials as an inseparable part of our humanity. The purpose of a trial is to neutralize our usual mechanisms, leaving us no choice but to tap into new sources of strength previously unknown to us and to bring them into our lives. The essence of a trial is the absolute faith of the Creator in us, for if it were not so, He would not test us. From this, we learn that a trial is inherently linked to faith.

How does the Tree of Life consciousness help us deal with difficult trials, complex crossroads in our lives, which are an inseparable and sometimes central part of our existence? Moreover, being a blessing is a profound wish for the tangible ability to bless the difficult parts of our lives. The Mishnah says: "A person must bless for the bad just as he blesses for the good."[1] This Mishnah touches on the riddle of life, and any attempt to understand and especially to live by it is a lifelong journey. How can one truly live this way? How can we bless the difficult parts of our lives just as we bless the good?

Maimonides adds an explanation:

[A person] should accept [the bad experiences] with joy. He should conquer his emotions and calm his mind when blessing "the true Judge" [blessing recited when we hear that someone has died] just as when he blesses "the good and the beneficent" [recited when hearing good news], etc. This is a rational matter among the wise, etc., because many things are considered bad at their outset, but

---

1 *Berachot* 9:5.

their end brings great good. And many things are considered good at their beginning but end up being very bad. (Commentary on the Mishnah, *Berachot*, chapter 9)

Maimonides adds a few points. Firstly, a person should react with joy in both cases.[2] He adds another aspect, stating that for the wise, this is a rational (logical) matter, because they understand that the concepts of good and evil are flexible and relative, and often things that appear bad turn into good, and vice versa. As usual, Maimonides follows the path of the Tree of Knowledge. However, as we know, objective reality does not always turn into good, even for "the wise." Perhaps the required process is not logical but rather consciousness-based, from elements of the Tree of Life.

As in our journey through this book, we embrace the blessings that we utter for both good and bad, rooted in Tree of Life consciousness, and not in any utilitarian understanding. This consciousness is primordial, transcending time and space, much like our soul. Its presence and movement are truly unaffected by the world and its events. Unlike our temporal bodies, the Tree of Life consciousness stems from the eternal realm – it is connected to our soul, which is beyond time. When this consciousness guides us in a world of the Tree of Knowledge, of good and evil, it allows us a different experiential interpretation of reality. At its core, it tells a person: everything that happens to you is truly yours. It is all part of your life story – both good and bad.

There is a good reason to mourn loss, to feel hurt, to experience the constriction of life, and of course, to confront death. We must undergo a phase of introspection around every loss. However, from the perspective of blessing and Tree of Life consciousness, our very existence is a call to live beyond the here and now. We are called to reach our full stature, to understand and especially to feel that all events are part of our life's journey toward reaching this unique height.

What Is "True" in "Blessed Is the True Judge"?

The concept of "*Baruch Dayan Ha'emet*" ("Blessed are You…the true Judge," the blessing recited when we hear that someone has died) involves acknowledging

---

2   Based on *Berachot* 60b.

and accepting the harsh realities and pain of life. This acceptance is a part of our world's judgment after eating from the Tree of Knowledge. Our world includes death, loss, illness, and loneliness.[3] Mourning these hardships is necessary, but it can also lead to opportunities for genuine renewal. This blessing serves as a reminder that there's more to our consciousness than just the negatives of life. It's not just about opposing evil but about recognizing the profound personal significance of our challenges.

These thoughts come in the wake of the recent horrific terrorist attack in Israel in October 2023. We face difficult days ahead, but we also have an opportunity to find deeper meaning and insights in our struggles. This ability to see the value while struggling enables us, at least to some extent, to bless the bad and accept our struggles in life.

The blessing "Blessed are You...the true Judge" over bad news[4] involves accepting a painful truth, stemming from Adam's consumption of fruit of the Tree of Knowledge, which introduced death and its emotional complexities into our world. This act marked the origin of all life's sins. Our life's essence involves grappling with this foundational sin.

However, we accept this harsh reality as a blessing. Recognizing life's crises, separations, and human mortality is a profound truth. It's a blessing in the sense that, similar to repentance, it involves a critical acceptance of our life's imperfections.

This acceptance should be infused with Tree of Life consciousness. Unlike the Tree of Knowledge, which denotes judgment and dichotomy, the Tree of Life symbolizes love and hope. Amidst the challenges brought by death, pain, anger, and division, the Tree of Life offers a perspective that encourages us

---

3   This is one of the reasons that halachah prohibits a mourner in the initial seven-day mourning period called shivah from engaging in marital relations. In their mourning, they must fully connect with the Tree of Knowledge, which is expressed in death. Mourning is about acknowledging death as well as impermanence and separation in the world, so it is not appropriate to unite during these days.

4   "One who hears bad news should bless 'Blessed [are You], the true Judge.' A person must bless for the bad with a good spirit, just as they bless for the good with joy, as it is said, 'And you shall love the Lord your God...with all your might.' Included in the abundant love in which we are commanded is that even in times of adversity, one should acknowledge and praise [God] joyfully" (*Mishneh Torah*, Hilchot Berachot 10:3).

to live fully. It invites us to transcend the punitive nature of judgment and embrace the possibilities of love and renewal in our lives.

Blessing and Abraham's Trials

Intriguingly, Abraham begins to encounter the trials of his life parallel to the initial command of *lech lecha* and the beginning of our forefather's journey, which is essentially the start of our path as his descendants. From the outset of his journey, there are few moments of respite. Firstly, the command *lech lecha* itself is a trial. Then, shortly after arriving in the Promised Land of Canaan, famine strikes, and Abraham descends to Egypt, facing complicated challenges with Pharaoh concerning his wife, Sarah. The words *ve'heyeh berachah* serve as a guiding principle in Abraham's journey, like a compass of consciousness for a path that is anything but easy. It's reminiscent of the fiddle in *Fiddler on the Roof* that accompanies Tevye and the people of Anatevka, or King David's harp that breathes life into its player.

The Sages relate Abraham was tested with ten trials.[5] These trials are vastly different from each other – some are internal and consciousness-based, while others are more practical. They touch upon many aspects of life, including wealth, his marriage to Sarah, tensions between his children, his wives, and more. These areas are familiar to us even today.

We may now focus on the question we asked at the beginning of this chapter. How does blessing consciousness, in which we are commanded to dwell, assist a person in the trials of life? We will try to understand how Abraham coped with this fate, focusing on the first trial, "Get you out of your country," and the last trial – the Binding of Isaac: "Get you into the land of Moriah; and offer him there for a burnt offering upon one of the mountains."[6]

In addition to the shared command to journey in both trials, there is another similarity. In the first trial, Abraham parts from his father, while in the last, he is required to part from his son. In both cases, we encounter the intra-family dynamic of parent-child relationships. Every person encounters these elements of separation in their lifetime.

---

5   Ethics of the Fathers 5c, and see Maimonides' commentary on this.

6   In this choice, we follow the Midrash: "The first trial [was] 'Go forth from your country,' [and] the last trial [was] 'Go forth to the land of Moriah'" (*Midrash Tanchuma*, Gen. 22:2).

Be a Blessing

I seek to touch upon the layer of blessing found in Abraham's conscious-ness that assisted him in coping with these trials – to see how they helped him both in dealing with the separation from his father's house and in confronting the command to bind his son, Isaac.

Abraham was commanded, "Go forth…from your father's house." Nachmanides provides one of the explanations for Abraham's difficulty in this first trial:

> The reason for mentioning "your land," "your birthplace," and "your father's house" is that it is difficult for a person to leave his land where he resides, the place of his loved ones and friends, especially when it is his birthplace where he was born, and all the more so when it includes his father's entire household. Therefore, he was required to leave everything for his love of God.

This portrays a familiar struggle with leaving one's parents' home, a phe-nomenon known to people who change their place of residence and leave their homeland. For many, this journey is remembered as a difficult transi-tion combined with new self-discovery. In the ancient world, without today's technology, this was a very challenging trial, as immigrants had to completely redefine themselves. The challenge exists today as well.

The Midrash adds another layer of difficulty, stating:

> "'To a land that I will show you' – He did not tell him a specific place; this is a trial within a trial. Is there someone who travels without knowing where they are going?" (*Midrash Tanchuma*, Lech Lecha 3)

God did not specify where Abraham should go. His initial journey was into the unknown, a "trial within a trial," adding a distinct layer of difficulty. The blessing helps one to walk toward the unknown in life. In this uncertainty, Abraham finds something new for himself. Heeding the command of *lech lecha*, he believes that he is called for a personal journey.

However, this journey is filled with challenges. As soon as Abraham arrives in the land of Canaan, he faces a famine. Canaan is not Haran. There might be a blessing in this land, but it is hidden from sight, lacking economic stability. He realizes that this land has a different economic secret regarding prosperity, a secret he does not yet understand. He lives in constant uncertainty. This is his blessing that supported him in leaving his father's house, toward a path where he would learn a new understanding of abundance in his world, and in our world as his descendants. His blessing in his journey is the ability to be in a state of unknowing, while feeling a personal sense of divine accompaniment. Abraham understands that significant learning about life awaits him.

We observe that in Abraham's trial of leaving his father's house and letting go of his past, he does not completely sever ties with his past. Upon arriving in the land, he finds that in heeding God's command, he also fulfills his father's wish to reach Canaan, but with a new and different perspective. Later, when Abraham seeks a wife for his son, the connection with his father's house is revisited. Eliezer, Abraham's servant, is instructed to bring a wife for Isaac from Abraham's father's land – Haran. It appears then that Abraham's blessing, which aided him in these trials, allows for a departure from his father's house while maintaining a connection. The ability to embark on a new path while retaining a positive link to the past is an expression of a blessing-oriented movement that embodies blessing. It's a connection to an ancient root, while establishing a new foundation.[7]

The Binding of Isaac

Undoubtedly, the Binding of Isaac is the most challenging trial in Abraham's life. How is it possible that "Yesterday you told me, 'For in Isaac will your seed be called,' and then you said, 'Take now your son,' and now you are telling me, 'Lay not your hand upon the lad'" (*Ta'anit* 10b)? As one Chasidic master said, "This is faith – beyond human understanding."[8]

This story carries an element of dread, and I find no explanation that eases the horror of this trial and the intensity of what was demanded of Abraham, despite its conclusion with the cancellation of the command.

---

7   See the introduction on the significance of blessing.

8   *Mei Hashiloach* on the Binding of Isaac.

The Binding of Isaac can be interpreted as a "journey of consciousness." This perspective does not explain the binding morally. It does not diminish the psychological or moral difficulty of the story, or the portrayal of the Creator as a fearsome deity. Instead, it seeks to show how this difficult trial, if undertaken with blessing consciousness, leads to the elevation of both Abraham and Isaac's souls.

A central verse spoken immediately after the Binding of Isaac reveals something about the purpose of the trial, beyond Abraham's willingness to bind Isaac:

> And he said, "Lay not your hand upon the lad, neither do you anything to him; for now I know that you fear God, seeing you have not withheld your son, your only son, from me." (Gen. 22:12)

This verse suggests that God sought to expand Abraham's previous identity toward being a God-fearing individual. This could only be achieved through his complete willingness to bind his son.

The *Zohar* explains that the purpose of the binding was the integration (*hitkalelut*) of consciousness between Abraham and Isaac – to "bind" their characteristics together. In integration, people merge aspects of themselves with each other. Through integration, each receives elements of the other's sub-traits, along with an awareness of their separate nature and will. This is likely seen in a good relationship. It's not a mixture of identities, but a tool for a new quality of connection. In the foundational story of our forefathers – Abraham, Isaac, and Jacob – this principle of integration was essential.[9]

Until this point, we've seen Abraham reveal his own distinct character, earning a son who embodies a unique and original nature. Now the binding demands a profound exchange. Abraham must absorb elements of Isaac's essence, and Isaac, in turn, needs to integrate aspects of his father's character. This isn't about imitation; it's about meaningful connection despite their individualities. Their separation actually fosters a deeper blessing, driven by a cognitive expansion that comes from this integration. This process is necessary for continuing their lineage into future generations. Just as in agriculture,

---

9   This also applies to the foremothers, Sarah, Rebecca, Rachel, and Leah.

where the old root nurtures the young branch, Abraham and Isaac must bond to solidify the foundation of the nation. As we emphasized regarding the relationship between Abraham and his father Terach, in which blessing lies in clarifying the acts of separation and connection, we see this even more forcefully in the relationship between Abraham and Isaac, the patriarchs of the Jewish people.[10]

The essence of the blessing in the binding lies in merging Abraham's qualities of kindness and love with Isaac's traits of awe and strength. Abraham is known as "Abraham, my beloved,"[11] emphasizing love, while Isaac is twice referred to as "the Fear of Isaac,"[12] highlighting reverence and strength.

In essence, this story rectifies the ancient sin of Noah and his son Ham. The ability to integrate is a healthy expression of intergenerational transfer, where there is separation between generations alongside the recognition of shared elements.

Almost every significant journey in a person's life requires touching upon a similar principle – a partial and temporary relinquishment of our familiar role, for the sake of a new path. After the Binding of Isaac, Abraham is not the same person he was before the event. From that point on, he carries the element of strength, alongside the centrality of kindness that characterized him until the binding.

The central change in his personality is recognized through the significant change in Isaac. The Sages often interpret the title Fear of Isaac as referring to Isaac's fear of God; however, some also connect it to the memory of the binding event itself.[13] The sweetening of Isaac's attribute of strength, while

---

10   Their shared journey toward integration is emphasized twice in the story of the binding, with the phrase "they walked together" mentioned twice in the narrative. This phrase signifies a form of unity as they approach a defining, challenging, and awe-inspiring event.

11   "But you, Israel, My servant, Jacob whom I have chosen, the seed of Abraham My friend" (Is. 41:8).

12   "Except the God of my father, the God of Abraham, and the Fear of Isaac, had been on my side, surely now had you sent me away empty" (Gen. 31:42); "And Jacob swore by the Fear of his father Isaac" (Gen. 31:53).

13   As Nachmanides wrote, "Some say that this fear is a reference to the day of the binding." In *Otzar Hamidrashim* (Eisenstein), we find: "The Fear of Isaac, the Father of Jacob, is the name of the attribute of our father Isaac, who was bound under the hand of Abraham."

internalizing some of his father's softer kindness, allows Isaac to act within reality. Typically, individuals with an introverted character like Isaac's keep their distance from reality. This might be why only after the binding does Abraham seek a wife for his son at a relatively mature age. Without the integration of Abraham's quality, Isaac might not have been ready for marriage and fatherhood. Only after the binding, which brought a soft element of kindness from his father's essence, was he able to recover and open up to love and connection.

Without this integration of Abraham's trait in Isaac, there is a likelihood that Isaac could have vanished from Abraham's family map. The trauma of the binding might have permanently distanced him from his family of origin, as in the narratives of Ishmael and Esau. This was also almost the case with Judah and Joseph, each separately. This integration helped Isaac to heal his life and become a unique father, continuing God's blessing to Abraham through his own path.

Abraham's journey, marked by a series of trials, reveals the profound role of faith in his life, much like in the Garden of Eden. However, unlike the garden experience, his life is not smooth but full of trials. The blessing helps him leave his parents' home in peace. It assists him through numerous and difficult crossroads, some practical and some existential. It even helps him through the most challenging trial of all – demonstrating the willingness to sacrifice his only son.

Abraham continually grows and evolves. His life's journey was underpinned by a blessed consciousness and a steadfast belief in divine guidance.

Questions for Reflection

- Try to recall a difficult trial in your life. How did the trial affect you?
- Did you find a blessing in it?
- Can you imagine today what tools of blessing you would want to build within yourself to help you face the trials of life?

PART FIVE

Modernity as a Call to Return to the Tree of Life

"Judaism is the only civilization whose golden age is in the future." (Rabbi Jonathan Sacks, *Future Tense*)

Chapter 17

The Land of Israel as a Mature Garden of Eden

I was born in the USA. My parents had gone to Israel after the Holocaust, then went to New York during the 1950s for medical reasons, with my two older sisters who were born in Israel. I grew up in the 1960s in a New York suburb, in a bubble where I thought the world only consisted of observant Jews and non-Jews. I was unaware of any other form of Judaism until I moved to Israel. This was despite the fact that right in the next room of my childhood home, my older sister Chava rebelled against the way we were being raised, from a young age.

Hebrew was the language of our home, and so, moving back to Israel felt natural for my parents, though for me at age nine, it was a challenging adjustment. Over time, I adapted, thanks to high-quality educational institutions, adventures in the Judean Desert, a passion for swimming in natural springs, involvement in a youth movement, meaningful Torah study, military service, and serving as a tank commander on the western front of the First Lebanon War. Gradually, my connection to my birthplace faded, and my Israeli identity solidified. This process was reinforced by my involvement in the establishment of Jewish study centers and engagement in Israel's political landscape, deepening my bond with the country. Yet to my surprise, over thirty years, I frequently traveled back to the USA, over a hundred times, to teach, forge partnerships, and raise funding.

In the late 1980s, my exposure to American Judaism opened my eyes to a form of Judaism vastly different from my childhood experience. On my first visit in October 1988, a friend took me to a ceremony for a Jewish teenager who had just received his driving license. The event was held in a luxurious apartment on Manhattan's Upper East Side, attended by the boy's extended family and his friends. A rabbi had crafted a Jewish ritual to mark the significance of obtaining a driver's license, which, in this case, was accompanied by the gift of a car from the boy's grandparents. Initially, I felt a sense of cynicism, typical of an Israeli perspective. "What kitsch!" I thought. "Here are the Americans with their schmaltz, creating a religious ceremony around getting a driving license!"

I listened to the ceremony, initially out of politeness, but gradually with an open heart. The parents blessed the boy with the Traveler's Prayer:

> May it be Your will...that You lead us toward peace, guide our footsteps toward peace, and enable us to reach our desired destination in life, gladness, and peace. May You rescue us from the hand of every foe, ambush, bandits and wild beasts on the journey, and from all kinds of punishments that rage in the world, and from the hard trials on the road, and grant us grace, kindness, and mercy in Your eyes and in the eyes of all who see us, for You are God who hears prayer and supplication...

The room was filled with a sense of seriousness and deep prayer. I suddenly realized that there was something very alive, relevant, and touching in this moment. It conveyed an awareness that the young man was about to control a powerful machine, bringing with it inherent dangers. I saw this as an important rite of passage for the modern teenager. It sparked the idea of a similar ceremony for soldiers upon receiving their weapons – not just an oath-taking event, but one that heightens the soldier's awareness of the power and responsibility that comes with holding a tool capable of taking life.

In time, I grew to deeply appreciate this form of Judaism. My first visit to a Conservative synagogue was to Bnai Jeshurun in New York, led by the late Rabbi Marshall Meyer, an Argentinean known for his meaningful approach to social justice and activism. I was struck by the community's commitment to social needs, with many volunteers hosting the homeless in the synagogue basement and their homes. Even the prayer service itself was a revelation. I remember during my first Kabbalat Shabbat there, surrounded by women,

African Americans, and various "others," suddenly realizing that I was the only one not praying. This is not what I was used to as an Orthodox Jew. It was an eye opener, and it led me to a new awareness. I recalled the words of our forefather Jacob, "Surely the Lord is in this place, and I knew it not" (Gen. 28:16). I was astonished.

Every time I returned to Israel, I would share with my children what I saw and experienced. I taught them new tunes I'd learned for Lecha Dodi, the traditional prayer recited in all Jewish communities on Friday night, and I told them about the fascinating Jewish creativity I encountered. They weren't as enthusiastic as I was, although they were happy for me. Family jokes emerged, along the lines of "There goes Dad again, getting excited about American Jews."

Babylon-Jerusalem

In those days, I and some friends established a group composed of Jerusalemites and New Yorkers, who studied the same topic for a year, and once a year we met to share insights. We called the project Bavli-Yerushalmi (Babylonian-Jerusalem), after the Talmuds that interpreted a common Mishnah, often through dispute. I felt that after seventeen hundred years, we were reviving a historically significant conversation. We received substantial financial support from various funds to expand the project. Later, this unique group adopted a Jewish community in Warsaw, worked with the Hillel organization in Riga, and aspired to be a leader of new dialogue between Israel and the Diaspora. Although I left the group in its early stages, it continues to operate to this day and has even served as a model for others.

During most of my trips to the USA, I returned with a new idea, whether big or small. I was fortunate to form deep friendships with various individuals. One who particularly touched me was Rabbi Rachel Cowan, of blessed memory, a convert and an extraordinary spiritual woman. Rachel and her late husband, who was Jewish, wrote a book titled *Mixed Blessings*, about the uniqueness and blessings of such a family. I saw her as a modern-day Ruth the Moabite, bringing blessings to the Jewish people she joined. She had the ability to accompany pain, be present, and create new structures in consciousness and soul. I have true soulmates from this Jewish world, people with a special and broad perspective that I unfortunately don't easily find in the Promised Land.

Be a Blessing

The commonality among these dear people I had the privilege to know is that they came from our modern-day "Babylon" – the United States. Something about their background, being Jews who chose to live in the Diaspora, contributed to them being unique individuals, in my perspective and for the people of Israel. Today's Babylon creates interesting life models and open-hearted people. This enduring bond with the Diaspora has been cultivated over many years through countless journeys, collaborative seminars, and fruitful partnerships.

Once, I was invited as scholar in residence to lead a Shabbat for the board of the New Israel Fund at a luxurious hotel in northern Israel. It was a quieter time in the relationship between the Fund and Israeli society, and they supported the Elul Beit Midrash I ran. On that Shabbat afternoon, the late author A. B. Yehoshua was invited to converse with the group. Known for his critique of the modern Jewish Diaspora, he spared no mercy in criticizing these individuals for choosing to live in the Diaspora when the State of Israel exists.

"How can one view the Jewish people's most significant endeavor, the State of Israel, from afar?" he challenged. He spoke with sharp, fervent Israeli passion, and upon finishing, checked his watch, stated there was no time for questions, and concluded with a metaphor: Jews in Israel are like fish in an aquarium, whereas American Jews are like fish outside of it. He ended with "Shabbat Shalom," and walked away.

Everyone was stunned, including me. The room fell into a stormy silence. The participants were bewildered, unsure where this had come from or why. They had never encountered a liberal intellectual who spoke in such terms. After several minutes of pained astonishment, they turned to me and said, "Say something. What do you think about his remarks?"

After a few seconds, I blurted out: "At least the fish outside the aquarium are thirsty for water." Diaspora Jews have to choose their Judaism every day, especially being outside the aquarium, unlike Israelis, who take their Judaism for granted. My words struck a chord with the audience, offering them some solace. Inside, I felt a sense of joy for "saving the situation," accompanied by a faint voice of unease. There was something in the Israeli author's unequivocal statement that touched me. Yet for a long time, I quickly silenced this voice within myself.

The Land of Israel as a Mature Garden of Eden

As years passed, participating in countless conferences, guiding Kolot delegations, and teaching in various settings, I slowly began to develop a profound concern about Diaspora Jewry, with a focus on American Jews. Amidst their immense creativity, pursuit of pluralism, and vibrant expression, a shift in my perception emerged. I noticed a disconnect among a whole generation of young Americans from this Jewish renaissance. They are grappling with distinct questions and existential needs that aren't addressed, even by the deeply moving Shabbat prayers crafted in unique synagogues across the United States. Even time spent in Jewish summer camps, once seen as pivotal for strengthening Jewish roots, seems quite insufficient against the secular, liberal, and humanistic values young American Jews encounter in college.

I've come to recognize that residing in Israel embodies a significance far beyond the post-Holocaust privilege of being part of a Jewish people consolidated in one secure, sovereign location. Rather, it's an integral part of understanding the essence and purpose of Jewish life. This realization spans from age-old Jewish prayers asking God to return His people to their land, to recognizing that something fundamental about the blessing of the Tree of Life – the actualization of Jewish life – is intrinsically linked to this land, Israel.

In recent years, I've listened more attentively to the younger generation of American Jews. Those I meet speak candidly about their deep connection to America – its culture and identity – alongside their love for Judaism, mainly expressed during Sabbaths and holidays. I deeply understand this dichotomy; it's so natural in our world. However, a life of division, rooted in the Tree of Knowledge, is tied to the expulsion from Eden and our dualistic lives ever since. It's challenging to forge a strong identity axis in this split. It feeds on the need and desire for survival, and certainly, passing it on to the next generation is no less challenging.

The Jewish Diaspora has a vital role in our times, and I'm not in favor of a mass immigration to Israel tomorrow. The Diaspora's daily choice to embrace Judaism fosters creativity and vitality. Jewish involvement in organizations supporting Israel is crucial, and rightfully, they should critique the state when needed. Further, Diaspora Jews can effectively represent and model the blessing of Jewish values to the world. But now, we must clarify the essence of our choice to live where we do. It's crucial to define our shared fate during challenging times and discuss the broader vision for the Jewish people. This vision should guide our actions wherever we are. The conversation must move beyond mere survival and the fear of assimilation. Discussing "ethnicity" without a meaningful purpose won't lead to any significant change. Even the term *continuity*, commonly used to emphasize the need for Jewish education, lacks depth. It raises the question: Continuity toward what end? Peoplehood toward what end?

In addition, the challenge of attempting to create new paradigms in areas such as economics, communication, family dynamics, and leadership intensifies when operating as a minority. It's difficult to offer meaningful alternatives within a Western world that clings to foundational beliefs, now in desperate need of reassessment. The ability of Western culture to introspectively examine itself is far from simple.

In the land of our forefathers, with all its issues and challenges, we have the opportunity to craft something unique and distinct. Israel as a sovereign state must ponder profound questions about human existence and propose innovative solutions. This necessity forms the core of its sovereignty and raison d'être: to evolve into a new model of being a blessing to the world!

However, it's clear that Israel is still a distance away from realizing this potential. The intense social divisions reflect a society in search of a fundamental reevaluation of its core values. The conflict forced upon Israel by terrorist organizations is an opportunity to redefine Israel's purpose afresh.

The question of Jewish nationalism's relevance might seem anachronistic in today's global village, where national boundaries blur as people migrate, intermarry across cultures, and digitally connect with distant places. This modern fluidity challenges the traditional concept of "place" in nationalism.

In the following discussion, we'll delve into the essence and tangibility of the place known as the Land of Israel, contrasting it with the ideology of the global village. What does this land represent beyond being a historical birthplace? How does it define the quality of life it offers? We'll link the Land of Israel to the Garden of Eden's setting and the biblical narrative of the trees. This exploration will illustrate how the Land embodies the deepest aspects of the biblical story, predating God's directive to Abraham to journey "to a land that I will show you."

Humans and Earth: Phases of Rupture

Rabbi Isaiah Halevy Horowitz, known by his initials as the Holy Shelah, immigrated to the Land of Israel long before the proclamation of Zionism. Born in Prague in 1558, he served as a rabbi in the community there for most of his life. In 1622, he moved to the Land of Israel, initially settling in Jerusalem, which at that time experienced a relative boom in Jewish immigration. He later lived in the Galilee, Safed, and finally Tiberias, where he passed away in 1630. While in the Land of Israel, he wrote his major work, *Shnei Luchot Habrit*, as a kind of testament to his family. The book addresses many areas of ethics and also discusses a unique relationship with the Land of Israel. Following is his description of the character of the Land of Israel:

> The person dwelling in the Land of Israel should always remember it as Canaan [*kna'an*], which implies servitude and subjugation [*hachna'ah*, from the same root]... The general principle is that in the land that the Lord your God seeks, all the more so must one be a submissive servant, as King David, peace be upon him, said, "I am a sojourner in the land" (Ps. 119:19), meaning I regard myself as a sojourner in the Holy Land.

The Shelah explains that the name of the land, Canaan, hints at a type of subjugation in the Land of Israel. He then describes the principle of sojourning that is required in the Holy Land. He continues:

> The general principle is that the inhabitants of the land must be submissive, like strangers, and should not make their main goal to settle in a sturdy dwelling.... When you wish to dwell in tranquility, you will be sojourners.

The Holy Shelah teaches that life in the Land of Israel should not be focused on bourgeois comforts ("in a sturdy dwelling"), but rather on cultivating a mindset akin to that of a sojourner. This mindset embodies humility, curiosity, and a soulful quest for meaning beyond mere materialism. He concludes:

The sign is "a land that eats up the inhabitants thereof" (Num. 13:32); it devours those who wish to settle in it comfortably and forcefully, to eat its fruits and enjoy it alone. The spies spoke this verse negatively; they turned words of holiness into the profane, profane for them. Whoever lives in the Land of Israel [according to the proper interpretation of] this manner is assured to enter the World to Come.

Here, the Shlah takes the pessimistic words of the spies about the Land of Israel, "a land that eats up the inhabitants thereof," and argues that there is indeed a true element to this for those who seek to "live in it comfortably and forcefully, to eat its fruits and enjoy it alone," that is, to live a "normal," bourgeois life. For such people, the land indeed consumes them from within. Interestingly, he posits a correlation: the more one seeks "normalcy," the more unrest and consumption will prevail in the land, and the more one lives in humility and submission, the more abundance and peace will be attained.

Israel is indeed a land of sensitivity. It bestows blessings on those who tread its paths rightly, while expelling those who traverse with force and might. Simultaneously a land of milk and honey, it is also one that consumes its inhabitants.[1] When we haven't yet reached it, it can be as beloved as in the Song of Songs, filled with yearning, a tender touch, moments of vanishing, and deep longing. Yet what unfolds when we do arrive? When we settle within, yearning for a normal life, sometimes even risking our lives for its cause?

In this chapter and the next, we'll explore the Land of Israel in its full manifestation as a "mature Garden of Eden,"[2] with Jerusalem embodying the Tree of Life essence of the garden. The land as a whole – and Jerusalem in particular – holds immense potential for being a source of blessing. Yet our current reality, far from this idyllic image, is marked by wars and societal

---

1   See Shelah, Parashat Lech Lecha, *Torah Or* 3:49, par. 11 (277, 2).

2   See Ez. 36:35–36: "And they shall say: This land that was desolate is become like the garden of Eden; and the waste and desolate and ruined cities are fortified and inhabited. ...I the Lord have built the ruined places, and planted that which was desolate; I the Lord have spoken it, and I will do it." The word for "that which was desolate," *haneshamah*, also means "soul." This recalls the act of creation when God infused the soul into humans.

division, far from the hallmarks of blessing. But it's within this very complexity, the ever-present chaos of our region, that the seeds of new hope are sown. What does it take to transform this chaos into blessing? What actions are necessary to shift from a discourse of violence to one of listening, encounter, growth, and joy?

To understand the unique nature of the Land of Israel, we must return to the biblical Garden of Eden story. The creation story in Genesis 2 begins with a description of the initial state of the universe, before the garden was created:

> These are the generations of the heavens and the earth when they were created, in the day that the Lord God made the earth and the heavens. No plant of the field was yet in the earth and no herb of the field had yet sprung up; for the Lord God had not caused it to rain upon the earth, and there was no man to till the ground. (Gen. 2:4–5)

This description emphasizes a state of "not yet," of waiting and absence. It conveys a sense of something raw and primal, seeking development:

- Vegetation: the plant of the field and the herb of the field had not yet grown.
- Irrigation: God had not yet sent rain.
- Humanity: there was no man to work the ground.

Just after this, the creative activity is described, clarifying what will complete creation and its purpose: to fill the initial void.

- Irrigation: "But there went up a mist from the earth, and watered the whole face of the ground" (Gen. 2:6).
- Humanity: "Then the Lord God formed man…and the Lord God took the man, and put him into the Garden of Eden to cultivate it and to keep it" (Gen. 2:7; 15).
- Vegetation: "And the Lord God planted a garden eastward, in Eden; and there He put the man whom He had formed. And out of the ground made the Lord God to grow every tree that is pleasant to the sight, and good for food; the Tree of Life also in the midst of the garden, and the Tree of Knowledge of Good and Evil" (Gen. 2:8–9).

On close examination, we discover an interesting point: there is still a gap between the opening verses that describe the deficiency and the description of the garden after its formation. Creation in the Garden of Eden is only a partial fulfillment of the lack in the opening verses.

- Vegetation: The Garden of Eden has only trees, whereas the plant of the field and the herb of the field mentioned in the "not yet" verses do not appear in the description of life within the garden.

- Irrigation: Mist and rivers characterize the conditions in the garden. It appears to have an abundance of water sufficient for watering the trees. However, the rain from heaven mentioned in the opening verses is not mentioned in the Garden of Eden. Apparently, the abundance of river water eliminates the need for rain in the garden.[3]

- Humanity: Man is created outside of the garden and brought into it. However, even after being placed in the garden, he does not fulfill the deficiency through his own toil. Instead, his interaction with the environment appears effortless – picking and feeding from the trees without the sweat and labor usually required for farming. In the garden, there is no relationship to the produce of the land from the man's labor. There is no real labor – no cultivation of the land.

The Garden of Eden apparently only partially addressed the deficiencies in the world as depicted in the creation narrative preceding its existence. Recognizing this gap is crucial to understanding the relationship between the Garden of Eden and the Land of Israel. The Land of Israel is envisioned as the complete rectification of the creation story, emphasizing human labor, rain from the heavens, and the cultivation of field crops. Thus, in the Land of Israel, we see a more comprehensive and profound fulfillment of the creation narrative, far surpassing the life in the garden.

Before entering the Land of Israel, however, the people of Israel descend into Egypt, which, aside from being a land of bondage, also possesses a Garden-of-Eden-like quality due to the Nile River that irrigates its fields.

---

3   "And so the land initially drank from below, as it is written, 'there went up a mist from the earth,' but the Holy One, blessed be He, changed it so that the land would not drink from below but from above...so that everyone would turn their eyes upwards" (*Midrash Genesis Rabbah* 13:9).

Indeed, Egypt features an abundance of field crops, in contrast to the growth of trees.

Although Egypt is strongly identified as a land of bondage, it became an object of profound longing for our people who left it. It seems the security offered by the Nile River, the lack of dependence on rain, and the frequent cultivation of field crops (such as squash and watermelons) created in the Hebrew slave a longing for stable and consistent nourishment, contrasting with the "challenge" posed by the Land of Israel, which threatened the Israelite slave's survival.

The Garden of Eden holds a uniquely significant place in our consciousness. In this garden, seeds of awareness were planted for the continuation of the human story in general and the Jewish story in the Land of Israel in particular.

In the primordial world of the garden, we lived in a secure and enjoyable emotional and physical openness. As humans are composed of both the breath of God and the dust of the earth, there was hope that humans would recognize they are not God, despite possessing a divine element. This unique aspect within us was supposed to help prevent eating from the Tree of Knowledge.

In this ideal state in the garden, humanity touched the roots of its creation: the dust of the earth and the divine breath of life, living in harmony. This represents the first image of innocence, a harmonious triangle between God, human, and earth.

However, Adam ate from the Tree of Knowledge and was subsequently exiled from the Garden of Eden. From this point forward, an interesting decline in the relationship within this triangle – human being, earth, and God – begins to unfold. Systematically, we observe how the relationship between humans and the earth becomes damaged, losing its quality and hence its innocence. This condition also affects the relationship with God. The disruption of harmony between humanity, the earth, and the Creator impacts the quality of all human life.

Let's examine the development of this decline.

Stage 1
After the consumption of the Tree of Knowledge and Adam and Eve's subsequent failure to take responsibility, the following verse appears:

> And to Adam He said, "Because you heeded the voice of your wife and ate from the tree of which I commanded you, saying, 'You will not eat of it,' cursed is the ground for your sake; in sorrow will you eat of it all the days of your life." (Gen. 3:17)

The focus of the change in the world, due to the sin of eating from the Tree of Knowledge, is on the relationship between humans and the earth. The earth is cursed because of the human action of eating from the tree, which violated the harmonious balance with the earth: "In sorrow will you eat of it all the days of your life." Compared to the sorrow mentioned previously for the woman: "In sorrow you will bring forth children" (Gen. 3:16), the man's sorrow is related to the earth;[4] thorns (*kotzim*) will separate man and the earth, perhaps reminding man of his end (*ketz*). From now on, humans will undergo laborious processes before producing "bread to eat." Instead of the abundance of picking fruit from trees in the garden, man struggles with "the herb of the field" close to the ground, forcing humans to lower their stature, like animals and beasts. This proximity to the earth will culminate in man's death, when he returns to the earth from which he was created.

The earth, instead of being a direct partner, becomes a source of toil in life and the place of burial in death. This change in the relationship between humans and the earth damages the innocence of Eden. The parts of the triangle within the garden, formerly in harmony, undergo a significant change and culminate in humanity's expulsion:

> And the Lord God said, "Behold, the man is become as one of us, to know good and evil; and now, lest he put forth his hand, and take also of the tree of life, and eat, and live forever." Therefore the Lord God sent him forth from the Garden of Eden, to till the ground from whence he was taken. (Gen. 3:22–23)

The Garden of Eden remains intact and unharmed, yet it becomes unreachable. Devoid of humanity to tend to it, the garden stands isolated. Meanwhile,

---

4   "And it repented the Lord that He had made man on the earth, and it grieved Him at His heart" (Gen. 6:6).

humanity, exiled from this idyllic setting, faces the harsh reality of the curse pronounced against them and the earth. The aspiration for a harmonious coexistence among the Creator, humans, and the earth is, for the time being, thwarted. As a result, humanity's bond with the earth gradually weakens, leading to a further breakdown in the relationship between humans and their natural environment.

Stage 2

Adam and Eve give birth to the first children of humanity, Cain and Abel, born into a reality outside the garden. Aware of the curse and the profound shift in human-earth relations, Cain and Abel choose their professions. Cain opts to work the land. Abel, on the other hand chooses shepherding. God prefers Abel's offering over Cain's.

Then Cain kills Abel. Here, as after the sin of eating from the Tree of Knowledge, the initial response focuses on the earth, which this time emits a cry. God challenges Cain:

> What have you done? The voice of your brother's blood cries out to Me from the ground. Now you are cursed from the ground, which has opened its mouth to receive your brother's blood from your hand. When you work the ground, it will no longer yield its strength to you; you will be a restless wanderer on the earth. (Gen. 4:10–12)

After the first murder in human history, we might expect a speech of rebuke from the Creator of the World about the horrific act of taking a life.[5] However, the focus of God's discourse is on the earth's cry following the murder: it cries out in protest at absorbing Abel's blood.[6] The earth is sensitive. It seeks to absorb other liquids, primarily rain, which would sprout life-giving seeds (akin to the Tree of Life). Instead, contrary to its nature, it reluctantly

---

5   Like the powerful verse further along in the text: "Whoever sheds man's blood, by man shall his blood be shed; for in the image of God made He man" (Gen. 9:6).

6   The next outcry is made by Sodom to God.

absorbs the blood of death (akin to the Tree of Knowledge). The result: "it will no longer yield its strength to you."

Cain gave the earth the blood of a murder victim; it will respond with a lack of vitality. This is another step in the breakdown of innocence. If after Adam's sin, the initial stages of estrangement began with the earth producing thorns and thistles, yet there was still a connection between effort and result, now there is no certainty at all in the relationship between effort, investment, and outcome!

This stage marks a dramatic breakdown of innocence. At this point, humanity truly becomes estranged from the earth. People will work the land, plow and sow, but may face drought and fruitlessness. It's not just about the hardworking person knowing there's a reward for such labor; it's about the laborer working without knowing if the labor will bear fruit at all.

This is a significant moment in human existence. From now on, people must live with a sometimes unbearable gap between expectation and outcome. God no longer trusts humanity's ability to "guard" the earth.

Cain is exiled and settles in the land of Nod, east of Eden. The biblical phrase "Cain went out from the presence of the Lord" (Gen. 4:16) signifies a distance between him and God. He builds the first city. Building a city is a clear symbol of despair in the relationship between humanity, the earth, and the Creator. A city, by definition, is disconnected from farming. The distance from the original garden is increasing.

Stage 3

The world continues to deteriorate. At the end of Genesis, the sons of God are described as taking the daughters of man. This passage depicts a kind of authoritative licentiousness by the "sons of God" – presumably those in power who felt entitled to take any woman they desired. This behavior represents one of the peaks of disconnection from the Garden of Eden, using power and status for personal gratification at the expense of the weak and exploited. The focus here is on the exploitation of women. The immense gap is evident between the intimate "This is now bone of my bones" in the garden and the degradation of women – "the daughters of man" – as merely objects for the powerful. Earthliness (dust) overcomes the breath of life, leading to the decree of the Flood, an eradication "from the face of the earth." The earth has a face, and it has been severely harmed by human behavior.

The birth of Noah brings hope for comfort from the hardship of working with the cursed earth that does not yield fruit.

> And he called his name Noah, saying: "This same will comfort us in our work and in the toil of our hands, which comes from the ground which the Lord has cursed." (Gen. 5:29)

Again, we find the phrase "toil of our hands, which comes from the ground which the Lord has cursed." The earth has transformed from a blessing to a curse.

Consequently, the Flood washing over the earth's surface represents a tangible and literal severance of the connection between humans and the earth.

This is a new stage in the breakdown of innocence. It's not just exile from the Garden of Eden or the disconnection between labor and its fruits, but a complete detachment of humans from their source. The earth beneath human feet vanishes under the turbulent waters, and in this detachment, humans find their death. Humans treated women as objects and, in return, faced total insecurity concerning the earth beneath them, becoming objects themselves in the void and chaos that engulfs everything.

After the subsiding of the floodwaters and the emergence from the Ark, it seems the world is heading toward a "reboot." The Creator, Whose position has seemingly evolved significantly since the days of innocence in the Garden of Eden, establishes a new principle:

> And the Lord said in His heart, I will not again curse the ground any more for man's sake; for the nature of man's heart is evil from his youth. (Gen. 8:21)

The clear implication here is that the Creator, weary of gambles and trials, distances humans from the earth. The Creator, Who initially wanted humans to enter the garden to cultivate and guard it, realizes that this connection between human and earth is unfeasible. The serpent has triumphed. The dust prevails over the element of the breath of life. The Tree of Knowledge leads.

If the Flood physically severed the connection between humans and the earth, God now severs any internal bond between them. The blessing or curse of the earth is no longer linked to human actions.

Stage 4

The next stage is the construction of the Tower of Babel. This story depicts an urban humanity building upwards, where the sky is not the limit:

> And they said, "Come, let us build us a city and a tower, with its top in heaven; and let us make a name, lest we be scattered abroad upon the face of the whole earth." (Gen. 11:4)

The Tower of Babel, among its other symbols, represents urban bourgeois and technological confidence. It claims that humans, like God, can create endlessly. It seeks to create a "name," implying an identity of limitless creation.

The builders of the Tower of Babel focus on endless human creation, disconnected from the earth below and often disregarding God above. This world is drastically different from the Garden of Eden. The consciousness of the people of Babel is far removed from that of humans in the primordial garden.

Here we witness the complete disintegration of the original innocence. If the Flood washed away the ground beneath humanity, the confusion at Babel restricted the heavens above.

The Tower of Babel marks a new and radical stage in the dissolution of the divine-human-earth triangle. This unique triangle completely falls apart. There is no longer a connection to God or to the earth. The story of the Tower of Babel concludes the universal chapters of the Bible. This ending is characterized by a sense that humanity has not lived up to its destiny. The pinnacle of creation – humanity – has not met expectations.

Place in Human Discourse: Location Matters

Here, surprisingly, amidst the complete disintegration of the Garden of Eden dream, a new hope emerges. The Creator of the world, Who initially created the Garden of Eden for humanity and then observed a steady decline from its original innocence, unexpectedly does not give up on His initial hope:

The Land of Israel as a Mature Garden of Eden

And the Lord said to Abram, "Go forth from your country, and from your kin, and from your father's house, to a land that I will show you." (Gen. 12:1)

In the depths of despair of His world, God introduces a hope for a second innocence.

Adam is replaced by Abraham (and later, the Children of Israel), and the Garden of Eden is succeeded by the Land of Israel, fostering a hope to establish a life of blessed quality there. Furthermore, the Land of Israel reveals itself as a more complete correction to the picture of deficiency in the creation of the world, as discussed at the beginning of the chapter.

Regarding the Land of Israel, a distinctly Edenic expression is stated:

A land which the Lord your God cares for: the eyes of the Lord your God are always upon it, from the beginning of the year even to the end of the year. (Deut. 11:12)

God watches and takes an interest in this land.

In contrast to the bleak picture of the severed connection between humanity and the earth post-Flood, in the Land of Israel, the yield of the land depends on human labor and God's perception of it. The land is "sensitive" to human action, offering its fruits as a "land flowing with milk and honey," but can also expel its inhabitants in extreme circumstances:

Do not defile yourselves in any of these ways, for by all these the nations I am casting out before you have defiled themselves. Thus the land became defiled; and I punished it for its sin, and the land vomited out its inhabitants. (Lev. 18:24–25)

In the Land of Israel, it's possible to return to the abundance and security that existed in the Garden of Eden:

If you walk in My statutes, and keep My commandments, and do them; then I will give your rains in their season, and the land will yield her produce, and the trees of the field will yield their fruit.

> And your threshing will reach to the vintage, and the vintage will reach to the sowing time; and you will eat your bread until you have enough, and dwell in your land safely. And I will give peace in the land, and you will lie down, and none will make you afraid; and I will cause evil beasts to cease out of the land, neither will the sword go through your land. (Lev. 26:3–6)

Here we have a description of eating bread to satisfaction and the trees of the field yielding their fruit ("Of every tree of the garden you may freely eat"), and dwelling securely without fear. But unlike the Garden of Eden, which was watered by a river, here there is abundant and timely rain. Additionally, this land provides produce from field grass, something not present in the garden. Here lies the possibility of a complete solution to the fundamental deficiency depicted in the creation story we began with, where the Garden of Eden was only a partial answer. In the Land of Israel, there is rain, field grass, and human labor. Rain, grass, and labor will be central elements in this second innocence, one associated with life in the Land of Israel.

In Moses's final speech before entering the land, he says:

> For the land, where you go in to possess it, is not as the land of Egypt, from where you came out, where you did sow your seed, and did water it with your foot, as a garden of herbs; but the land, where you go over to possess it, is a land of hills and valleys, and drinks water as the rain of heaven comes down. (Deut. 11:10–11)

The significant difference between the Land of Israel and Egypt lies in the method of irrigation. In Egypt, there is an abundance of water. Irrigating the land involves a small movement of the foot to open a water gate, enabling the waters of the Nile to flow into the fields. In contrast, the Land of Israel depends on rain from heaven. This reliance on heavenly rain is considered a blessing compared to the abundant waters of the Egyptian Nile.

As we've seen in the opening chapters, Lot's separation from Abraham stemmed from a fundamentally different perception of the essence of economy and blessing. Lot chose the region of Sodom, described as "like the garden of the Lord, like the land of Egypt" (Gen. 13:10). This implies that

Sodom was a representation of the Garden of Eden (like the garden of the Lord), a unique place in the Land of Israel that didn't depend on rain – "that it was well watered" (ibid.). Lot saw this and was tempted. However, the people of Sodom were "wicked and sinners before the Lord exceedingly" (Gen. 13:13). In our post-Fall world, there is a significant danger of forgetting God amidst abundant wealth generated by human effort.

Lot thought it was possible to return to the Garden of Eden. This also explains the longing of the Israelites in the wilderness for Egypt, where they had regular meals, the Nile, and stability. The slave mentality is challenged to comprehend journeying to a land dependent on heaven's rain. Living in reliance on rain, as a way of life, is deeply connected to profound freedom. It involves the ability to lose control over life, to breathe deeply, and to believe.

A central question I've been asking businesspeople in recent years is how they understand the notion that dependency on rain is a hallmark of blessing in the Land of Israel, a concept that seems to contradict simple economic logic. This dialogue and the emerging responses are part of the essence of the new Jewish discourse I envision in our times about a blessed economy.

The experience of life in the Land of Israel differs from that in the Garden of Eden. In cultures where a river – such as the Nile in Egypt – is the primary source of abundance, it often attains a deity-like status. However, the concept of second innocence in Israel ties closely to the blessings from God, which descend from the heavens. This blessing is contingent upon the individual who diligently works the land, remains conscientious of duties toward others, and regularly gazes skyward, acknowledging the divine. Here, the earth, humanity, and God reforge the ancient triangular bond of the garden, but with a renewed and mature understanding, emerging from the historical phases of rupture we've seen.

Farmer and Shepherd, Israel and the Diaspora

Many have questioned Cain's sin. He first brought an offering of the earth's fruits to God. About Abel, it is said he also brought "of the firstlings of his flock" (Gen. 4:4), following Cain's initiative. The biblical story does not make it clear why God did not accept Cain's offering.

Hillel Zeitlin, a journalist, thinker, and mystic from Warsaw, who was murdered in the Holocaust, determined:

The Holy Scriptures almost always favor the shepherd over the farmer.... Noah is described as "a man of the earth," and not in a praiseworthy way.... The patriarchs were shepherds. Jacob was "a dweller in tents," and Esau was "a man of the field".... This is because the work of the earth is tied to the concept of private ownership by the worker, and the Holy Scriptures do not recognize the right of a private individual to the land, except under specific limitations and conditions (sabbatical year, jubilee, gleaning, forgotten sheaves, the corners of the field, etc.).

Rabbi Samson Raphael Hirsch develops a similar idea:

Agriculture demands all of a person's physical strength.... Through the sweat of his brow, he cultivates his land, and it becomes his supreme value, becoming part of his personality.... Agriculture arouses and develops culture. Most of the inventions and arts are credited to it. Settlement creates society, the state, and legal relations. When man was decreed to work the land, the door to human development was opened. On the other hand, the farmer becomes a slave to his field, and his land draws him to it.... He may easily turn to worship the forces of nature, as the flourishing of his field depends on them. The belief in God and the dignity of man first disappeared among agricultural nations. There, slavery and idolatry first developed.

In contrast, a greater virtue is found in the life of a shepherd. Their main occupation is with living creatures. Caring for them awakens human emotions and empathy for the suffering of creatures.... But their existence is not in human hands. Thus, the shepherd is saved from the danger of exaggerating the value of self and property. The work of his hands does not occupy all his strength. His spirit is not so completely harnessed to work, and it remains free for divine and human values. Therefore, our forefathers were shepherds.... The Torah anticipated the dangers inherent in agriculture and established laws against the deification of property: the Sabbath and the sabbatical year.... (Commentary on Gen. 4:2)

These two Jews, Zeitlin and Rabbi Hirsch, lived in Europe toward the end of the Jewish Diaspora there, before the horrific Holocaust. According to them, God's preference for Abel's offering is related to his being a shepherd, thus showing God's preference for the shepherd over the farmer. They cite as evidence the fact that central leaders in our history, such as Moses and David, began as shepherds. They also justify this preference by the special quality found in caring for sheep and their mobility, as opposed to the spiritual dangers faced by farmers, who might strengthen their sense of ownership and authoritarianism.

I would like to offer another interpretation, an almost opposite approach. Indeed, working the land can be the height of egotism, creating a sense of ownership between the person and the land, with no regard for the heavens, as in the Sages' saying, "by my power and the might of my hand." However, the farmer can also lift his eyes to the heavens, in awareness of his dependence on rain. This act renews the triangle between the earth he just cultivated and his turning toward the Creator. This upward gaze is key to understanding the blessing of the Land of Israel, as we have seen.

In the Land of Israel, the stakes are higher. From Passover to Sukkot, the farmer takes responsibility for his land. He plows, plants, and sows. During Sukkot, after the harvest, he turns to the heavens as if to say to the Creator of the world, "I have done my part, now do Yours" – a profound existential movement of responsibility and release. Farming can be the peak of authoritarianism and egoism, but it can also be the pinnacle of blessing, where a person knows that not everything is under his control.

From this perspective, shepherding seems a necessary stage leading to the cultivation of land, which represents the pinnacle of the Creator's hope for humanity.

This tension between the shepherd and the farmer can be seen as a kind of debate between the Judaism that resides in the Land of Israel and that of the Diaspora. The Diaspora represents shepherding – constant movement, a lack of connection to the land. This movement allows for unique creativity, as evidenced throughout our years in exile. Shepherding reveals new worlds to the shepherd. Indeed, significant Jewish works were created in the Diaspora – in contrast to the inhabitants of the land, who are focused on place, sovereignty, and power.

Some post-Zionist thinkers believe that the connection between Israel and the land and sovereignty has already failed in the past and will fail again in the future, arguing that our existence is fundamentally rooted in the Diaspora.

I believe differently. The farmer was the fundamental hope in the Garden of Eden, a hope that has not faded from the Creator's world even after humanity's expulsion from the garden. The hope for the renewal of connection with the Land of Israel embodies a special invitation to cultivate the land and what it represents in our modern lives. The hope for the return to Zion in our times is a profound request for the right balance between belonging to a place, creativity, and power, and between humility and being a blessing. It is an invitation to a unique dance.

These principles are true for all sectors of the economy; even in business and high-tech, there should be "a heaven."

The Western world tends to grasp control and responsibility, while the Eastern world expresses much of the realm of liberation and lack of control. The Jewish world seeks a special dance between responsibility and liberation. Thus, the debate between shepherds and farmers continues in its modern form, even in our times.

To return to the Israel-Diaspora relationship – the challenge I raise is: Can Diaspora Jewry create a shared vision with the State of Israel around the hope of being a blessing, despite the difference of location, which, as we have seen, is significant? This mission can reinvigorate the relationship and give new vitality to nationhood, rendering it not just a partnership of fate, but a partnership of mission.

Between Haran and the Land of Israel

We are familiar with the opening verses where God says to Abraham, "Go forth from your country, and from your kin, and from your father's house, to a land that I will show you" (Gen. 12:1). We usually think this is Abraham's first appearance in the Bible and in our world. Interestingly, before the command to Abraham to go, it was Terah, his father, who began the journey to Canaan: "And Terah took Abram his son, and Lot the son of Haran, his son's son, and Sarai his daughter-in-law, his son Abram's wife; and they went forth with them from Ur of the Chaldees, to go into the land of Canaan; and they came to Haran, and dwelled there" (Gen. 11:31).

The Torah does not explain why Terah and his family set out. Perhaps he was of middle-class status and sought to improve his economic standing. It's likely that a poor family could not afford such a journey in those times. On their way to Canaan, Terah stopped and essentially ended his journey in Haran, which is located in what is today southeastern Turkey. Why did Terah stop his journey in Haran? This can be understood from the verse in Abraham's journey: "And Abram took Sarai his wife, and Lot his brother's son, and all their substance that they had gathered, and the souls that they had gotten in Haran; and they went forth to go into the land of Canaan; and into the land of Canaan they came" (Gen. 12:5). In Haran, Terah's family acquired wealth and people. He stopped there because he reached his own "promised land," a place where he could grow in wealth, a successful relocation from an economic standpoint. Therefore, there was no need to continue the journey to Canaan. Haran was economically powerful.

Within this successful scenario of Terah's family, God's command to Abram, his son, to leave Haran for Canaan is heard. God invites Abraham to transition from one economic approach to another, linking the pursuit of good livelihood with a gaze toward the heavens, a unique feature of the Land of Israel. And Abraham understood that there is a broader realm of abundance beyond the enrichment experienced by his father's household. There's something in God's personal call to him that invites him to a higher consciousness in relation to the mystery of abundance in the world. God invites him on a life journey filled with blessing and abundance, yet fundamentally different from his father's endless pursuit of wealth in Haran.

Political Debate and Blessing Consciousness

The concept of a blessed world requires being aware of reality. The current return to Zion has confronted us with a difficult reality. While liberating historical regions and seeking to apply sovereignty there, we encounter people who are also connected to the Land of Israel but do not desire Jewish rule, let alone sovereignty.

Zionism as a second form of innocence, with a Garden of Eden consciousness and the desire to be a blessing, must be openly aware of the difficulty
that began with the very emergence of Zionism and all the more so with its
expansion during the Six-Day War.

The dominant paradigm for solving the Palestinian problem is fundamentally Western. It seeks a resolution through negotiations over sovereignty, independence, and trust via legal formulations. Many in Israeli society strongly
intuit that Western tools are not relevant as central means to resolving this
conflict. Western-style negotiation did not succeed in the past, and there is no
reason to think that it will succeed in the future.

There is room to propose a different approach, not one that separates and
divides. In the conflict between Jews and Palestinians, there is a clear reli-
gious-spiritual element. The current war that began on October 7 strengthens
the understanding that this conflict has powerful religious roots. Perhaps this
language, which seems difficult to decipher, is the key to peace. If religion is
the major source of the tension, it also holds the solution.

Rabbi Menachem Froman, of blessed memory,[7] a prominent figure in the
Tree of Life mindset, held a firm belief that only interfaith dialogue, delving
into the roots of faith, the nature of God, and the connection between violence and love could resolve the conflict. He envisioned that such a perspective could foster a new dialogue and pave the way for peace. His approach
wasn't about dividing authorities but about fostering a conversation around
an inner vision that creates meaningful encounters. His efforts were significant, especially after the assassination of Rabin, when I closely accompanied him to various meetings. We visited hostile villages in Egypt, Gaza, and
Jordan, engaging with religious figures who had supported suicide bombings
of buses filled with innocent civilians. These meetings, which merit further
exploration, created an opportunity for a profound encounter with God.
Through mutual surrender, a doorway to love and a longing for life opened.
These encounters achieved relative success, though they did not visibly impact

---

7   Rabbi of the settlement of Tekoa, a spiritual leader who believed that deep faith-based
     dialogue contained the solution to the conflict between Jews and Muslims and was very
     active in promoting this view.

mainstream politics. The current war is an expression of the challenges of this approach, alongside the hope it offers.

I wish to add another layer to this approach.

Abraham, the father of Isaac and Ishmael and a patriarch of many nations, was commanded to "go forth" and was promised to become "a blessing." Can we envision a new dialogue that collectively explores what a blessed life means for both Jews and Muslims? Could discussing significance and purpose foster new trust? Might regional peace stem not just from separation but from a conversation about a vision of blessing in our world?

The crisis with Hamas and terrorist organizations, drastically inflamed since October 2023, could potentially undermine all trust in Jewish-Arab relations. Yet I still believe that the descendants of Abraham can and should create a new regional model.

The methodology proposed in this book is not satisfied with just addressing the distinct fates or clarifying separate narratives. It focuses on the question of purpose: *Why sovereignty? What does this land tell you? What does it ask of us?* I believe we can initiate a new dialogue about the essence of blessing, which can then be applied to our actual reality.

In February 2022, I led a seminar in Dubai focused on the blessings of Abraham's descendants for our world. The event was attended by prominent figures from both Israel and the Muslim world. My partner in this initiative was a Muslim leader of international standing, with whom I had established a meaningful connection a few months earlier.[8] A highlight of the seminar was the study of the story of Sarah and Hagar, in which Hagar flees from Sarah after being mistreated. The story goes on to describe Hagar's thirst in the desert and the miracle by which God provides her with water and foretells the birth of Ishmael. A Muslim participant asked, "Do you teach this story to your children?" expressing her shock at the level of violence endured by Hagar. The room fell silent and was filled with embarrassment, until Rabbi Yuval Cherlow, one of the participants, cited Nachmanides:

---

8   I wish to thank Rabbi David Rosen, who introduced me to the Muslim world and put me in touch with leading individuals. Rabbi Rosen identified the shared destiny of blessing as embodying a new potential for future solutions.

"And Sarai dealt harshly with her, and she fled from her face."
Our mother erred in this harsh treatment, and Abraham also erred
by allowing it. God heard her affliction and gave her a son who
would be a wild man, afflicting Abraham and Sarah's descendants
with various sufferings. (Nachmanides on Gen. 16:6)

This poignant interpretation by Nachmanides paved the way for a healing
process between the moderate descendants of Ishmael, who acknowledge the
descendants of Isaac and their connection to the Land of Israel, leading to a
different future. This healing involves deep religious dialogue.

Can we imagine a joint conversation between Jewish and Arab residents of
the land about the concept of Shemittah (the sabbatical year), a biblical principle that suggests the absence of ownership over the land, as a foundation
for creating a peace dialogue for those who seek this land? The Land of Israel
belongs to God, as no person truly has "title" to it. Removing the element of
ownership might lead to more humane solutions and open surprising options
for peace. This is true for the Land of Israel as a whole and particularly for
Jerusalem and the Temple Mount.

Perhaps a dialogue focused on the blessings among the descendants of
Abraham, relinquishing the discourse of ownership and taboos, knowing that
God is the true owner, could lead to a new dialogue in our modern State of
Israel, seeking stable and genuine peace.

Judaism and the Jewish people experienced tremendous flourishing in the
Diaspora. Jewish communities established unique structures of life, deeply
connected to Jewish tradition and values. Significant spiritual creativity
unfolded throughout the years of exile.

Similar to Cain – who was exiled from the garden, built a city, and developed human culture in various fields – the Jews also created in many areas.
The survival and flourishing of the Jewish community over two thousand
years are unparalleled among other nations.

Yet it turns out that place does matter. The longing for the Land of Israel
was an important part of Jewish vitality. From the very first appearance of
Abraham, the phrase "to a land that I will show you" holds a central place
in the destiny of "being a blessing." In this chapter, I have tried to show a
bit of the psychological and existential mystery of the Land of Israel for its

inhabitants, as a place that is above and beyond Jewish sovereignty after years of exile. This is the place where essential parts of a blessed life can and should exist. Transforming the State of Israel into a blessed and mature Garden of Eden is the challenge that we face today.

Questions for Reflection

- What is the role of "place" in your life? What is the role of the Land/State of Israel in your existential experience?
- What is the content and essence for you of the covenant between the Jews of the Diaspora and the Jews of the State of Israel?

Chapter 18

⌒

Jerusalem: The Tree of Life

In 2003, I had the opportunity to study with Nir Barkat. At that time, he had just left his successful business career and was considering running for mayor of Jerusalem, against Uri Lupolianski.[1] His advisors believed it would be beneficial for him to learn about the city's significance in Jewish texts. He arrived at my office at Kolot in Jerusalem, and I was favorably impressed.

Our study sessions were brief. As the election drew closer, his time became increasingly limited. During our final meeting, I asked him what was the most meaningful insight that he was taking away from our study sessions. He responded: "What we learned in the Babylonian Talmud, that 'Jerusalem was not divided among the tribes.'"[2] Essentially, unlike other parts of the land which were allocated to different tribes, Jerusalem belongs to God, and no tribe has ownership over it. Curious, I asked why this struck a chord with him. He explained: In a place without disputes over ownership, there's an opportunity for deep listening. Letting go of ownership fosters creative thinking where all parties might feel satisfied. Relinquishing ownership is the path to peace.

I was moved by his words and told him that if he wished, we could study a powerful Talmudic story about Jerusalem that addressed the city's inherent chaos, the balance of power, and peace. He replied, "After I become mayor." Unfortunately, we never got to study that precious story together. This story will conclude our chapter and serve as a kind of summary for the entire book.

---

1 Nir indeed became mayor of Jerusalem, after which he became a member of Knesset, representing the Likud Party as Minister of the Economy.

2 "The houses in Jerusalem are not rented out because they are not [owned by anyone]" (*Yoma* 12a and *Megillah* 26a, with a slight variation).

Jerusalem is one of the most emotionally charged cities in the world. No one can remain indifferent to it. Some ascend to it joyfully, others out of necessity, but all acknowledge that it has a special aura.

Beyond its ancient history, just in the last hundred years, Jerusalem suffered the pogroms of 1929 and also became the base for the Second Intifada. Jerusalem Day is a complex holiday for many Israelis. Some celebrate it, while others, feeling its difficult political complexities, choose not to celebrate.

Jerusalem is a central city for various religions, evoking strong memories, some painful. For some, it represents a great hope for a form of world peace. Undoubtedly, this city encapsulates a unique energy and profound mystery.

As a blessed city for all its inhabitants, Jerusalem invites a different kind of dialogue. Due to its nature and location, the usual Western discourse cannot succeed in this city, where the essence of chaos and deep religious feeling is part of its very being.

In Jerusalem, solutions derived from the knowledge of good and evil; discussions of ethics involving "occupation" or "liberation" that come from conventional wisdom will not succeed. These languages reduce its essence. They do not touch the hidden secret of the city, the root of its blessing. "Pray for the peace of Jerusalem," urges the verse in Psalms (122:6). Our personal peace is intimately tied to its peace.

This is the basis for the connection to blessing consciousness and the discussion of the trees in the garden. Jerusalem is an expression of the Tree of Life within the garden; we will expand on this later.

The following Midrash sharpens Jerusalem's position relative to humanity:

> Just as this navel is placed in the center of a person, so too the Land of Israel is situated in the center of the world...and from it, the world is nourished. The Land of Israel is positioned at the center of the world, and Jerusalem at the center of the Land of Israel, and the Temple at the center of Jerusalem, and the Holy of Holies at the center of the Temple, and the Ark at the center of the Holy of Holies, and the Foundation Stone before the Ark, from which the world was created. (*Midrash Tanchuma*, Kedoshim 10)

Jerusalem: The Tree of Life

The Midrash describes a spiral that begins with the centrality of Israel as the focal point of the world and gradually narrows down to Jerusalem, the Temple, the Sanctuary, and the Ark, culminating in its most inner point – the Foundation Stone, from which "the world was founded." According to this Midrash and ancient Jewish traditions, the world was created from the innermost point of the Temple, the Holy of Holies. Isaac was bound on the Temple Mount, and the request for the Creator to dwell again within it has been a fundamental element of Jewish prayer throughout the generations. According to this view, Jerusalem is the most appropriate and fitting place for God to dwell in our world. Jerusalem in general, and the Temple within it, represent a profound longing and a desire that demand exploration and interpretation.

Imagining Jerusalem, and certainly the Temple, as the Tree of Life in our times may seem like a far-fetched fantasy. The volatility of the Temple Mount and the tensions throughout the city do not reflect the positive energy of this tree, which is concerned with giving life, abundance, and a sense of security. However, upon deeper reflection, we may identify a true connection between them.

The commandment of the pilgrimage to Jerusalem three times a year fundamentally expresses a longing to touch a broader consciousness. It reflects the human desire to touch hidden dimensions of ordinary existence, dimensions within oneself that seek revelation.

As we've seen, a person expelled from the Garden of Eden yearns for the foundational senses that were active there. Consequently, there's a human longing for a renewed encounter with the infinite, in the tangible space on earth. Sometimes this happens in the dimension of time, on the Sabbath, or during a festival, and sometimes it happens in the spatial dimension. Jerusalem, as a physical place, expresses this longing.

Similar to the symbolic meaning of the Sabbath and Jerusalem is the transient dynamic of advancement and retreat. Just as every Sabbath is a movement in time that has a beginning and an end, we also experience movement in the spatial dimension. It is difficult to constantly dwell near the most sensitive point of human existence. The humanity within us demands the movement of touching a place and then releasing. This movement of advance and retreat creates longing.

Our world that is saturated with processes, longing, and yearning seeks a home and stability, a sense of having reached the destination. Perhaps this is what King David seeks when he is settled in his house, while God does not have a house:

> And it came to pass, when the king dwelt in his house, and the Lord had given him rest from all his enemies round about, that the king said to Nathan the prophet: "See now, I dwell in a house of cedar, but the ark of God dwells within curtains." (II Sam. 7:1–2)

The desire for God to have a house on earth reflects a longing for stability, a reconnection to the quality of encounter that existed in the Garden of Eden, providing a sense of security and peace. This was King David's wish. King David plays a central role in understanding the mystery of Jerusalem, which we will expand on later.

In the description of the Temple, there are many hints to the Garden of Eden and the Tree of Life at its center. Let's examine the similarities between these places, both in their earthly and spiritual aspects.[3]

The Physical Landscape

The Garden of Eden is abundantly watered:

> And a river went out of Eden to water the garden; and from there it was parted, and became four heads. (Gen. 2:10)

A similar reality is described in the vision of the end of days concerning the Temple in Jerusalem: a spring of living water will flow from the Temple and water the world.[4] This motif appears in several books of the Prophets. It hints at Jerusalem's connection with the Garden of Eden, giving the city a

---

3   I would like to thank my son, Rabbi Eitan Bar-or, who pointed out many similarities between the garden and Jerusalem.

4   In addition, we find in the prophecy of Zechariah (chapter 13) a description of a river that flows out of Jerusalem and revives the Dead Sea. See also Ez. 47; Joel 4:18; Zech. 14:8.

mythic dimension that links the beginning of creation to its end. On one hand, it's rooted in the primal garden, and on the other, its branches spread to the end of days.

The garden is abundant with trees that are notable for their beauty, the quality of their fruit, and their marvelous properties:

> And out of the ground made the Lord God to grow every tree that is pleasant to the sight, and good for food. (Gen. 2:9)

Jerusalem has the same characteristic:

> The cedars in the garden of God could not hide it; the cypress-trees were not like its boughs, and the plane-trees were not as its branches; nor was any tree in the garden of God like to it in its beauty. I made it fair by the multitude of its branches; so that all the trees of Eden, that were in the garden of God,[5] envied it. (Ez. 31:8–9)

From the garden, a river flows – this river divides into four heads that water the world. And in the future:

> And it shall come to pass in the end of days, that the mountain of the Lord's house shall be established at the top of the mountains, and shall be exalted above the hills; and all nations shall flow to it. (Is. 2:2; Micah 4:1)

Here, there is a connection between the river as a source of water and the movement of flow, symbolizing ecstatic experience. In the garden, the rivers flow out and irrigate, while all humanity will flow toward Jerusalem. In this sense, Jerusalem is an expression of the universality that characterized the garden and is destined to be a point of attraction for the nations.

---

5   The garden of God is a motif in the Tanach that expresses God's most intimate dwelling place. See Is. 51:3.

The Spiritual Landscape

Regarding the garden, the verse says: "And they heard the voice of the Lord God walking in the garden toward the cool of the day" (Gen. 3:8); and regarding the Tabernacle, it is said: "And I will set my dwelling among you... and I will walk among you" (Lev. 26:11–12). Both in the garden and in the Tabernacle, there is a sense of presence and security associated with the divine walk.

After the expulsion of man from the garden, cherubim guard the way to the Tree of Life; in the Tabernacle and the Temple, cherubim guard the cover and the Ark, to prevent anyone who is not prepared from approaching the intensity of the encounter. According to mystical interpreters, the tragic story of Aaron's sons Nadav and Avihu expresses their desire to return and eat from the Tree of Life, yet they did not heed the cherubim. This powerful encounter is possible only within boundaries.

What is the significance of the similarities between these two sacred places?

Firstly, the Temple's similarity to the garden demonstrates that the Temple embodies life's profound essence. It's not just part of an abstract spiritual world, but signifies a place that is a source of immense power for earthly life.

The practice of pilgrimage, the desire to draw near to the Temple, is fundamentally a profound yearning to rejuvenate the forces of life. The multitude of laws related to entering the Temple stem from the need for caution when engaging with these potent forces.

The modern aspiration for rebuilding the Temple is complex, beyond the political or halachic controversies. Humanity carries a fracture from eating from the Tree of Knowledge, and a similar fracture exists since the Temple's destruction. Rebuilding the Temple without addressing the internal axis of human beings is not feasible. Individuals and society must acknowledge the fractures of life and build an internal sanctuary. No external place can heal our duality and wounds. It can aid, provide direction, but not resolve the fracture. Similarly, the experience of exile of the Jewish people, seeking a time of healing before redemption, reflects this understanding. The knowledge that the Garden of Eden is inaccessible, while the construction of the Temple is a future vision, demands creating a unique consciousness within oneself. This consciousness strengthens the Tree of Life within us.

The ability to precisely balance an honest, existential personal image and an expansive future vision is one of the secrets of blessing consciousness.

The Garden, The City, and Exile

An additional parallel between the garden and the Temple relates to sin. Adam's sin can be divided into two aspects. On a simple level, eating from the Tree of Knowledge violates a divine command. However, there is a deeper layer of sin – the disconnection of man from the root of his soul.

This disconnection is more of a transgression than the sin itself. God doesn't punish Adam immediately after the act but invites him to a deep self-reflection through the question "*Ayeka?*" (Where are you?). Adam's refusal to introspect in response to this question is a key reason for his exile from the garden. The question "*Ayeka?*" is not just about accountability for the act. It's an existential inquiry about one's inner place. God is asking: *Do you understand what you have missed? Do you realize that by eating from the Tree of Knowledge, you have disconnected from the Tree of Life within you?*

> The sin of Adam is his estrangement from his essence, his inability to provide a clear answer to the question of *Ayeka*! (Rabbi Kook, *Orot Hakodesh* 3:140)

When we examine human downfalls that include sins, we may do so in a similar manner as we viewed the fall of Adam in the garden: a person who sins disconnects from the Tree of Life within.

Similarly, in the Temple, sacrifices are one of the primary means of atoning for sins. The sacrifice or *korban*, derived from the root *kuf-resh-bet* (*k-r-b*), which means "to come near," is meant to create closeness between the person and God, and consequently between the person and his or her inner self and personality core, providing rejuvenation for healthy living. When the service of sacrifices is performed without inner change, the purpose of the Temple is missed. The prophets of Israel frequently warned about this issue. Similarly, in our lives outside the garden, correction begins with an act of approaching. It involves a request to come back to life with a broader consciousness, stemming from a new self-awareness.

The punishment for the sin of eating from the Tree of Knowledge, and similarly for the sins of the Israelites in the land, was exile, from both the Garden of Eden and the Land of Israel.

The exile of the Jewish people mirrors the exile of Adam. It signifies an inability to be centered and understand the purpose of inhabiting the land. Similarly, for an individual, the lack of a place results in constant movement. Without the ability to pause, engage, and introspect, one becomes consumed with pursuit, achievement, and conquest. In such a state, an individual is essentially running from the existential question *Ayeka* that haunts us throughout life. Exile, therefore, is a fitting response – a reflection of the internal state. The inability to confront *Ayeka* signifies an internal exile; the ensuing physical exile merely sharpens and completes this picture of a disturbed and unsettled state of mind.

Jerusalem: A City of Awe and Vision

Another aspect of eating from the Tree of Knowledge that is worth exploring is the senses involved.

> And the woman saw that the tree was good for food, and that it was pleasing to the eyes. (Gen. 3:6)

Eve's vision was flawed. She was attracted to the immediate appeal and consequently, to her desires. She viewed the forbidden tree as edible, lacking the discerning vision that leads to awe. Profound awe fosters a kind of separation, the ability to recognize and establish boundaries. Incorrect vision leads to a craving for a taste, which then opens the eyes to awareness and discernment, along with all the consequences of eating from the Tree of Knowledge. In the Garden of Eden, the humans failed to heed God's voice, mainly because they misused their sense of sight.

Jerusalem, too, is deeply connected to the sense of sight.

In the Torah, the nation of Israel is commanded to make pilgrimages: "Three times a year shall all your males appear before the Lord your God" (Deut. 16:16). The Sages interpreted the word *appear*: "Just as he comes to see, so he comes to be seen" (*Chagigah* 2a). This means that the pilgrimage to the Temple involves both the individual pilgrim's vision and God's vision.

The balance between the pursuit of life and proper awe is achieved in the Temple.

Unlike the vision in the Garden of Eden, which created an encounter of desire, here the vision combined with holy awe provides a deep perspective. The focus is on the interior, not the exterior. The initial vision was a narrow one, linked to self-gratification, while the second vision extends from the past to the future, beyond the self.

"Jerusalem" is composed of the words *yir'u shalem*, "complete vision."

King David and the Secret of the Focal Point

Ever since I can remember seeking meaning in my Judaism, the figure of King David has fascinated me. The richness of his stories and the eternal nature of his character always stirred me. With this enchantment came questions about his personality – his ascents and descents, and their meanings.

I never accepted the apologetics that I sensed from some of my teachers and rabbis. The discourse of "good and evil" – even the Talmudic attempt to extricate him from the magnitude of his sin[6] – did not satisfy my soul.

Back then, I couldn't articulate it, but I knew the answer would come from the language of the Tree of Life, a language that sees a broader perspective, touching on the secret of a unique existence.

I wish to conclude this chapter with an analysis of a cherished and unique story, concerning the mystery of King David and the enigma of Jerusalem. This mystery is intertwined with the essence of the Tree of Life, which we can never truly touch or completely understand.

Throughout his life, from his youth to his later years, David perceived himself as a messenger of God. This was evident in his confrontation with Goliath as well as in his encounters with Saul, who sought his life. He saw himself as a vessel for God, acting on divine command. Even when acknowledging his sin of taking another man's wife (Bathsheba) while sending her husband (Uriah) to his death, David declared, "I have sinned against the Lord," though it is evident that there were earthly figures more directly affected by his deeds. The earthly sin pertains to the nature of the Tree of Knowledge. The sin against God relates to the nature of the Tree of Life.

---

6   For instance, "Anyone who says that David sinned must be mistaken" (*Shabbat* 56a).

David reached a significant crossroads in his life when he finished his military campaigns. Part of celebrating this transition involved bringing the Ark of God from the land of the Philistines to Jerusalem. After the Ark's arrival, he expressed a desire to build a house for God on earth, specifically in Jerusalem.

> And the king said to Nathan the prophet: "See now, I dwell in a house of cedar, but the ark of God dwells within curtains." (II Sam. 7:2)

God refuses the request without explanation. However, in the Book of Chronicles, the refusal is explained:

> The word of the Lord came to me, saying, Thou hast shed much blood, and hast made great wars; thou shalt not build a house to My name, because thou hast shed much blood upon the earth in My sight. (I Chron. 22:8)

To which bloodshed does the scripture refer? Is it to the very wars that David fought on behalf of God, or does the emphasis on "much" imply unnecessary bloodshed, with a clear hint to the murder of Uriah?[7]

David's awareness that he would not build the Temple is the backdrop to the story before us. In the biblical narrative, David does not plead. Like Moses, who was not allowed to enter the Promised Land, David also did not achieve his life's goal of building the Temple as God's earthly dwelling place. However, in the Midrash we will analyze, he takes action by digging the foundations of the Temple.

The background of the story is the Simchat Beit Hasho'evah (Celebration of the House of Water Drawing) ceremony during the Sukkot festival, a ceremony of mythical intensity. A nation of farmers ascends to Jerusalem, seeking rain from the Creator for the upcoming winter. The climax of the ceremony is the pouring of water drawn from the Silwan spring onto the altar. "The Holy One, blessed be He, said: 'Pour water before Me during the festival, so that the rains of the year may be blessed for you'" (*Rosh Hashanah* 16a).

---

7   This follows the Malbim's explanation of "much blood."

There is a connection between the earthly pouring and the heavenly pouring, represented by rain.

This ceremony is unique in Jewish culture. The Mishnah emphasizes: "Whoever has not seen the joy of the Beit Hasho'evah has never seen joy in his life" (Mishnah, *Sukkah* 5:1).

The ceremony is described thus:

> The devout and men of action would dance before them with flaming torches in their hands, reciting songs and praises. The Levites would play on lyres, harps, cymbals, trumpets, and countless other musical instruments. The musicians would stand on the fifteen steps leading down from the Court of Israel to the Women's Court, corresponding to the fifteen Songs of Ascents in the Psalms, upon which the Levites stood with their instruments and sang. (Mishnah, *Sukkah* 5:4)

This ceremony had primal – even erotic – foundations. It was a sort of earthly arousal, aiming for a heavenly awakening, through the pouring of water drawn from the depths. Not coincidentally, this ceremony is where the Talmud mentions the first partition between men and women. The energy, rooted in the desire for life and sustenance, created a great emotional storm, necessitating the separation of genders to avoid any mishap.

As they approached the altar, the song of the Levites in the Temple, sung on the steps descending from the Court of Israel to the Women's Court, is described. There is a correspondence between the number of these steps – fifteen – and the number of Psalms beginning with the words Shir Hama'alot (A Song of Ascents). This connection forms the basis of the story.

The story in the Talmud begins with the question: In response to which event did David write the fifteen Psalms of the Song of Ascents in the Book of Psalms?

> Rav Chisda asked… "Have you heard, corresponding to what did David recite these fifteen ascents?" He replied: "Thus said Rabbi Yochanan: When David dug the drainpipes [looking for the foundations of the Temple], the abyss rose and sought to inundate the

world. David recited fifteen Psalms of Ascents and caused them to subside."

Rav Chisda asked, "If so, should they not have been called 'fifteen descents'?"

Rav Chisda continued: "Now that you have reminded me of this matter, this is what was [originally] said: When David dug the drainpipes, the abyss rose and sought to inundate the world. David asked: 'Is there anyone who knows if it is permitted to write the sacred Name on a shard and cast it into the abyss to calm it?' There was no one who could answer him. David then declared: 'Anyone who knows and does not speak, may he choke in his throat.'"

Then Ahithophel raised an a fortiori argument of his own and said: And just as in order to make peace between a man and his wife [in the case of *sotah*, when the husband suspects his wife of having committed adultery (Num. ch. 5)], the Torah said: My Name that was written in sanctity will be erased on the water to establish peace for the whole world in its entirety, all the more so it is permitted. He said to David: It is permitted.

He wrote the sacred name on an earthenware shard and cast it into the depths, and the waters in the depths subsided sixteen thousand cubits. When he saw that they subsided excessively, he said: The higher the waters, the moister and more fertile the soil of the world. He recited the fifteen Songs of the Ascents and elevated them fifteen thousand cubits, and established them at a depth of (minus) one thousand cubits. (*Sukkah* 53a)

The story begins with David digging the foundations of the Temple despite any divine command, leading to the eruption of the abyss, which threatens to inundate the world. David then composed and prayed the Songs of Ascents to lower the abyss and restore it to its original state. In this interpretation, the function of these psalms is to lessen the intensity of the abyss, to calm it. The prayer stands in opposition to the abyss's force, aiming to return it to its initial place. However, in typical Talmudic fashion, a question is raised: If this is the case, why are the chapters called "Songs of Ascents"? Shouldn't they be "Songs of Descents," given that they caused the waters of the abyss to recede?

Yet the story that ultimately prevails is a bit different: David excavated the drainage of the Temple, and chaos rose, threatening to engulf the world. What is he ultimately seeking? He is aware that he is prohibited from building the Temple.

We might say that David was looking for a creative solution to his desire to participate in the construction. He would excavate the foundations, an act that apparently was not forbidden to him.

However, it seems the answer is deeper, more "abyssal."[8]

David understood that in this sacred place, in the most inner and sensitive point of Jerusalem, there lay some primal secret, a foundational point of meaning and interpretation. The place where David dug the drainage channels for the Temple is indeed the site from which the world was established. The Foundation Stone is the spot where, according to tradition, God sealed the abyss with the explicit Name at the beginning of creation.

This was the primordial abyss of pre-creation: "Now the earth was unformed and void, and darkness was upon the face of the deep" (Gen. 1:2).

Although David accepts the decree against building the Temple, he can't let go of his yearning to touch the focal point, that foundational essence of the very nature of life and its meaning. This place holds the secret of divinity, where it all began. This longing isn't born from the intellectual curiosity of the Tree of Knowledge, but rather from the existential core of the Tree of Life. As David nears the end of his life, he seeks to grasp a life secret he has yet to comprehend. This secret is tied to the innermost point of Jerusalem, perhaps of the universe – for the Foundation Stone is at the heart of the world just as the Tree of Life stands in the middle of the garden.

The connection to *tohu* (chaos) is integral to the mystery. It propels the rivers of Eden, rooted deep within the Tree of Life. The Foundation Stone,

---

8   "When the Holy One, blessed be He, created His world, He created it like the birth of a woman. Just as the birth of a woman starts from her womb and extends here and there to the four directions, so too did the Holy One, blessed be He, begin to create His world from the Foundation Stone, and from it the world was established. And why is it called the Foundation Stone? Because from it, the Holy One, blessed be He, began to create His world" (*Midrash Tanchuma*, Parashat Pekudei 3).

and the subdued abyss beneath it, embody profound complexity. On one hand, they hold the world's life and vitality within their nourishing waters, and on the other, they represent the world's peril when those same waters rise and threaten to engulf.[9]

With this revelation comes danger. David, overwhelmed by the discovery, fearful and concerned about the consequences of his digging, seeks help. He asks: Is it permitted to write the explicit Name on a shard and place it upon the opened abyss?

What is this shard? The *Zohar* relates:

> When the Holy One, blessed be He, created the world, He cast a precious stone from beneath His throne of glory, which sank to the abyss. One end of that stone is embedded in the depths, and the other end is above...and this stone is called the Foundation Stone from which the world was branched out to all sides. (*Zohar* II 71a–b)

It appears that even the Holy One, blessed be He, grapples with chaos and placed a stone – the very Foundation Stone – upon the earth to separate the outer world from the inner one. David follows in the path of his Creator, seeking to place a shard with the explicit Name upon the abyss to return it to its original place.

Gripped by a sense of responsibility and perhaps guilt, David seeks help from Jewish scholars, but no one responds to his plea. Perhaps his companions are tired of his dynamic personality, one that creates extreme movements. David threatens strangulation, an interesting threat given the rising waters of the abyss that threaten to choke everyone. Then Ahitophel, a wise and truthful biblical figure,[10] is called upon to make a halachic ruling. He

---

9   "Only when a person recognizes himself as created by a Creator who made both light and darkness, good and evil, does his 'self' reveal itself as a totality...connecting, like the divinity, all contradictions. And only then...can a person live in this world without that dangerous rift that frays the unity of creation and the unity of a person's being." Erich Neumann, Jung's prominent student, in *Depth Psychology and a New Ethic* (New York: Schocken, 1964), 74.

10   The Tanach describes Ahithophel as a skilled advisor, and his advice was proven correct after the fact. "And the counsel of Ahithophel, which he gave in those days, was as if a

decides that if for the sake of peace between a man and his wife, the Torah says that the divine Name may be erased in the water, how much more so to make peace for the entire world. Ahitophel permits the act,[11] using *kal va'chomer*, one of the hermeneutical methods for interpreting the Torah that allows one to infer that rules for a lighter case must be even more applicable to a more severe case.

What is the story that prompts this *kal va'chomer*? The story from chapter 5 of Numbers of the *sotah* – a woman suspected by her husband of adultery. She is brought to the Temple, and the High Priest prepares a drink for her. The mixture contains water from the basin, earth from the ground, and the erasure of God's explicit name, which is dissolved from parchment into the water. God is personally involved in the woman's examination. She drinks from the cup, and if she has indeed strayed, her belly swells, a sort of self-destruct mechanism that occurs in her abdomen. If she has not committed adultery, she will be cleared and bear offspring, a symbol of domestic peace and its blessings.[12] David wants to know if it is permissible for him to use the same magical power, now writing the explicit name of God on a shard, hoping that the waters will recede and calm down. Ahitophel says it is permitted – by the principle of *kal va'chomer*.

A tale of a woman's suspected boundary violations sets the stage for the narrative of King David's own boundary transgressions.[13]

Indeed, David inscribes the explicit Name on a shard, and the abyss returns to its original state.

This is where our story finds its core. The waters recede deep into the earth, to a depth of sixteen thousand cubits. God's magical intervention

---

man inquired of the word of God; so was all the counsel of Ahithophel, both with David and with Absalom" (II Sam. 16:23).

11 Some explain that Ahithophel's support for Absalom was driven by a desire to avenge David for the affair with Bathsheba, who was the daughter of Eliam, Ahithophel's son. If so, there is a hint here to his personal pain in bringing the request for peace between a man and his wife.

12 This story is difficult for the modern reader to digest, but the Sages have offered revolutionary interpretations that resonate with today's consciousness. See Moshe Halbertal, *Commentary Revolutions in the Making* [in Hebrew] (Jerusalem: Magnes, 1997).

13 We could expand on the connection between the two stories, particularly on the issues of male (David's) and female boundaries.

works effectively, so much so that there is a risk of drying up the world. Previously, the surging waters posed a threat to the world, but now the danger has reversed. Such a drastic reduction in water levels prevents the earth's surface from receiving moisture from within. This extreme measure could lead to the drying up of the earth. The mist that once rose from the ground in the second act of creation now faces the threat of annihilation.

David then created the fifteen chapters of the Song of Ascents. With each chapter he sang, the abyss rose one thousand cubits, until it reached the level of minus one thousand.

"Minus one thousand" – this is the crux of the entire story. Above this level lies the risk of flooding; below it lies the danger of drought and desiccation.

This measurement – recognizing the abundance and the life forces within us – is pivotal to a life of blessing. "Minus one thousand" serves as a benchmark for a blessed existence.

The storyteller might have concluded the tale with the casting of the shard inscribed with God's explicit Name into the abyss, causing the waters to drop straight to minus one thousand cubits, preventing the threat of flood. However, a different path was chosen. The shard with the explicit Name does not create balance! Were the world solely based on divine power, it would be excessively rigid. The "energized" shard drives the waters to an extreme point of dryness. Balance in the world is attainable only through a synergy between God and humanity.

This juncture is the story's pinnacle. God relies on human beings to mend a parched and unbalanced world. This presents a novel aspect to blessing consciousness. One who understands the equilibrium between the sometimes boundary-breaking physical force and the influence of words and prayer forges a new, vibrant boundary. The Creator engaged Abraham to have his progeny establish a society, a nation adept at harnessing abundance and life forces. A lack of vigor leads to scarcity that cannot adequately moisten the earth. Humanity requires living water for its sustenance. Conversely, we face the peril of flooding. An excess of force – the result of an unbalanced utilization of life forces – can engulf humanity. What is required is a blessing mindset that serves as a channel for abundance, a consciousness that discerns the point of minus one thousand.

David began his day as his biblical character suggests – a tempestuous man busy with breaking boundaries. Later in the story, he seeks help from scholars. The ability to ask for help, recognizing our limitations, is an important step in human maturation. After receiving assistance from Ahithophel and facing a new crisis of the earth's barrenness, David encounters a gentler aspect of his personality. In a single day, David transforms from an active boundary breaker into the psalmist of the Book of Psalms. Thanks to him, the abyss reaches the balanced state of minus a thousand. On an archetypal level, David in the morning is a "masculine" figure who tests boundaries. By day's end, he is a "feminine" figure, using words to compose the Psalms and raising the abyss to the right balance.

In this story, David achieves significant rectification. He is not consumed like Aaron's sons who breached the sacred. Moreover, he gains a profound insight. He no longer needs to build the Temple. He has touched its innermost foundations. He understands that the Temple indeed sits upon the human existential abyss and learns the secret of the minus-one-thousand dance, which is the essence of this unique city. Perhaps it's even the secret of human existence.

At a workshop I once held at Israel's National Security College, we studied this story. I asked the officers: What is your "minus-one-thousand" measure? These were people engaged in combat training, who had experienced the battlefield – had they encountered balance in the military power under their command? We discussed ways to achieve this on the battlefield and in commander training.

This fascinating dance takes place in all areas of life: economy, communication, relationships, sexuality, rectification, and forgiveness.

Jerusalem of 2024 is a city of chaos and void. There's a feeling that someone has moved the stone atop the abyss. It's certainly far from the minus-one-thousand balance point. At any given moment, the waters of the abyss might burst forth and flood the world. The discourse about Jerusalem must touch upon the drainage, the connection between the foundations of chaos and the greater quest for peace in existence. Any other conversation won't touch the essence. The insight from the story of King David could lead to a new dialogue among the inhabitants of the land. We all want to feel strength and abundance, and everyone might be interested in the secret of the minus-one-thousand dance, because it touches the foundation of our existence as human beings.

A new discourse on the city could transform Jerusalem not only into the capital of Israel but also into the heart of the world.

Jerusalem invites a different consciousness approach that can lead to a unique quality of life. Such an understanding could also bring about a different conversation about its centrality as a house of prayer for all nations, as a model of "and in you will all the families of the earth be blessed."

Chapter 19

Being a Blessing – A Vision

"Where there is no vision, the people cast off restraint." (Prov. 29:18)

The Jewish people underwent a seismic shift in the past century. One-third of it was annihilated. Yet this nation recovered, strengthened Jewish communities worldwide, established a unique economic status, and founded a state in the Land of Israel. This state has made the desert bloom, gathered the exiles, revived an ancient language, created a unique culture, and achieved significant economic and technological advancements. Many trees from the original garden have found growth and a place in the Land of Israel.

The State of Israel experienced a seismic shift on October 7, 2023, seventy-five years after its establishment. As I complete this book, Israel is fighting a tough battle in Gaza and in the north. This war, beyond its local context, touches upon fundamental questions of the world. In the twenty-first century, there are leaders, nations, and thinkers who cannot distinguish between good and evil. In a somewhat unexpected turn of events, we are witnessing the resurgence of antisemitism in the Western world.

These circumstances demand a reexamination of our identity. We should strive to redefine who we are as a community and our underlying purpose. We should not bear responsibility for antisemitism. However, there are moments when I perceive that some individuals harbor antisemitic sentiments due to an unspoken inquiry we pose to ourselves and the world: *Who are we, and what constitutes our essence and mission?*

Professor Viktor Frankl taught us that especially during our hardest moments, we must demand of ourselves and those around us to ask the question of meaning, going beyond mere survival.

It is precisely in these difficult times that we must address the purpose of the Jewish people in the world and in Israel. It's time to ask: *What can Jews contribute to the fundamental questions of humanity in this era?*

In this new reality, it is essential to build bridges between the Judaism of the past and the Judaism of the future. Concurrently, we should open our arms and be receptive to approaches and movements in the world aimed at a healed future for all humanity. The uniqueness of our era lies in the opportunity – or rather, the necessity – for the particular Jewish story and the universal human story to meet.

The Jewish people as a whole, and the State of Israel in particular, are moving toward a future without a meaningful vision to guide them. Yet a vision is vital to personal and public resilience. Unfortunately, I am experiencing the truth of this as I support families who have lost loved ones due to the current war in Israel, attempting to find solace and meaning in their bereavement experience.

There is a need to build an additional layer to Jewish existence, fostering hope for the realization of an old-new vision of blessing consciousness. From this broader perspective, a practical plan, a structured strategy for constructing a complete picture can be derived.

In the following lines, I propose a vision for the Jewish people in the spirit of blessing consciousness. I seek to stimulate a discussion about this vision of the future.

Blessing Consciousness – A Proposal

Education
We must hold a renewed discourse on the essence of education – defining the foundational elements that equip our children to build meaningful, creative, and satisfying lives. We must additionally explore the partnership between the educational roles of home and school. Education should focus on nurturing the individual's inner world, where the Tree of Life qualities of vitality and creativity can flourish. It must teach deep listening to others and promote face-to-face dialogue, in a culture that accommodates differing views.

Education should explore the blessings of abundance and wealth, probing the concept embodied in the Sages' saying "Who is rich? He who rejoices in his own lot."[1] It should equip individuals with tools for healthy, loving relationships.

These are foundational principles that precede the study of core curriculum subjects and are intended to shape them. Jewish studies should integrate essential principles from historical Jewish tradition along with a meaningful appreciation of the life celebration that Judaism offers to address the challenges of the current era.

Economy and Business

The Jewish people have played a significant role in creating innovative economic models. Jews were integral in the formation of early communism and are prominently involved in leading models in the Western world. The start-up nation has a considerable presence (relative to its size) on the American stock exchange, and part of the dream for many young people is to be part of this movement. However, a thriving economy and the growth of the start-up nation have not yet solved the deep economic disparities between the poor and the rich, resulting in social tensions, marginalization, and many living below the poverty line.

A blessed economy suggests a new consciousness, from which an understanding emerges that at its core, the economy seeks to serve society's needs and recognize its weaker members. In such a world, we would create new standards for business and economic success, where success is measured by its positive impact and contributions to society. Western economies, despite their significant achievements, have not addressed questions of meaning, seeing the vulnerable, and the ability to be content with one's lot.

In a society with blessing consciousness, workers feel a deep sense of meaning in their work, not measured solely by the profit margin. In such a society, there is a balance between home and work. A blessed society grapples with the commandment of Shemittah every seven years, translating its spiritual foundations into modern life.

---

1   Ethics of the Fathers 4:1.

Communication and Media

In the twenty-first century, human capabilities for self-expression and communication with others through technological means have greatly expanded. Alongside its abundance, the media is also filled with empty, often aggressive and forceful speech; it blurs the line between truth and falsehood and diminishes the ability to create real, deep, and meaningful connections between people. The blessing consciousness vision seeks to strengthen the power of the word and interpersonal communication. It will aid in developing tools for effective listening, enabling healthy debate, the ability to live with questions, and creating conditions for creation through the power of words.

In a society with blessing consciousness, media bodies operate according to these principles. The goal of writers, broadcasters, and interviewers is to expand dialogue, clarify positions deeply, and not to sharpen conflicts for the sake of sensational headlines or to highlight extremes. In such a society, interpersonal and public communication is a reflection of creativity and the quality of life of its members.

Recognizing the Other

Today's world suffers from a widespread phenomenon of invisible people – those we don't meet or notice in our daily lives. This group includes the vulnerable, such as those struggling for their basic survival, foreign workers far from their home countries, minorities under our jurisdiction, and many isolated individuals living just a stone's throw away. Sometimes, these individuals have no loving relationships in their lives.

In a world blessed with insight, we cultivate an empathetic and not a covetous gaze. This caring and inquisitive look, finding grace in others, is crucial in forging personal connections.

Blessing consciousness advocates for being present and bearing witness. In such a world, technology serves only as a tool, without replacing the value of face-to-face interaction. The commandment of "seeing," as referenced in the context of Temple pilgrimage, applies to all life stages, as we engage with others in their true form.

In a blessed nation, the cultivation of life and the economy are intertwined with the obligation of seeing. This vision becomes integral to the pursuit of abundance and the definition of success.

Restoration and Forgiveness

A healthy society is measured by its ability to honor the processes of repair and the search for forgiveness. Those who have erred and fallen must acknowledge their mistakes and take responsibility for their actions. However, falls and mistakes are the foundations for growth and creating meaningful lives. Failure is a necessary stage in development, like a seed whose decomposition allows for growth. A person living with blessing consciousness is in a state of continuous development. Such a society has the capacity for forgiving failings and constructs frameworks that facilitate healing and repair.

This kind of society believes in the human capacity for change. It opens gates for those seeking transformation and needing new tools. It welcomes the ability to admit mistakes, with its leaders serving as examples of this capability. It believes in a person's return to his or her true self and even creates appropriate systems that allow individuals to heal themselves.

Family

The intimate bond between partners is a confluence of powerful life currents representing almost opposite movements: the need for self-empowerment and personal satisfaction versus the need for meaningful connection. The ability to bridge these aspects lies at the heart of life and is the essence of blessing.

The family plays a central role in blessing consciousness. Couple communication, parent-child relationships, and even sibling connections form a fundamental structure linking individual growth with societal healing. A blessed family connects these vital circles, serving as a source of support and strength for its members. A blessed family demonstrates a healthy integration of personal growth, professional development, and fruitful family life.

A blessed society invests resources in strengthening family life and couple communication, viewing the family as a central resource, the heart of individual and societal repair.

Nutrition and Body Care

The food we consume is a central foundation in our lives. A blessed person strives to strengthen the divine image within while preserving the physical body and its sanctity. This includes feeling good about our bodies and being aware of what enters and exits them. In such a world, we are required to have at least enjoyable food, and even more so, food that brings *oneg*.

Such a perspective must assist the hungry as well as individuals who are challenged to maintain a healthy body.

Holiness

One of the foundations of being created in the image of God is an awareness of the divine aspect within us. This divinity calls upon individuals to relate to others as subjects, not objects. This principle is especially true in close relationships, employer-employee relationships, and many other contexts explored in the book. Recognizing oneself as a subject gives one a sense of value and self-worth.

In a blessed society, education in both homes and educational institutions is directed toward understanding the concept of holiness and its application in life. The Sabbath day is the weekly day set aside to infuse holiness into life, touching on the most earthly aspects of our lives: food, sexuality, personal communication, and more. From such a face-to-face encounter, one can build a life nourished by the holiness of life.

Leadership

In contrast to the ambitious model of the leader with the masses behind him, Judaism presents an alternative model of leadership: the shepherd. In this model of leadership, the leader operates with a sense of mission. As public emissaries, leaders are required to lead their communities with responsibility and sensitivity to their well-being, rather than as rulers who govern people's lives. As conduits, they understand the secret of balancing the blessings of power and wisdom with the modern-day equivalent of the restrictions on "wives, horses, silver, and gold" the Torah spells out as limitations on the king.

According to the book of Deuteronomy, the leader "writes for himself a Torah scroll" and acts in accordance with it. This scroll is an expression of their consciousness and their perception of the purpose they serve.

These are just examples, and the list can be expanded. The main principle is to engage in an ongoing dialogue about the personal and societal purpose of our lives.

Blessing Metrics

A significant part of the world around us operates based on success metrics. Measurement allows us to understand and evaluate the relationship between effort and outcome, providing a relatively clear picture of the bottom line of our endeavors.

Usually, these metrics are objective and not dependent on the subjective interpretation of the measurer or the measured. A good metric is one that inspires and promotes the project, aligning it with the participants' or organization's overarching goals.

The blessing promised to Abraham is one of economic abundance, a blessed family, and inheritance of the land. These are tangible, real things. If Tree of Life consciousness is an internal, spiritual process, then blessing consciousness is a story of success in the practical world.

In light of the blessing consciousness vision, I wish to share some preliminary thoughts on metrics of blessing. These metrics will be developed in the future by partners in this vision, as many of them come from the practical world and have a more natural ability to translate education and consciousness into metrics. Following are a few examples.

Work-Family Relations

Workers and their families will speak about the balance between these worlds. The metric will include physical and emotional presence at home, the ability to share, bringing the blessing of work into the home, and bringing the blessing of the home to work. Tools will be developed to report and reflect this reality.

Workers' Feelings in the Workplace

Tools will be developed to ascertain the level of employees' satisfaction at work. This includes how happy they are at work or if they are constantly thinking about leaving. It also measures how involved they are in creative issues and how much they feel seen. The metrics will also address the issue of layoffs, one of the painful areas in the world of work. The metric will examine the process of dismissal of employees and how the employer assisted them at this difficult juncture.

Economic and Social Relations

Metrics will be created to assess the impact of business success in terms of social contribution. All partners on the economic side are initially aware of the areas of social contribution and can even influence their end results. The bottom line of income is accompanied by an additional dimension of the direct impact of the business on the broader society, which becomes part of the metric of its success.

Media

Metrics will be developed to evaluate the success of leaders and media personalities based on their ability to create constructive dialogue, bring a positive perspective to reality, maintain respectful language, and similar considerations. The developed metric will be published periodically, and it will be an important consideration for those in the field to aim for the top of the list. A similar approach will be taken with various media channels. A channel will be evaluated not only by ratings but also in terms of emotional and spiritual interest, broadening of knowledge, culture of debate, and more.

Technology

Technology will not only be evaluated by its efficiency but also by the level of blessing it brings. A metric will be developed to examine issues of loneliness, the joy of those who benefit from its services, and their level of independence versus dependency. Part of the success of technology will be its users' ability to disconnect from it from time to time.

Family

A tool will be developed for individuals to assess the quality of blessing in their families. This includes their relationships with parents, children, and spouse. Additionally, tools will be developed for sibling relationships. These metrics will enable a person to seek practical tools to build bridges with family members where the flow is not easy. Although this is a sensitive area, metrics may help people understand their place and ability in this important system.

Leadership

Leaders will also be evaluated based on their ability to balance power with humility. The modern equivalents of the Torah's prohibitions on accumulating excessive wealth, gold, women, and horses will be examined, as well as what constitutes the values they believe in and are judged by.

Ability for Forgiveness and Rebooting

A social metric can be developed to ascertain where criminals, sinners, or people who have fallen stand in their journey of correcting their ways. This metric will evaluate the sincerity of their process and its effectiveness. Additionally, this metric will assess the ability of the organization, society, or community to forgive such individuals and even provide tools for their rehabilitation.

These are just examples, and the beginning of a process that requires expansion, depth, and precision.

Blessing measures are a kind of social ethics of the era in which we live. They may join the global discourse on quality-of-life dimensions, with an additional and unique Jewish statement.

Vision and being a blessing, along with blessing measures, represent a crucial stage in our internal model as a people and in fulfilling the destiny of Abraham – "and in you will all the families of the earth be blessed."

"Is There a Tree in It?"

During the wandering of our people in the desert, tribal leaders were sent "to spy out the land" and share their experiences. In Moses's instruction to the spies before they departed, he told them to check if there was a tree in the land: "Is there a tree in it, or not?" (Num. 13:20).

The *Zohar* asks: Moses knew that the Land of Israel was a land flowing with milk and honey, containing grapevines, figs, and pomegranates, and he shared this beautiful image with the desert generation. So what tree was Moses referring to? The *Zohar* explains that Moses wanted to know if the Land of Israel had the Tree of Life: Was there an element of abundance, heralding a different quality of life? When they returned with a cluster of grapes, the spies' testimony revealed that the answer was negative. The *Zohar* adds that Moses then knew he would not enter the land, because "a person's emissary is like himself," and although he apparently had elements of the Tree of

Knowledge necessary for the desert generation, they were not sufficient for the leadership that the Land of Israel required.

The State of Israel faces significant and existential questions, including on the security level, social issues, and the future of the Palestinians. The severe social crisis that emerged in November 2022 and the war that began in October 2023 present a unique opportunity to address foundational questions.

What is the Land of Israel of the Tree of Life? It is a region with a unique quality of life. This state is not satisfied with just being modern, creative, and ethical. It also embodies deep listening, a special vision of others, the ability to forgive, and personal and public communication that expands the heart. A land that invites its inhabitants to seek meaning, connecting family, work, and community circles with a consciousness of being a blessing – and much unconditional love.

A land with the Tree of Life creates a covenant among those sheltered in its shade, as they seek a common destiny determined for Abraham of being a blessing. The connection and mutual responsibility are not just moral values but stem from an exciting and shared vision of the future. It also invites a new layer of faith, and a sense of God's presence – "Is the Lord among us, or not?" (Ex. 17:7).

Can we imagine such a land? A land that invites us to a different and bold way of life? A land in which God wishes to dwell, in today's spirit? A land that creates abundance, making all its inhabitants feel a part of it? A land whose inner quest is to heal a broken world with Tree of Life consciousness? Such a land could forge a renewed covenant with the Jews of the Diaspora, working together toward a Jewish model of blessing and *oneg* – a model of celebrating life for meaningful and successful living in this era.

Personal Story, People Story

[Rabbi Chaim of Sanz] used to say in his later years, when he was ignited with the love of God, that he thought he could rectify the whole world and bring them back to properly serve God. When he saw that this was not within his power, he thought that at least he could rectify all the inhabitants of his city. He toiled in this endeavor. Yet again, he saw that this too was impossible.

He then thought that at least he could rectify all the members of his household to be true servants of God. Once more, upon reflection, he realized this was impossible and that at least he should strive for himself to be a servant of God. He toiled much in this and saw that even this was not simple.[1]

Recognizing the Personal Story in the Path of Blessing

The Tree of Life vision and the mission of blessing consciousness that underlie this book move in the spectrum between personal and social repair. Knowing one's personal story – what is open in me, what is wounded, what I actually seek from life – is vital for a change in consciousness and from there, the hope to heal a broken world.

Indeed, without personal change, societal change is not sustainable. This is why a significant part of the book deals with personal consciousness related to the Tree of Life, which will guide our movement and actions in the world.

---

1   Martin Buber, *Or Haganuz* (Tel Aviv: Schocken, 2005), 172.

Be a Blessing

It is impossible to talk about a blessed economy without a change in personal consciousness regarding the desire for money and property. Change in the media and mass communication is not possible without a change in the quality of personal speech and listening on the part of each and every one of us. Nor can we discuss the concept of brotherhood without examining our relationship with our biological siblings. These principles are true for all aspects of our lives that seek personal blessing on the way to societal blessing. Similarly, it is not relevant to discuss employee-employer relations or relations with others without examining object-subject relationships in life in general, and in personal relationships in particular. On the same note, it is not right to talk about a general educational perspective without accurately examining our relationship as parents to our children, alongside a renewed understanding of honoring parents on the part of our children.

In each of our personal stories, there is the potential to touch the Tree of Life within us, that foundation of being a blessing. For this reason, throughout the book, I have shared a little of my journey in various areas of life that the book addresses. As I approach the closing of the book's pages, I want to expand a bit on this journey, without which the insights and invitations in the book would be incomplete.

The Holocaust in Europe had a profound impact on the home in which I grew up. My late father was the son of the village rabbi of Ştefăneşti in Eastern Romania. He was a man with a warm and expansive heart. My father and I were very different in many ways. Yet despite this, I was fortunate to have a good relationship with him, as did my children and some of my grandchildren who had the privilege of knowing him and feeling an emotional closeness to him. He had a great love for people, a subtle sense of humor, and a love of books. I remember how he would often ask: "How is your heart doing?" He showed genuine and deep interest in me, my children, and people close to him.

And there was pain in him.

During a roots visit to his childhood village of Ştefăneşti, my father climbed a small hill near his house, which used to be the rabbi's house (my grandfather's), and with tears, he pointed to an altered football field that was there. It remained as it was fifty-five years later, with only a minor change – faded wooden goalposts, instead of rusty metal ones. As we looked at the field together, Romanian children were playing on it, and my father said, "Every day, as I watched my friends playing football, my father, the village rabbi, would grab my ear and pull me to study Mishnah with him." He so wanted to play with them. This was a childhood image my father often revisited with pain throughout his life. During the Holocaust, all the village's Jewish families were uprooted to the larger city of Botoşani, never to return, and their houses were taken by the non-Jewish residents.

My father passed away at the age of ninety in Jerusalem from a heart attack, while watching the Israeli national team play a soccer game. It was a rare game in which the team won. I have wondered about the connection between the hill near his house and the circumstances of his death.

My late mother survived the Holocaust days in Bratislava, the capital of Slovakia. She was the middle child in a family of eleven children, three of whom were murdered in Auschwitz. Her father, Rabbi Moshe Zinger, was the city's ritual slaughterer. He suffered torture at the hands of the Nazis and died of a heart attack in 1944.

My mother began sharing Holocaust stories relatively early in my life and never stopped. There were two main stories she often revisited. One was about the damp, cramped cellar where she hid with part of her family and the Steiner family during the winter of 1944, after the Nazis had rounded up the remaining Jews of the city. A wet cellar, just two hundred square feet (20 sq m), sheltered two families through the winter, including my mother, then fifteen years old.

The second story was about how at eighteen, she took responsibility for her young nephew Menachem, a motherless orphan (my aunt was murdered), and brought him to Israel on an overcrowded ship. This story was pivotal in my mother's inner world. This story involves much pain, as my late father refused to keep Menachem in their small, new home in the kibbutz for long, and Menachem was placed in an orphanage. Menachem never forgot this abandonment. Despite my mother's self-sacrifice and literal saving of his life, he chose to distance himself from Israel and went to live in Toronto, Canada. He passed away a few months after my mother.

My parents' marriage did not survive the hardships of the Holocaust and postwar generation, and after forty-five years of marriage, they divorced. My father remarried at sixty-five and enjoyed many years of contentment in his later life before passing away in late 2015. He loved Torah, taught, and was instrumental in founding the Har Etzion Yeshiva, a yeshiva where I had the privilege to study and grow. My father achieved a form of repair in his later years – reconciliation with himself and his children. Indeed, he was blessed with love and a good partnership. His memory is a blessing for me and my family. "Better is the end of a thing than the beginning thereof: and the patient in spirit is better than the proud in spirit" (Ecc. 7:8).

My late father is an example of someone who experienced a new lease on life in his older years. He learned to listen to his heart, care less about what the outside world might say, and believe in love, connection, and dialogue. He shared these changes with us, his three children, and we found in him new strengths of support and giving.

My mother passed away in Jerusalem after years of dementia, oddly paired with an extraordinary vitality. She survived a severe and stormy infection, and up until the days of COVID-19, she visited the Yakar synagogue every Saturday morning. As she used to say, she was very connected to prayer at Yakar, not because of belief in God, Whom she didn't quite believe existed, but because of the songs. The music was one of the brightest and most vivid parts of the service for my mother. Despite the tribulations of dementia, she remembered every word, every note, and every nuance of songs and melodies. It was the only time she would close her eyes and drift to realms of pleasure. She was full of life and optimism and had great appreciation for living in Jerusalem.

Growing up in my parents' home was not easy, yet I am deeply grateful to them. The love I received, the Chasidic tunes of Shabbat meals, and their zest for life – all these instilled in me faith and positivity. Healing childhood pains is an amorphous, elusive process; there are moments when it seems you have touched upon change, only to find yourself reverting to old patterns. Nonetheless, I felt a spiraling movement in these years, something shifting, even amidst the occasional fall down the circular ladder.

Writing this book was enjoyable and difficult. Attention and concentration challenges were not conducive. Yet those daily minutes and hours began to create foundation stones in the inner home I sought to build.

A New Torah like a Planted Tree

In the Garden of Eden, there were two central forces of abundance that the Creator made manifest: the river and the trees. The image of a river flowing out of Eden from the depictions of the Garden of Eden's infrastructure always spoke to me. When my sons Eitan and David were younger, we would go every Thursday evening to dip in a spring in the Jerusalem area. Summer and winter, we would count to three and jump into the water, which was sometimes freezing cold.

The imagery of rain in the Land of Israel, from the Scriptures through the literature of the Talmud and Chasidism, holds a central place in my life to this very day. I remember the year of studying the topic of rain at the Elul Beit Midrash as a wonderful year for me. Water in all its forms – realistic, mythical, and psychological – has always inspired me and stirred ancient elements within me. I feel especially connected to the mystic rainmakers in our culture, as related in Talmudic stories and the *Zohar*.

During my sabbatical, I sought to explore the second nourishing element in the garden: the trees. Contrary to what might seem apparent, there are common lines of similarity between water and a tree. Water, like a tree, has hidden roots in the form of the deep waters. In fact, they are much deeper than the roots of a tree. Water, like a tree, also has a higher element. The clouds and the upper waters (the rain) rise far above the treetops.

But still, as the tree represents me and my roots, with slow and hidden movement, it emphasizes uprightness and blessing. Perhaps this is where its true power lies. Maybe the tree is a masculine image, and the river a feminine one.

The Book of Psalms begins with a description of an individual using a unique expression of the meeting of tree and river:

> And he shall be like a tree planted by streams of water, that brings forth its fruit in its season, and whose leaf does not wither; and in whatever he does, he shall prosper. (Ps. 1:3)

As opposed to a powerful river, the tree is planted by streams of water. Its leaves do not wither, and it bears fruit. Being a tree planted by streams of water is an image of personal uprightness, amidst a reality that sometimes swirls around us stormily. To me, this verse is an emphatic expression of a person connected to the Tree of Life within – and thus blessed.

The parts of the tree have parallels in the soul. The root represents an awareness of the living layer that constitutes the soul; the trunk symbolizes the body; the leaves that do not wither conjure the realization of our potential qualities. The fruits are our creation, our unique contribution to the world. "Brings forth its fruit in its season" is an expression of precise giving, which is a sign of blessing.

Beyond this impressive image of the tree, the end of the verse describes the earthly success of the person likened to this tree. This is not the Tree of Knowledge, by which man chooses between good and evil, but a depiction of the Tree of Life in its glory. The ideal of the planted tree takes me back to the description of the trees in the garden:

> And out of the ground the Lord God made to grow every tree that is pleasant to the sight and good for food; the Tree of Life also in the midst of the garden, and the Tree of Knowledge of Good and Evil. (Gen. 2:9)

I asked myself: What is the quality of the Tree of Life beyond the biblical description of a tree that gives life? I recalled a visit I made with my friend Rabbi Dov Berkovitz to Professor Yehuda Liebes at his home in Jerusalem that year. Yehuda is one of the greatest Kabbalah researchers of our generation, wholly devoted to the love of myth and mystery. A recipient of the Israel Prize, he is deeply connected to the *Zohar*. We asked him: What is the role of the Tree of Life in the *Zohar*? His eyes sparkled with enthusiasm despite his age, and with great excitement, he said: *"Ilana dechaye?"*[2] It is not just the essence of the entire *Zohar*, but also the foundation of the entire Torah." Then he clarified to us that the Tree of Knowledge is called in the *Zohar ilana demuta* – the Tree of Death. He added without explanation: "Do you understand the significance of this linguistic choice?"

At that time, we were left without a precise lexical definition for the Tree of Life. In the course of my life, I endeavored to delve into the nature of this

2   The Aramaic term used in the *Zohar* for the Tree of Life.

tree, and I realized that the more I try to define it, the more elusive it is; there will always remain some mystery, just as in life itself.

Since then, I have been trying to clarify the conscious quality of the Tree of Life. I realized that it is related to a person's ability to connect to an inner core that revives from within, not to the love and appreciation we receive from external worlds. Our roles as parents, partners, children, and professionals do not define us; rather, it is our most primal existence within ourselves. This is not an easy task – shedding the external garments, the facade, and touching our pure nakedness.

In a world connected to the Tree of Life, we strive to bless the adversity that meets us, just as we bless the good in our lives, because good and evil are inseparable parts of the tree planted by streams of water. In these waters, there is no good and evil. They flow in our lives regardless of knowledge. This quality of the Tree of Life touches a place in the soul that is beyond choice, beyond duality. In this consciousness, there is an ability for self-forgiveness and interpersonal forgiveness, faith and courage in healing pains and accepting our shortcomings. It embodies a longing for rectification, the most fundamental essence of human beings and an expression of the life within us. And yes, in the Tree of Life consciousness, a person may touch the experience of *oneg*.

In the workshops we conduct in the Ve'heyeh Berachah project, we ask people when they feel connected to the Tree of Life and when they sense the Tree of Knowledge in their daily routine. Most people find it easy to identify aspects of the Tree of Knowledge. They share moments of control and management, decision making, complexity, and success. It becomes apparent to participants that much of our lives are lived in the shadow of the Tree of Knowledge of good and evil, sometimes for the better, sometimes for the worse, and most of the time with a lot of "knowing."

During the workshop, people gradually open up to the areas of the Tree of Life in their lives. For many, these are expressions of a sense of real life, of a pulsating inner abundance. Expressions like a sense of precision, something simple happening, experiencing a deep touch, an experience indescribable in words. In the experience of the Tree of Life, there is an ability to balance between receiving and giving, connecting to an experience that touches the soul directly. These are moments when a person says: *I am alive*. For such moments, life is worthwhile.

During my trip to India, I encountered for the first time the words of the *Zohar* that form the basis of this book:

> "Of every tree of the garden you may freely eat" – this refers to the Tree of Life from which Adam was allowed to eat. Yet he sinned [by eating] from the Tree of Knowledge of Good and Evil – from which he was commanded not to eat (*Zohar Chadash* 1:31b).[3]

I was very moved by the thought that the main transgression in the garden was the failure to eat from the Tree of Life! I started to imagine what the world would have looked like if the first man had eaten from the Tree of Life before eating from the Tree of Knowledge. I understood that in this image lies a world full of life, of correction and renewal. In such a world, where eating from the Tree of Knowledge is managed by eating from the Tree of Life, man has the ability to repair evil through healing and even elevating it. Guilt and blame are replaced by faith and compassion. Material life seeks *oneg*, not just enjoyment. This is a mature Garden of Eden, not shying away from the responsibility to heal the world. It is led only by the axis of the Tree of Life within us, while the Tree of Knowledge is sheltered in its shadow.

The Holocaust, Knowledge, and Life

During my youth, I was deeply engaged with the Holocaust. I asked my uncle Simcha, of blessed memory, to tell his version of my mother's stories. I watched films, but mostly I read a lot of books. However, like many, I always felt an existential void around the Holocaust. I began to get used to this and understood that the Holocaust is an existential hole in life and consciousness. I gave up the quest for resolution.

In those days in India, I recalled what Uzi Weil wrote about the Holocaust. Uzi is an Israeli satirist, journalist, and author, a Tel Avivian. I paraphrase his words as follows:

---

3   I found a similar source in *Midrash Tanchuma*: "God said, I placed you in the Garden of Eden so that you would labor in the Torah, and eat of the Tree of Life" (Buber edition, Genesis, section 25).

Since the Holocaust, time has been moving backward.... The pain of exile is unbearable. For every person, and especially for a Jew, because we know it should have been different. This is the greatest pain of all: that there is no connection between how things seem and what they really are....

Without absolving anyone of blame, of course, and without claiming, heaven forbid, that I have found any solution to the pain, I make the following argument: that the Jews could no longer bear the suffering of exile, the humiliation of being the exiled prince, draped in rags. They could no longer endure one more day in a life whose meaning is not apparent to the eye. And so, they brought the secrets out....

This is what I claim: that subconsciously, the Holocaust was an invitation of the Jewish collective subconscious. It could no longer endure another day in a world where good is not apparent to the eye. And so, it went and brought out the secrets of creation. It said to the Holy One, blessed be He: "Let's see how this works in the world." This caused a great confrontation between good and evil.

Since the Holocaust, time has been moving backward. Backward, toward repair.

Uzi's words deeply resonated with me, as they directly engage with the concept of the Tree of Life. The exile from the Garden of Eden created a significant wound in human existence, just as the exile from the Land of Israel deeply wounded the Jewish people. This injury highlights the unbearable gap between living under the shadow of the Tree of Knowledge of Good and Evil and the quest for a life of true substance under the Tree of Life. It's about the profound existential pain that lies between mere survival and a life filled with meaning and vitality.

The exile from the Land of Israel and the Tree of Life sparked numerous movements of liberation. The Sabbatean movement ignited a fire in the Jewish heart with its quest for a shortcut to Eden and to override the Tree of Knowledge. The Enlightenment, followed by secularism, sought to liberate Jews from the ghetto. Zionism aimed to reclaim Jewish honor from the exile and establish equality on a political level. Even God was seen as part of the exilic past. Those who maintained their faith and did not rebel largely clung to an image of God from the Jewish past: Our Father in heaven. If there was ever any doubt about the potency of the longing for life versus the reality of exile, the Holocaust came and definitively said: *No more!*

Uzi Weil views the Holocaust as a mirror, reflecting a people striving to introduce the message of life to the world. In the terms I have defined in this book, the Holocaust marks the end of a period in which Judaism was dominated by the separation of the Trees of Knowledge and Life. After two thousand years, post-Holocaust Judaism demands reunification of the approaches signified by the two trees.

As a nineteen-year-old student at Har Etzion Yeshiva, I approached Rabbi Yehudah Amital, of blessed memory, the *rosh yeshivah* (dean), on Holocaust Remembrance Day. Rabbi Amital, a distinctive figure among *roshei yeshivah*, had come to Israel directly from the Holocaust of Hungarian Jewry. The Holocaust profoundly influenced his Torah teachings, as well as his political and social outlook. Approaching his room that morning, I felt a deep sense of reverence. Rabbi Amital was known for his impatience with trivial matters. I had an agreement with my study partner: if I didn't return within fifteen minutes, he should start to worry and come looking for me. We decided on the question: "How can one pray a regular prayer today, on Holocaust Remembrance Day?" It was the innocent query of a young student. I knocked on the door. Rabbi Amital was busy preparing a lesson. I asked if I could pose a question, and he invited me into his room.

After I stammered my question, Rabbi Amital looked at me and sharply responded, "The Holocaust was the greatest desecration of God's name in human history," and then he escorted me to the door. The total time he allotted for me was about two minutes. I remember feeling disappointed. I had expected something heart-opening, some kind of resolution. But over the years, I realized that he had said something profoundly meaningful.

Let me explain.

God is an expression of the fundamental essence of vitality and life in the world. The knowledge of good and evil, connected in its essence to the element of death, is far removed from God. It is no coincidence that the Creator commanded Adam not to eat from the Tree of Knowledge. The very existence of God is the unfolding of life in its fullness. Therefore, the horrific and bizarre deaths that characterized the Holocaust are the greatest expression of a void of godliness, and consequently, a desecration of His name. If the Holocaust represented a contraction of God's presence in the world, then Judaism must renew itself after the Holocaust by expressing the greatest life forces as a manifestation of living divinity.

However, the transition from the life contraction experienced during the Holocaust to a life of sovereignty and freedom cannot overlook the deep wound embedded in both the individual and the nation.

After returning from India, I realized with great clarity that the path to healing and healthy engagement with life passes through the foundational experiences of my family in the Holocaust and examining what remains in me from that pain. Generally, in recent years, I've come to understand that everyone has a wound. As this understanding expands within me, I find greater capacity for listening and forgiveness. The more this understanding expands on a human level and the more we dare to touch the wound in human discourse, the more we feel the fullness of a person. Vulnerability is an essential part of intimacy. Indeed, this is a gift I discovered in being a second-generation survivor.

This visit to India, which was a journey to the realm of the Tree of Life, expanded various areas of my life. I came to see God's image as accompanying us in our lives, as long as we dare to lift our heads, look, and feel. The living God created us to enjoy the pleasantness of this world with all its trees and rivers. I felt clearly that He indeed is a King Who desires life, *Melech chafetz b'chayim*, as we say in the prayers.

I realized that a couple's bedroom is essentially the laboratory of the earthly dwelling that the Creator seeks. The quality of intimacy in all its aspects is a crucial part of God's desire for us, as the Divine Presence is drawn to these spaces. I felt a change in my Torah study. I sought in Judaism not only the correct and safe way of life but also its life-giving essence. I found myself looking at the Torah in a new way, at the debates of the Sages, and of course, I found real comfort in the realms of Chasidut. A significant part of its philosophy draws from the Torah of the Tree of Life.

I felt a change in my understanding of the concept of "teacher." In the foundational study of the Tree of Life, the teacher and the student are partners in a long-term journey, in which we all strive together to strengthen the foundations of the tree.

There was also a change at a societal level. I noticed that while I may have many acquaintances, I sought a few true friends. These people bring with them honesty, pain, and desire, alongside the quest for life.

I felt a change in my attitude toward partners and investors I wanted to work with in the future. I sought people who would be partners in a journey – not just those who trusted me, but those genuinely seeking significant change in their lives. Beyond being economically blessed, they possess the courage for new beginnings. I wanted their contribution to come from a stream of life that is curious about the path. I envisioned the investor as someone who influences from a space of abundance, like a blessed conduit.

The Need for a New Paradigm

The English version of this book was prepared during a severe Israeli societal crisis, an existential war for the State of Israel, amid a worldwide rise in antisemitism, and at a time when significant global changes seem to be unfolding. Many share the concern that a paradigm shift is needed in relation to several pillars of our lives.

A foundational source for this perception and feeling appears in the following passage:

> The Rabbis taught: Forty years before the destruction of the Temple, the lot [for the Yom Kippur scapegoat] did not come up in the right hand, nor did the strip of crimson wool turn white, nor did the westernmost light burn, and the doors of the Temple would open by themselves,[4] until Rabban Yochanan ben Zakkai rebuked them, saying: "Temple, Temple, why do you alarm yourself? I know about you that you are destined to be destroyed..." (*Yoma* 39b)

Forty years before the destruction of the Temple, long before the political crisis and the Roman entry into Jerusalem, we witness Rabban Yochanan ben

---

4   These were signs that something was amiss in the Sanctuary.

Zakkai's visit to the Temple. It seemed like just another day in the routine of the Temple. However, the Temple was filled with signs that something fundamental was no longer functioning.

The greatness of Rabban Yochanan ben Zakkai lay in his addressing the Temple, clarifying to it, and to us, that the Temple's paradigm had reached its end, at least for his time. This was not related to the impending Roman conquest or even to the internal Jewish conflict that led to significant bloodshed during the siege and destruction. Rabban Yochanan ben Zakkai's leadership was expressed in his understanding that the destiny of the people of Israel would no longer be manifested in the Temple service, with all its implications. In time, the study hall would replace the Temple, and the Torah scholar would replace the High Priest. Prayer would substitute for the service of sacrifices, and the quest for God would be expressed in the study of Torah and the work on character traits – for the time being. This revolution enabled the Jews to survive for two thousand years, despite drastic changes in their way of existence.

The ability to identify a paradigm whose time has passed, long before a crisis arises, and even to propose the necessary change, is a hallmark of the Tree of Life. People living such a life are attuned to themselves. They do not need an external crisis to become enlightened and awakened. This special ability is an expression of leadership over oneself. It is the ability to honestly identify the sources of the river and joy, and also to part with what no longer gives life. In contrast, people living in the shadow of the Tree of Knowledge need an external crisis to awaken and lead change.

I begin the first workshop in the Ve'heyeh Berachah project with this story of Rabban Yochanan ben Zakkai. I ask: What paradigms of our time, seemingly dominant or present in reality, have reached their end? This fundamental question is central to a living consciousness. It also pertains to the role of the Jewish people today – to identify necessary changes, ask questions, and propose new directions.

Jewish history is marked by moments of crisis, each leading to the creation of new paradigms within the Jewish world. The aftermath of the Second Temple's destruction revolutionized all aspects of Jewish life. Similarly, the expulsion from Spain led, among other things, to the sixteenth-century renaissance of the Kabbalists in Safed and more. The dramatic events of the twentieth century, including the Holocaust and the establishment of the State of Israel, call for a Jewish revolution on a much larger scale than what we currently see. This change has the potential to add new depth to the meaning of being Jewish and the purpose of the Jewish people in our times. This dynamic could broaden the sense of personal and societal potential, revealing a new level of meaning in our lives as Jews.

This book was completed during difficult times for the Jewish people in general and the State of Israel in particular. Humanity as a whole is also going through a significant and challenging period. Paradigms are shifting before our eyes, and much mystery still lies ahead. "Blessing only resides in that which is hidden from the eye."[5] I hope that the book provides some meaning to our lives and our future.

Rabbi Jonathan Sacks said, "Judaism is the only civilization whose golden age is in the future."[6] The Jewish future depends on each one of us. In a rapidly changing world, we have the power to revive personal, familial, and communal Judaism, preparing for the many challenges ahead.

Yehi ratzon – May it be His will that we merit becoming blessings for ourselves, our loved ones, and for all the people of this world.

---

5   Talmud, *Bava Metzia* 42a.

6   Jonathan Sacks, *Future Tense: A Vision for Jews and Judaism in the Global Culture* (London: Hodder and Stoughton, 2010), 113.